*Also by Christopher Turner*

London Step By Step
Paris Step By Step

Christopher Turner

# BARCELONA
# Step by Step

St Martin's Press – New York

First published in Great Britain 1991 by Pan Books Ltd

First US Edition 1991
10 9 8 7 6 5 4 3 2 1

© Christopher Turner 1991

Drawings © Christopher Turner 1991

Maps by Ken Smith
Design by David Pelham and Leigh Brownsword

ISBN 0 312 07487 5

Photoset by Parker Typesetting Service, Leicester

Printed and bound in Great Britain by
BPCC Hazell Books, Aylesbury, Bucks
Member of BPCC Ltd.

Library of Congress Cataloging-in-Publication Data
Turner, Christopher, 1934–
    Barcelona step by step / Christopher Turner.
        p.      cm.
    ISBN 0–312–07487–5
    1. Barcelona (Spain)—Description—Tours.    2. Walking—Spain—
    Barcelona—Guide-books.    I. Title.
    DP402.825T87    1991
    914.6′720483—dc20                                                    91-2859(
                                                                                CIP

*Acknowledgements:* For their kindness and help in Barcelona, I am grateful
to the Patronat de Turisme de Barcelona; David Mackay of the
architectural partnership, Martorell, Bobigas and Mackay; Professor Juan
Bassegoda-Nonell of the Faculty of Architecture of Barcelona; Rosa
Garicano, cultural co-ordinator of the Palau de la Música Catalana and
Magdalena Guel, Director of the Picasso Museum.
In particular, I should like to thank Juan Soriano, my Catalan friend now
domiciled in England, for his advice and provision of great quantities of
information on all aspects of Barcelona.

# Contents

# Introduction

Barcelona, rated by many as the finest of all Mediterranean cities, poses two basic problems for visitors. The ancient Gothic core is made up of a formidable warren of winding streets and passageways, whilst the modern 'Eixample' is laid out to a grid pattern of tiring thoroughfares, with the magnificent but hard to locate Modernist buildings of Gaudí and his contemporaries widely separated. It is to overcome these problems that I have written this book.

More than two hundred locations are grouped into twelve separate itineraries, each beginning and ending at a Metro station. Like all other European art cities, Barcelona can only be explored properly on foot; explicit directions are given for walking from one location of interest to the next and for viewing the exterior, and where possible, the interior, of each one precisely as it is reached. To minimize fatigue, the routes are planned so that long uphill stretches are avoided. Specially drawn large-scale maps clearly pinpoint each location.

A separate 'R' key on most of the maps identifies refreshment facilities – bars, bodegas, coffee houses and restaurants, to suit all tastes and pockets. Every establishment referred to is described in the Food and Drink in Barcelona section and, wherever possible, correlated with the maps. Comprehensive menu vocabularies in the Catalan and Spanish languages will prove an indispensable aid.

With this book in hand the visitor will miss nothing, never get lost and avoid going round in circles wasting precious vacation time.

Christopher Turner

# Barcelona and the Barcelonans

**The City**

Barcelona is different. Different not only from practically all other Spanish cities, but very different from the other great art cities of Europe. The prime reason for Barcelona's uniqueness is the survival, almost intact, of a large medieval city comprising street after street of Gothic buildings. There are several reasons for this good fortune. Due to its decline from the sixteenth to the eighteenth centuries, the city suffered little Renaissance or Baroque remodelling; there was no wholesale nineteenth-century modernization as in Paris; little damage to buildings, apart from church interiors, occurred during the frequent periods of strife; and Spain resisted Hitler's blandishments to enter the Second World War, thereby escaping the devastation suffered by so many other countries. An additional reason, suggested by H. V. Morton, is the sheer difficulty and expense of replacing most of the buildings, as they are constructed from great blocks of extremely hard stone.

When the modernization and extension of Barcelona eventually began, in the nineteenth century, it took place on virgin land outside the area formerly enclosed by the medieval wall. There are, therefore, few examples in the old city of unsympathetic modern architecture.

It should be borne in mind that the name of the famous Gothic Quarter (Barri Gòtic) was thought up as recently as 1926, and only refers to the central section of the extensive Gothic area. However, the 'quarter' does include many of the city's most important Gothic buildings and has helped to ensure the conservation of the streets around them. It has also promoted tourism.

Barcelona is probably the only true art city to be sited actually on the Mediterranean but, here again, its treasures are different. Very few old master paintings are exhibited and those who seek the works of Velázquez, El Greco, Zurbarán, Murillo and Goya are better served in Madrid, Toledo and Seville. Conversely, admirers of Romanesque and Gothic art will find unsurpassed examples in the Museum of Catalan Art. Modern art enthusiasts are equally well catered for. Picasso, although born in Malaga, spent his formative years in Barcelona, and the Picasso Museum in Carrer Montcada, a street of preserved medieval palaces, includes many rare examples of his early work. The world's most extensive collection of Joan Miró's paintings is also to be found in the city, housed in an outstanding modern gallery, a work of art in itself, designed by Josep Lluís Sert. Antiquities, most of them discovered in Catalonia, are displayed in the Frederic Marés Museum, although some visitors derive the greatest pleasure from its unique collection of ephemera throughout the ages.

Music lovers will discover that many of the world's leading singers and dancers perform in the operas and ballets at the Liceu. However, the theatre closes during the hot summer months. Newly installed air conditioning has meant that concerts at the magnificent Palace of Catalan Music now continue throughout the

year, and many more tourists can therefore attend them.
Regarded as the epitome of Modernist architecture, Domènech i
Montaner's building also possesses outstanding acoustic qualities.

Like the English, the Spaniards have never been addicted to long
unbroken city vistas, preferring greater intimacy, and Barcelona
possesses few examples. A notable exception, that should not be
missed, is the view of the Sagrada Familia church from Avinguda
de Gaudí. Due to the lack of space within the walled city and the
absence of large estates, no extensive park or garden exists in
central Barcelona, the only 'lungs' being provided by the
occasional large square and the waterfront, although the latter is
directly faced, in the city centre, by moles and dockyard buildings
that preclude a view of the open sea. All the major parks
surround the city, occupying hillside locations, but the most
central, Ciutadella, is low and easily approached on foot: the
parks of Montjuïc and Tibidabo may both be reached by road or
funicular. Alone of the great Mediterranean cities, Barcelona has
its own sandy beach, currently being extended and improved,
although most visitors never learn of its existence as it is
concealed by the triangular spur of Barceloneta. Sunday lunch
here, at a beachfront fish restaurant, is one of the liveliest culinary
experiences that the Mediterranean has to offer.

Although shops of interest may be found in most areas, the
leading fashion stores are concentrated in the Eixample,
particularly along Passeig de Gràcia, Rambla de Catalunya and
sections of Gran Via and Diagonal; many of them will be passed
on excursions to the Modernist buildings. Overseas visitors will
find virtually all the internationally known fashion houses
represented, but the prices charged will rarely be lower than in
their own countries and sometimes higher – things have changed a
great deal since the days of Franco, who virtually excluded foreign
goods from the country and kept the cost of locally made items
low. It should be emphasized that Barcelona's best known
thoroughfare, La Rambla, is for rambling rather than shopping.
Many visitors will find that Spanish food, generally unobtainable
outside the country or in the tourist resorts, is the best buy. Food
and drink in Barcelona is covered in a separate section (pages
205–25) and all that need be said here is that, like other Spanish
provinces, Catalonia possesses its own unique specialities which
most will find delicious.

### The People
Due to Barcelona's importance as a centre of employment, many
of its citizens are as likely to hail from Granada, or even Algiers,
as from ancient Catalan stock, and a cosmopolitan mix has
ensued. Nevertheless, it is still the Catalan with whom visitors will
most frequently come into contact. There is, of course, no 'typical
Catalan' but certain traits may be noticed, many of them
emanating from an intense national pride which has been
amplified by recent persecution. Although practically always
kindly and helpful, the Catalan possesses a greater seriousness
than most Mediterranean people, and some visitors find them
bland, in a Swiss or Swedish manner. Don't, therefore, expect the
back-slapping jollity of the Greek or the vocal brio of the Italian.
An expressed interest in Catalan culture, particularly its language
and cuisine, usually proves to be a good ice-breaker, but be
careful; some Catalans opt for complete integration with the rest
of Spain, a prime example being the painter Salvador Dalí, an

enthusiastic supporter of Franco. In particular, do not discuss the Civil War with elderly strangers: you can never be sure on which side they fought and memories of its horrors are still bitter. A great advantage of the Catalans' seriousness is that it inspires application and a capacity for hard work. In consequence, Barcelona is an efficiently run city, where everything generally operates to time, even though overseas visitors will find that most locations of tourist interest shut during the exasperatingly long lunch hour/siesta, apparently still inviolate throughout Spain. Catalan seriousness is rather amusingly expressed in its national dance, the Sardana, a stately jig in which participants rarely betray the vestige of a smile; it is believed to have evolved in Sardinia, once part of the Catalan empire.

Gifted and artistic as well as hard working, the Catalans organized Crafts Guilds in the Middle Ages, whose members were amongst the most talented in Europe. When the industrial revolution arrived, Barcelona was the first city in Spain to adopt the new inventions, thus laying the foundations of its position, which it still maintains, as the wealthiest manufacturing city in the country. Barcelona is today a leader in the field of graphic design, and only Paris and Milan surpass it as a fashion centre.

Since the return of democracy, Catalan nationalist aspirations have come to the fore, expressed, in particular, by their language, which once more has been given equal status with Spanish. On every possible occasion, the red and gold flag of Catalonia is waved, most enthusiastically by football fans celebrating a victory by their beloved 'Barça', the richest soccer club in the world. The Catalan national flag, created in 1082, is the oldest in the world, preceding Portugal's by a century. ˙

Conservatism is another Catalan trait, but it is shared with the rest of the country and is one of the reasons why Spanish cities remain, fortunately, so 'Spanish'. Until the development of Modernism, new architectural styles had been regarded with suspicion, and were late to be adopted in Barcelona. This same conservatism, however, has imbued the Catalans with a great sense of civic pride, a pride that has led to so much tasteful conservation in their cities. For a similar reason, the Catalan cuisine is in no danger of disappearing. In spite of Barcelona's proximity to France, her membership of the EC and the influx of immigrants and tourists from other countries, foreign specialities are still rarely found in the shops. Reminiscent of many Englishmen, the Catalan knows what he likes and likes what he knows.

Unfortunately for tourists, the Catalan does not differ from other Spaniards, in that he appears to believe that the onset of night has a blanketing effect on sound and that the decibels must, therefore, be turned up in order to be heard at all. From a quiet soul, he metamorphoses into a shouting, singing, ghetto-blaster-playing, engine-revving extrovert. He doesn't want to sleep and cannot imagine why anyone else should. Try to ensure that your hotel room doesn't overlook a street with late-night venues – or else go native and become nocturnal.

# The development of Barcelona

Barcelona's history may be summarized briefly as two five-hundred-year periods of stability under the rules of, respectively, the Romans and the medieval Catalan counts/kings, followed by complete or partial subjugation to Castile. Evidence of human occupation can be traced back five thousand years, a neolithic tomb of c.3000 BC having been discovered in Carrer Muntaner. It was the Iberians, however, who first established a settlement on Mons Taber, the low hill from where the streets of the old city still radiate. Greeks, Phoenicians and Carthaginians in turn conquered the enclave until, by tradition, Hamilcar Barca founded the city c.230 BC, naming it to commemorate his family, rulers of Carthage.

The Romans colonized Barca in 133 BC, and eventually the Emperor Augustus renamed it Colonia Favencia Julia Augusta Paterna Barcino, a name that, not surprisingly, was generally shortened to Barcino. Typically Roman in layout, the city was divided into quarters by two main streets, Cardo and Decumanus, which still exist but under several other names. At their intersection stood the forum and, on the summit of Mons Taber, a pagan temple, part of which survives *in situ*. Frankish raiders appear to have sacked Barcino in the third century and a defensive wall with watch-towers was built, much of which may still be seen. Excavations have revealed some of Roman Barcelona's streets, and these are now incorporated in the basement level of the City's History Museum.

After the Roman withdrawal in the fourth century the Vandals seized the city, but they were soon replaced by the Visigoths, led by Ataulf, in 419. By the sixth century, the Visigoths had adopted Roman Catholicism. However, evidence of their churches in Barcelona is limited to reused fragments and parts of the paleo-Christian basilica that lie beneath the Frederic Marés Museum.

From North Africa, the invasion of Europe by the Moors spread steadily northward, reaching Barcelona in 715. Their stay was brief, Charlemagne pushing them back in 801, and because of this, no Moorish buildings have survived in the city. Nevertheless, the influence of the Moors was not lost, as many became Mudéjar Christian converts and remained. Features of their architecture were often incorporated in later styles: stepped pyramid battlements, ceramic tiles and multi-lobed windows, reminiscent of North African kasbahs.

In 878, Guifred el Pilós founded the Catalan dynasty that was to rule for more than five hundred years. Complete independence from the Franks was established in 985 after they had failed to assist the city against the Moors under Al Mansour. Although the incursion only lasted six months, many churches were destroyed or badly damaged.

Barcelona's important buildings at this time were designed in the Romanesque style, introduced from southern France in the ninth century. Like the rest of Spain, Catalonia has always been conservative in its architecture, and Romanesque, with its massive walls, small round-headed windows and Lombard friezes, seems to have had a particular appeal, many of its features lasting well into the thirteenth century. Ramon Berenguer III rebuilt the Visigothic basilica in this style, 1046–58, but all that survives above ground level is its ceremonial portal, reused as a subsidiary doorway of the present cathedral.

Although more than 1,000 Romanesque churches may be seen in Catalonia, few exist in the city itself. The most important of these are the Chapel of Santa Llúcia, the Chapel of Marcus and the monastic church of Sant Pau del Camp. Secular buildings include the fabric of the Tinell Hall, part of the Bishop's Palace and the Palace of the Countess of Palamós. Some vernacular buildings retain their round-headed windows, particularly within the former Jewish quarter. In addition, Barcelona is fortunate to possess, displayed in its Museum of Catalan Art, a collection of Romanesque works, mostly from surrounding village churches, which is unsurpassed in the world.

In the eleventh century, Provence and Tarragona were incorporated in Catalonia, and in 1137 the kingdom was united with Aragon. The acquisition of Valencia, Ibiza, Majorca, Sicily, Sardinia, Greece and southern Italy followed, and by the fourteenth century the Catalan empire was the most extensive in the Mediterranean. The thirteenth century witnessed the beginning of Barcelona's medieval period of greatest prosperity, partly due to the development of the textile trade. New townships were built outside the Roman wall and Jaume I commissioned a new wall to encompass them. Alfons II established the Generalitat in 1289 and for the first time in Europe the absolutism of a monarch was effectively limited.

Gothic architecture reached Catalonia in the twelfth century, initially adopted by Cistercian monasteries, but it was not until the fourteenth century that all vestiges of the Romanesque style completely disappeared. Castile favoured northern European Gothic, but Catalonia was more influenced by Italy and developed its own version. In the warm, sunny south there was less need for the large window areas so desirable in the north, and the emphasis was on wide, open 'halls' with slender columns, thus providing maximum visibility; wherever possible, aisles were completely avoided. In order to permit wide, clear-span roofs, internal buttresses became an important feature, supporting a series of great arches in many secular buildings, including the Tinell Hall, the Stock Exchange, the Archives of the Crown of Aragon and the Hospital of Santa Creu.

The pointed arch, normally the most typical Gothic feature, was usually reserved for churches in Catalonia, as though it had some religious significance. Apart from Barcelona Cathedral, with its modern Gothic Revival façade, many other great churches in the Gothic style have survived, most notably Santa Maria del Mar, Santa Maria del Pi and Santa Anna. The external emphasis is on the horizontal line, rather than the vertical as in northern European Gothic. Although the main façades of Catalan Gothic churches, featuring deep portals, rose windows and flanking bell towers are satisfying enough, the remainder of their exteriors is plain to the point of dullness, largely because of the lack of visible buttresses and exotic tracery. Santa Maria del Mar, with its high vaults and delicate wide-spaced columns, is generally considered to possess the finest interior of all Barcelona's churches, including the cathedral.

The most impressive secular buildings to survive from the Middle Ages are undoubtedly the Generalitat and the Ajuntament, the seats, respectively, of provincial and city administration. In both, the pointed arch was employed, possibly because chapels were incorporated. An extraordinary Gothic survival is the Drassanes, begun in the thirteenth century for the construction, repair and dry-docking of ships, and now housing the Maritime Museum.

Barcelona retains more Gothic domestic buildings than any other city in the world, although some original features have been lost due to later remodelling. Many houses can only be differentiated easily from their Romanesque predecessors by the addition of a central lobe at the head of the windows. The basic structure, built around an arcaded patio, of a wide round-arched portal, roof-gallery and tower remained unchanged. 'Ajimez' windows, of two or three vertical lights separated by colonettes, continued to provide the main decorative feature of the façades; the type is believed to have been developed by the Visigoths.

The Catalan dynasty ended in 1410 when Martí the Humane died without an heir: henceforth, Castile was to dominate most of Spain. By inheritance, Ferdinand II and his consort Isabella, 'the Catholic Monarchs', became joint rulers of both Castile and Aragon in 1479, thus unifying the two great regions. Their religious zeal promoted the Inquisition throughout the land, including Catalonia and Aragon, where it had never previously been a burden. Dominican inquisitors were appointed in Barcelona, the main victims, as elsewhere in Spain, being converted Jews who were believed to have reverted to their original faith. Those convicted of irredeemable heresy against the Roman Catholic church were publicly burned to death at the stake, following trial at the ritual *auto-da-fé* (act of faith). In 1492, all unconverted Jews were banished from Spain, and Barcelona, in particular, lost many of its most gifted citizens.

With the expulsion of the Moors from Granada, their last Iberian stronghold, and the discovery of the New World by Christopher Columbus, 1492 was a great year for Spain as a whole, but not so good for Barcelona. Eleven years later, Seville was to be granted the monopoly of trade with America and the seeds of Barcelona's decline as a trading post were sown. The sixteenth century is known as Spain's 'Golden Age', due to the wealth and power that it gained from South American gold; however, this was a stagnant period for Barcelona, which is reflected by the almost complete lack of Renaissance architecture in the city, the richly decorated Spanish version of which, Plateresque, is particularly noticeable by its absence.

Philip II (1556–98) presided over the greatest empire that the world had ever seen but much of the wealth acquired from America was frittered away on indulgences and pointless wars. The defeat of Philip's Armada by the English in 1588 was a blow from which Spain never fully recovered, and the nation began a steady decline. Also a religious zealot, Philip gave further impetus to the Inquisition; this time, Protestants were considered to be the main heretics and their persecution continued in Spain until the Inquisition was finally suppressed in 1834.

Three major wars inhibited Catalan progress between 1618 and 1715: the Thirty Years War, the War of the Harvesters and the War of Succession. Philip V, having captured Barcelona, dissolved the Catalan kingdom in 1716, demoting it to provincial status. He also demolished most of the Ribera quarter of the city for the construction of a citadel, the largest in Europe. Due to this period of strife, little of importance was built in Barcelona in the Baroque style which was so dominant in other parts of Spain at the time. However, many existing buildings were remodelled: deep, balconied windows replaced their Gothic predecessors, and the façades were plastered to disguise the alterations. It became fashionable to create sgraffito designs on the façades by scratching the painted surface of one coat of plaster to reveal another in a contrasting colour. Sgraffito lasted from the late-seventeenth until the early-nineteenth century when it was replaced by terracotta decoration, which required far less maintenance. In the second half of the eighteenth century, Charles III ended the monopoly of trade with America that had by then passed from Seville to Cadiz, and Barcelona's long-established textile trade, in particular, began to prosper from this new market.

In spite of the Peninsular War with Napoléon, it was the nineteenth century that saw the establishment of Barcelona's modern prosperity, the city being the first in Spain to embrace the Industrial Revolution: the country's first railway line opened in 1848, between Barcelona and Mataró. Monastic establishments were dissolved in 1835 and their treasures dispersed: vast areas of land were thus made available for development, particularly around La Rambla. Even more significant was the demolition of the great medieval wall and its gateways in 1854; only a short fourteenth-century section, beside the medieval shipyards, survives. No development between the wall and the village of Gràcia to its west had been permitted, for defence reasons, but in 1859, with the great expansion of the city's population, a comprehensive building plan by Ildefons Cerdá was accepted. Thus was born the Eixample (extension), as the modern part of Barcelona is still known.

Barcelona's industry prospered, and immigrants from the agricultural areas moved to the city. Their working conditions were appalling, however, matching those of the United Kingdom a century earlier. In the 1830s the 'Renaixença' (Renaissance) of Catalan culture, initially literary, had crystallized into a movement that eventually became Modernism. Modernism was a philosophy linked with nationalism, rather than a Spanish version of the contemporary Art-Nouveau style as many believe. However, it is in the field of architecture that it is best remembered. Functional planning, the adoption of new structural techniques and the application of craft materials, preferably local, were the guiding principles. Architectural styles were eclectic, with an early emphasis on Catalan Gothic Revivalism, but frequently incorporating themes from other periods. Many architects became Modernists, although the leaders were unquestionably Lluís Domènech i Montaner, Josep Puig i Cadafalch and Antoni Gaudí i Cornet. Gaudí, as he is generally known, is by far the most famous Spanish architect internationally, although he eventually drifted away from the mainstream of Modernism, developing his own highly personal style based on the Art Nouveau principles of structures and forms taken from nature. Gaudí's idiosyncratic methods and their high cost limited his direct influence on others, and 'Gaudíism' never became a movement. Many buildings erected for the Universal Exhibition of 1888, held at Ciutadella, were Modernist and gave an immediate impetus to the movement, which lasted until 1914. Modernist buildings are generally recognizable from the multiplicity of materials that are employed, notably bricks, tiles, stained glass, ceramics, stone, mosaics and ironwork. Important examples by the three main exponents, all described in this book, include, by **Gaudí**: The Sagrada Familia, Casa Milà (La Pedrera), Güell Park, Güell Palace, Casa Batlló, Casa Calvet, Casa Vicenç, Güell Gatehouses and Colonia Güell; by **Domènech i Montaner**: Hospital de Sant Pau, Palau de la Música Catalana, Casa Fuster, Palau Montaner and Casa Thomas; by **Puig i Cadafalch**: Casa Terrades, Cuartel de Policia Nacional, Casa Quadras, Casa Serra, Casa Martí, Casa Macaya and Casa Company.

By 1908, Modernism had peaked and was gradually replaced by Noucentism, which was marked by a return to Classical themes. The buildings created for the Great Exhibition of 1929, at the foot of Montjuïc, were designed in this style and most of them remain as exhibition venues or museums.

For much of the present century, Barcelona was a hotbed of anarchy and, as the church was always closely linked with the establishment, it repeatedly suffered at the hands of dissidents. Much of great value was lost through arson in the 'Tragic Week' of 1909 and even more in July 1936, when very few of Barcelona's churches escaped extensive internal damage.

Catalonia was granted a high degree of autonomy in 1914, that lasted until 1923 when Primo de Rivera insisted on complete rule from Madrid. This autonomy was revived eight years later, following the dictator's fall and the abdication of Alfonso XIII. At the outbreak of the Civil War many Catalan priests were assassinated, including Irurita, the Bishop of Barcelona. Once more the city was on the losing side, and autonomy was again taken from Catalonia when, in 1939, General Franco came to power. During his dictatorship, Catalan culture was repressed and its language forbidden for any but private use.

Juan Carlos, grandson of Alfonso XIII, became head of state on Franco's death in 1975. General elections were held three years later and Catalonia became one of seventeen Spanish autonomies. The Generalitat and Catalan Parliament were reestablished and pressure is being maintained to gain even wider powers of self-determination. The hosting of the Summer Olympic Games in 1992 has led to the remodelling and extension of the sports facilities on Montjuïc, and the complete regeneration of the beach area east of Barceloneta, where the Olympic Village has been created. Barcelona's wealth has attracted another wave of immigrants from Spain's agricultural south and North Africa, many of whom have been unable to find work. Poverty, intensified by drug addiction, has led, not surprisingly, to crime. It is to be hoped that increasing prosperity and improved social welfare, promoted by EC membership, will solve this problem, one of the gravest to mitigate against the city's current 'Olympic' euphoria.

Meanwhile, work on Gaudí's Sagrada Familia church, the emblem of Barcelona, laboriously continues!

# Practical information

### Timing a visit

Barcelona boasts a typical Mediterranean climate, with very little rainfall between mid-May and mid-September. It is rarely cold, but July and August are almost always very hot and airless; it is then, of course, that the nearby beaches come into their own.

### Airport

Between 1989 and 1991 Barcelona's international airport, Aeroport del Prat, was virtually rebuilt, and is now one of the finest in Europe. Unlike most airports, it is not far from the city centre. Buses and, of course, taxis will transport visitors to Barcelona, but the speediest means of reaching the city is the RENFE train, which runs every thirty minutes throughout the day, arriving at Sants Station in just a quarter of an hour. Buses arrive at Plaça de Espanya.

### Accommodation

New accommodation, to cope with visitors to the 1992 Olympic Games, has greatly increased the supply of luxury hotel rooms, but there is still a shortage of middle-grade accommodation. Cheap rooms in *hostals* are in greater supply, although the very cheapest can be alarmingly basic. It is recommended that visitors stay close to the centre of the old city, as this is where most of their time will be spent. Unfortunately, the majority of the top-grade hotels are sited near the commercial areas in the Eixample, notable exceptions being the Almirante Colón, Rivoli, Ramada Renaissance and Royal. La Rambla itself is a good centre for moderately priced hotels, such as the Montecarlo, Oriente, Continental and International. The spring and autumn fairs put a great strain on the city's hotels as, of course, do international sporting events, and it is preferable that rooms be booked well in advance at such times. Since Spain entered the EC, prices have increased rapidly, but are still generally cheaper than most in Western Europe. They are always quoted per room, not per person, and vary widely according to season; visitors must expect to pay more when Barcelona is staging international events such as World Cup Football, World Cup Athletics or the Olympic Games.

### Trains

Sants Station is the most important railway terminal in Barcelona; in addition to its link with the airport, trains also leave from here for all major Spanish cities and for France via Gerona. Many will find it more convenient, however, to travel to Tarragona or Sitges from the RENFE Station at Passeig de Gràcia, which is linked with the Metro station of the same name. Prices of all train tickets are reduced by 25 per cent on 'Blue Days' and details of these are given at any station or information office.

### The Metro

The Metro system is the easiest method of travelling round this city of suffocating traffic jams. Although large areas of Barcelona are not covered by it, particularly within the Eixample, most locations of interest to tourists are within easy walking distance of a station. Lines are numbered L1, L3, L4 and L5. Tickets for individual journeys are sold, but it is much cheaper to buy, at any of the stations, a *tarjeta multiviaje* T2 ticket, valid for ten journeys anywhere on the system plus the FFCC Generalitat lines, although use of the latter entails a further cancellation of the ticket; also included are the bus and funicular to Tibidabo and the funicular and cable car to Montjuïc; again, each entails a further cancellation. Tickets must be inserted in the machines on entering the station, but not on leaving it. If the ticket has been folded it may jam, and the attendant will then cancel it manually. At Liceu station, there is no link between the two platforms, and passengers must ensure that they have entered on the correct side for the direction in which they wish to travel before purchasing or cancelling a ticket.

Trains are invariably clean, and lengthy delays are rare. Strangely, in such a late-night city, the last trains leave the centre by 23.00 Monday to Friday, although this is extended by two hours Saturday and Sunday nights. Most trains are now air-conditioned and each forthcoming stop is announced over the intercom. Illuminated panels in the compartments make the system even easier to follow.

The chief disadvantage of the Metro is that in spite of the limited number of lines, almost all connections between them necessitate lengthy treks along airless corridors, punctuated by short flights of steps. One wonders if the engineer responsible mislaid his compass! A dearth of 'down' escalators compounds the problem, and travellers with heavy luggage are recommended to splash out on a taxi, particularly when Sants Station is involved.

**Buses**
Nobody has yet devised a method of communication whereby city bus routes can be understood easily by those unfamiliar with them. Barcelona is no exception, and as it is subject to lengthy traffic jams for much of the day, most visitors ignore the system in favour of the Metro. On occasions, however, buses are more convenient; it is far easier, for example, to reach the beach at Barceloneta and most of the long Avinguda Diagonal by bus. Throughout this book, details of bus numbers and stops are given where appropriate.

Single-journey tickets are purchased on the vehicle, each being valid for the entire route taken by the bus, but not, as on the Metro, for interconnections. Because of this, some journeys will be more expensive than their Metro equivalents. As with the Metro, a *tarjeta multiviaje* T1 ticket for ten journeys is available, valid for bus or Metro, and may be purchased from the transport office on the west side of Plaça de Catalunya, facing Carrer Bergara.

Bus 100, operated by the Patronat de Turisme from the last week in June until mid September, is an exceptionally useful service for tourists linking, as it does, the city's peripheral locations of interest at an inclusive price. Tickets, purchased on the bus, are valid for either full-day or half-day (after 14.00) use and include the funicular and bus to the summit of Tibidabo and the funicular and cable car to Montjuïc. The service runs at half-hourly intervals, 09.00–19.30, and passengers may alight and depart at any of the stops as often as they wish. In one day, for example, the tourist is able to visit, in order: Güell Park, Tibidabo, Pedralbes Monastery and Montjuïc Park, thus saving much time and money. The most generally convenient points for joining the bus are in Plaça de Catalunya (outside the El Corte Inglés store) and Plaça Sant Jaume (facing the Generalitat).

## Taxis

Barcelona's taxi fares are more economical than most in
European cities; even a journey to the airport won't break the
bank as long as the traffic is not too heavy. Saturdays, late-
morning, early-afternoon and late-evening are when the traffic is
lightest and fares, in consequence, lowest. When free, a cab
displays the 'Libre' sign above its windscreen, which is augmented
at night by a green roof-light. Supplements are charged for
luggage, journeys after 22.00, Sundays, public holidays and
journeys to stations, the port or major sporting fixtures. Unless
fluent in Spanish, write out your destination clearly. A few drivers
are still unfamiliar with the recently restored Catalan street names
and if you can discover their former Spanish equivalents from
your hotel so much the better.

## Public holidays in Barcelona

On the following days virtually all buildings of public interest,
except churches, will be closed: 1 January, Good Friday, Easter
Monday, 1 May, 24 June*, 15 August, 11 September, 24
September*, 12 October, 1 November, 6 December, 8 December,
25 December, 26 December.

*Subject to change

## Orientation and directions

Due to the layout of the streets, which tend to run parallel with,
or at right angles to, the coastline, practically every map of
Barcelona is designed to run vertically from north-west to south-
west, rather than the usual north to south. The maps in this book
follow the same rule but, for simplicity, where directions are given
in the text the four cardinal points of the compass are adopted as
if north-west were true north, and so on. Exceptions are only
made to avoid confusion.

The medieval area of the city, which was enclosed by walls, lies
between the hillside parks of Montjuïc and Ciutadella, stretching
from Plaça de Catalunya to the sea. Although the walls have
gone, the obviously greater age of the buildings and the winding
nature of the streets still act as a visual barrier. Roman Barcelona
lay in the centre and much of its fourth-century wall survives.

The modern grid-plan city, still known as the Eixample
(extension), is most dramatically approached at Plaça de
Catalunya. Due to the chamfering of corners at intersections
(originally a traffic safety measure), to progress in a straight line is
a tiring business for the pedestrian, who must make a series of
semi-circular detours or else risk life and limb by ignoring the
crossings. It is preferable, therefore, to plan routes in the
Eixample that avoid too many long straight stretches, and this
principle has been followed throughout the book. Fortunately,
two of the leading shopping streets overcome this problem:
Passeig de Gràcia having right-angled corners and Rambla de
Catalunya a central promenade.

## Churches

Virtually all churches of interest to tourists are described in this
book. Every church in Barcelona, with the exception of Gaudí's
Sagrada Familia, is closed during the afternoon, generally from
13.00 to 17.00, but sometimes even longer: Santa Maria del Mar
rather puzzlingly closes at 12.00! When entry to a church is greatly
restricted, specific details are given. Return visits to some will

almost certainly have to be made if their interiors are to be seen. Understandably, visitors are not expected to tour a church during services. With the exception, again, of the Sagrada Familia, no entry charge is made for churches, but payment must be made to visit the interior of the cathedral's choir and museum.

## Museums/Art Galleries

In general, Sunday and Monday are best avoided for museums due to closures and, as with other public buildings, they usually shut during the afternoon: specific details are given for each one throughout this book. Although an admission charge is generally made it will be much more reasonable than in most other countries. However, municipally run museums charge only foreigners, a practice that I have never come across before outside third-world countries. It seems unlikely that EC regulations will permit this to continue to apply after 1992.

## Shops

The department stores and fashionable shops in the Eixample remain open throughout the day, but many will close early on Saturday in the summer, as well as, of course, all day Sunday. Smaller, non-specialist shops, particularly in the old city, generally close between 14.00 and 16.30 and for most of Saturday. Even on Sunday, however, some food shops, particularly bakers, will remain open.

## Banks and currency exchange

Opening hours are Monday to Friday 08.30–14.00; Saturday 08.30–12.00 or 13.00. Unfortunately, many Spanish banks continue to follow bureaucratic methods of changing money, involving form-filling and queues. Many branches refuse to accept Eurocheques. Passports and the customer's address in Spain are almost always requested, but I have not yet been asked my mother's maiden name! Try to avoid Monday mornings or days following public holidays when queues will be longest. Eurocheques, and travellers cheques issued overseas by the Banco de Bilbao in pesetas (generally at advantageous rates), are a good buy, because of the high minimum charge involved in changing travellers cheques in foreign currencies. If travellers cheques are taken, American Express offer by far the best replacement service; card membership is not necessary, and they may be purchased from Lloyds Bank and many building societies. An additional advantage is that no commission is charged when the cheques are changed at the Amex branch.

## Tipping

Spanish bars, restaurants and hotels always incorporate the service charge in their bill and an additional tip is not expected. It is usual, however, to add 10 per cent to a taxi fare as long as the meter has been used.

## Telephones

Grey-painted public booths are found in important streets and three five-peseta coins are sufficient for most local calls. Coins fall automatically from the top channel as needed. Many bars in the city provide telephones for public use and this, although usually a little dearer, is often the simplest way of telephoning. Calls made from hotel rooms are always much more expensive. International calls at a standard rate may be made from the Telefónica in Carrer Fontanella, facing Plaça de Catalunya, open Monday to Saturday 08.00–21.00. Here, English-speaking operators will make your connection and charge you at the end of the call without a supplement. Credit cards are accepted for reasonably expensive bills. Lower rates apply after 22.00. Direct dialling codes are 0744 for the United Kingdom and 071 for the United States.

## Toilet facilities

Although Barcelona is not well endowed with public toilets, restaurants, bars, hotels, cinemas and department stores must, by law, offer their facilities to anyone without charge. Railway and bus stations and department stores also provide them. A few plastic pay-on-entry units exist in particularly busy locations, such as Plaça de Catalunya and the port end of La Rambla. It is prudent to carry a small supply of toilet paper with you.

## Food and drink

Information is to be found in the separate section (pages 205–25).

## Language

The Catalan and Spanish (Castilian) languages have equal status in Barcelona, although whereas everyone speaks Spanish, fewer than half are fluent in Catalan.

All buildings and thoroughfares in Barcelona originally had Catalan names, but were changed to Spanish by decree of Franco. The Catalan versions have now been restored and it is these that appear on signs and up-to-date street maps. Most references in this book to Catalan people and places, therefore, are given in Catalan rather than in Spanish. However, Catalan places and non-Catalan personalities that are already well known to English-speaking visitors in another language are given in that form, unless used for identifying a location, e.g. Gerona rather than Girona, Ferdinand and Isabella rather than Fernando and Isabel, St Peter rather than Sant Pere.

Frequently, although not always, a Spaniard's name is formed by those of his father and mother, linked by *y* (and). In Catalan, the link-word is *i*, also meaning 'and'.

The Catalan language is thought to have originated in Provence, now a Department of France but once part of the Catalan empire, and similarities with the French language will be noted: *Si us plau* for please and *Merces* for thank you are commonly used examples. In spite of tales to the contrary, only a very unusual Catalan objects to speaking Spanish, particularly with non-Catalans, and the visitor with a modicum of Spanish will find it most useful. Older people may also speak French, but English is currently favoured among the young, and most students have at least a smattering of that language.

In view of the city's attraction for tourists, it seems strange that so many important notices at museums and art galleries are given in Catalan only, thus making them incomprehensible to most. The same criticism applies to those restaurants that only display a Catalan menu in their windows. It is to be hoped that pragmatism will eventually overcome such misplaced nationalism. The following brief vocabulary should overcome most general difficulties of this nature, and many more examples are given at the end of the Food and Drink section. The list basically comprises Catalan words that appear on notices, and Spanish words (shown in Italic) for use in conversation.

| Days of the week | | Seasons | |
|---|---|---|---|
| Sunday | Diumenge | Spring | Primavera |
| Monday | Dilluns | Summer | Estiu |
| Tuesday | Dimarts | Autumn | Tardor |
| Wednesday | Dimecres | Winter | Hivern |
| Thursday | Dijous | | |
| Friday | Divendres | **Questions** | |
| Saturday | Dissabte | What | *Qué* |
| | | Where is | *Dónde es* |

Apart from Gener for January the names of the months are easily understood

| Questions | |
|---|---|
| What | *Qué* |
| Where is | *Dónde es* |
| When | *Cuando* |
| How much | *Cuánto* |

| Opening details | | Polite terms | |
|---|---|---|---|
| Open | Obert | Good morning (or day) | *Buenós días* |
| Shut | Tancat | Good afternoon (or evening) | *Buenas tardes* |
| Until | Fins | Good night | *Buenas noches* |
| From | Des or de | Yes | *Sí* |
| After | Després | No | *No* |
| | | Please | *Por favor* |
| | | Thank you | *Gracias* |

**Christian names**

| Carles | *Carlos* | Charles |
|---|---|---|
| Ferran | *Fernando* | Ferdinand |
| Jaume | *Jaime* | James |
| Joan | *Juan* | John |
| Pau | *Pablo* | Paul |
| Pere | *Pedro* | Peter |

**Numbers** (Spanish are universally understood)

| 0 | *cero* | 10 | *diez* | 20 | *veinte* |
|---|---|---|---|---|---|
| 1 | *uno* | 11 | *once* | 21 | *veintiuno* |
| 2 | *dos* | 12 | *doce* | 30 | *treinta* |
| 3 | *tres* | 13 | *trece* | 40 | *cuarenta* |
| 4 | *cuatro* | 14 | *catorce* | 50 | *cincuenta* |
| 5 | *cinco* | 15 | *quince* | 60 | *sesenta* |
| 6 | *seis* | 16 | *dieciséis* | 70 | *setenta* |
| 7 | *siete* | 17 | *diacisiete* | 80 | *ochenta* |
| 8 | *ocho* | 18 | *dieciocho* | 90 | *noventa* |
| 9 | *nueve* | 19 | *diecinueve* | 100 | *cien* |

**Toilets**

| *Lavabos* | Toilets – mixed |
|---|---|
| *Servicios* | Toilets – mixed |
| Serveis | Toilets – mixed |
| *Aseos* | Toilets – mixed |
| *Señores* | Gentlemen |
| Senyors | Gentlemen |
| *Caballeros* | Gentlemen |
| Dames | Ladies |
| *Señoras* | Ladies |
| Senyores or | |
| *Senyoretes* | Ladies |

# Information offices

**Barcelona information only**
Sants Station  daily 08.00–22.00
Conference Centre, Avinguda Reina Christina  during conference periods.
La Virreina Palace, 99 La Rambla.  Summer only, Monday–Saturday 10.00–21.00
Ajuntament, Plaça Sant Jaume.  Summer only, Monday–Friday 08.00–20.00, Saturday 08.00–15.00

**All Spain information, including Barcelona**
Barcelona Patronat de Turisme, 35 Passeig de Gràcia  Monday–Friday 08.00–15.00
658 Gran Via,  Monday–Friday 09.00–19.00, Saturday 09.00–14.00
Airport,  daily 07.00–23.00.

Information officers wearing Red Jackets may be found during July, August and September in the Gothic Quarter, Passeig de Gràcia and La Rambla

**Crime or accident**
A special office for assisting visitors who become the victims of criminals, or meet with an accident, has been set up at 43, La Rambla (Tel. 3019060). The service operates 24 hours a day. English-speaking personnel offer legal and medical advice, provision of temporary replacement documents and an international telephone facility.

# 1

## Cathedral and Roman Wall

The area skirting the Roman wall, almost half of which survives, provides many of Barcelona's outstanding historic viewpoints. Practically all the wall is passed on this route before entering the ecclesiastical core of the city, which radiates from the medieval cathedral. Also visited is the Frederic Marés Museum, with its outstanding collection of works of art from the Roman period to the nineteenth century.

*Timing:* The patio of the Bishop's Palace closes at weekends.

The Frederic Marés Museum is closed Sunday afternoon, Monday and 14.00–16.00.

Barcelona Cathedral and the Santa Llucía Chapel are closed 13.30–16.00.

The 'Gothic' antiques market is held in Plaça Nova every Thursday.

Passers-by join in the Sardana, Catalonia's national dance, in Plaça de la Seu, Sunday from 12.00.

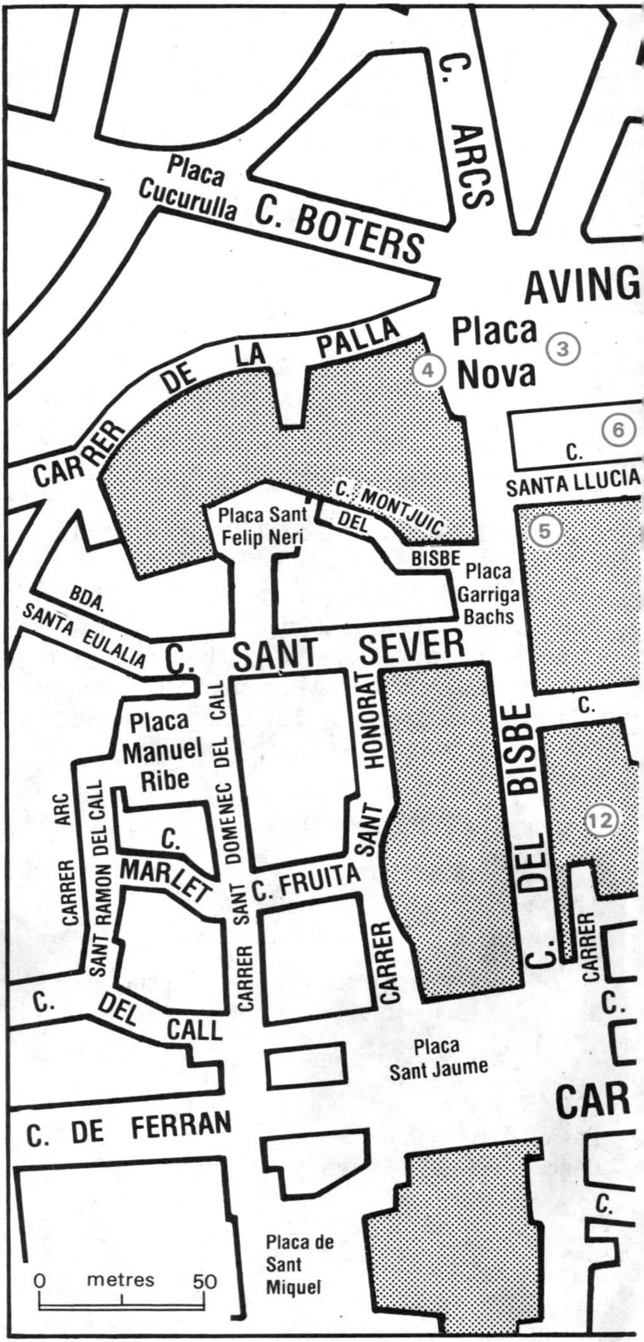

Placa
Cucurulla    C. BOTERS

C. ARCS

AVING

DE   LA   PALLA
Placa ③
④ Nova

CARRER

C. ⑥
SANTA LLUCIA

C. MONTJUIC
Placa Sant   DEL
Felip Neri
BISBE   Placa
⑤
Garriga
Bachs

BDA.
SANTA EULALIA   C.   SANT   SEVER

Placa
Manuel
Ribe

C. DEL

CALL

DOMENEC DEL CALL

SANT HONORAT

ARC

CARRER

SANT RAMON DEL CALL

C.
MARLET   C. FRUITA

CARRER

CARRER

C.   DEL   CALL

C. DEL BISBE

C.

⑫

CARRER

C.

Placa
Sant Jaume

CAR

C. DE   FERRAN

C.

Placa de
Sant
Miquel

0   metres   50

**Start:** *M Jaume I, line 4. Exit ahead to the west side of Plaça de l'Àngel.*

| Location 1 | **PLAÇA DE L'ÀNGEL** |
|---|---|

During the Roman period, this square formed part of a field that faced the east gate of the wall. The gate, flanked by cylindrical towers, was later surmounted by the Viscount's Castle, which eventually became a prison. One tower survived until the 18C and the other, together with the prison, was demolished in the late 19C. From this gate ran Decumanus, the most important Roman road within the city. Outside the wall the road continued south-eastward to the port, cutting diagonally through the field.

By the 10C, a village had evolved around the field, which became its square and was called the Plaça del Blat (wheat) due to the covered grain market built in the centre.

A medieval legend that St Michael miraculously appeared in the square was commemorated by placing a figure of the angel on the Viscount's Castle. This was removed in 1616 when, following the Italian fashion, an obelisk was erected in the centre of the square, surmounted by a new bronze angel. The city council ordered the removal of the obelisk in 1823, but the angel (always wingless) was transferred to a niche in the building on the north side of the square. It has since been replaced by a copy and the original is displayed in the City's History Museum.

*Exit from the square at its north-west corner and follow c Tapineria northward.*

**Carrer Tapineria** runs parallel to the most impressive surviving stretch of the Roman wall. Its name, a medieval word, refers to the many shoemakers who formerly had premises in the area.

| Location 2 | **ROMAN WALL** |
|---|---|

Barcelona, settled by the Romans between 15 and 7BC, suffered a major attack, probably by the Franks, in the 4C, which led to the immediate construction of a defensive wall, with a perimeter of approximately 1,200 yards, enclosing the relatively small area of Mons (Mount) Taber. Half of the wall appears to have been demolished 1837–77, but good stretches survive to the north and east and other remnants may remain, incorporated in existing houses.

A cornice throughout indicates the height of the Roman structure, which was built of hewn stone to a width of approximately 12 feet. No indentations or superstructures to it were permitted until the 13C, when Jaume I erected a new city wall, enclosing a much larger area. All the round-headed Romanesque detailing, therefore, dates from the early 13C. Subsequent Gothic work is apparent, notably the lobed windows and the great curved arches, which were built during the Middle Ages to support new superstructures. Missing Roman sections have been replaced with red bricks, thus making the original work immediately apparent.

Rising above the Roman wall is the gallery of the **House of Clariana-Padellàs**, a 14C structure originally sited in Carrer Mercaders but re-erected on its present site in 1930.

*➥ Continue ahead to the equestrian statue in pl de Ramon Berenguer el Gran.*

This small square faces the most spectacular section of the Roman fortification. The entire wall was punctuated at regular intervals by rectangular watch towers, originally 50 feet high, but subsequently heightened. An example, ahead, supports the bell tower of the royal chapel of Santa Agata, rising above the wall, which was built over it in the late 13C.

Three of the original four small Roman windows survive (two blocked) at the base of the bell tower.

Protruding from this building towards the square is the Queen's Chapel, added in the mid 14C. Its two rosette windows are original.

A much smaller, gabled chapel, with one rosette window, projects further to the north. This was added by Martí I and his consort Maria de Luna *c.* 1400.

The 'perfect Gothic' building, R of the Santa Agata Chapel, is a 1952 reconstruction of work that had been demolished in the 19C. It links the royal chapel with the great hall (Tinell) of the palace.

*➥ Follow the perimeter of the square anticlockwise and continue northward.*

The bronze equestrian statue of Ramon Berenguer III (1096–1131) is a modern work by **Josep Llimona**.

Carrer Tapineria now passes 19C houses, which were built when the wall here was demolished.

The stretch of wall that follows is composed almost entirely of modern brickwork.

*➥ Continue past bda Canonja (first L).*

Immediately L is the gabled rear of the House of Pious Alms, built in the mid 15C.

At a right angle to this building, lying back, Romanesque features above wall level indicate the rear of the Canons' house that served as the residence of a fraternity of Augustinian Canons until they were disestablished in 1369.

Each of the four angles of the Roman Wall was marked by circular or polygonal towers, and the example ahead stood at the north-east angle.

In its north face, the two-light Romanesque window was inserted early in the 13C.

*➥ Cross to the north side of av Catedral. Turn L and proceed westward. Immediately L is pl de la Seu, dominated by Barcelona Cathedral. A further major stretch of wall follows.*

Two rectangular towers, both heightened, survive in this section of the wall, which supports part of the Archdeacon's House.

All the gateways were originally flanked by cylindrical towers. The two R, the only remaining examples, guarded the entrance to the second major Roman street, Cardo, which ran north to south, crossing Decumanus at right angles, thereby dividing the city into quarters.

Both towers were heightened and remodelled in the
12C and windows were inserted in the 16C.

In the Middle Ages, the entrance was known as the
Bishop's Gate, as it adjoined the Bishop's Palace to
the west. However, at that time both towers were
linked by an archway and incorporated in the
Archdeacon's House. The arch and its roof-gallery,
added in 1614, were demolished in 1823 to permit the
passage of higher vehicles, and the north tower R,
now separated from its twin, was integrated with the
Bishop's Palace.

Until the present century, these towers were the only
part of Barcelona's Roman wall that were exposed,
an indication of the tremendous clearance and
restoration that have taken place in modern times.

●● *Cross to the south side of av Catedral and proceed
to pl Nova, facing the cylindrical towers.*

| | |
|---|---|
| Location 3 | **PLAÇA NOVA** |

*'Gothic' antiques
market, Thursday.*

Like Plaça de l'Àngel, Plaça Nova was a field until
the early Middle Ages. It was extended in 1353 by the
acquisition of the orchard belonging to the Bishop's
Palace, which closed its west side.

The triangular square was gradually built up, but in
1939 lost its enclosed character when Avinguda
Catedral was laid out. Until recently, houses built in
the 19C formed its east side, clustering around and
concealing the wall at the rear of the Archdeacon's
House, but these were demolished in 1960 and
replaced by the present gardens, thereby increasing
the openness of the square.

●● *Proceed ahead towards the cylindrical tower L.*

Behind a glass-fronted niche, a gilded figure
represents St Roc. On 16 April, the Saint's feast day,
the figure is adorned with flowers, the square
decorated and the Sardana danced.

Immediately L of the niche survives a remnant of the
Roman aqueduct that brought water to the city.

Every Thursday, a 'Gothic' antiques market is held in
the square. This is transferred on occasions to Plaça
del Pi.

●● *Proceed R to the Classical façade of the Bishop's
Palace, which still occupies the west side of pl Nova.*

| | |
|---|---|
| Location 4 | **BISHOP'S PALACE (PALAU DEL BISBE)** |

1 Plaça Nova

*Patio open (from c
del Bisbe)
Monday–Friday
09.00–14.00.
Admission free.*

The severe 18C façade to Plaça Nova is of little
interest, but Romanesque and Gothic detailing may
be seen in the patio, approached later from Carrer
del Bisbe.

The earliest episcopal palace had been sited in Carrer
dels Comtes and survives as the nucleus of the
Frederic Marés Museum. Work began on a new
palace on the present site in the late 12C. Although
Gothic windows were inserted in 1482, the entire
Plaça Nova façade was rebuilt in 1784 in Classical
style.

Within a niche R, beside the gate, stands the figure of
Manuel Irurita i Almándoz, Bishop of Barcelona,
who was assassinated in 1936. To commemorate him,

the street was renamed Calle del Bisbe Irurita during the Franco period; Irurita was officially dropped in 1989.

•● *Follow c del Bisbe southward.*

Simple sgraffiti were added to this section of the Bishop's Palace in the 18C.

•● *First R enter the patio.*

The patio gained its present appearance in 1928, when the south wing L was built. During construction work, remains of the Romanesque gallery on the north and west sides were discovered and restored.

The range R is all that survives of the late-12C building. Original features include the entrance arch at the head of the steps and, R of the steps, two further arches, followed by traces of three more, now blocked but with two of their capitals exposed.

To their right is the outline of another Romanesque arch, which was filled and partly replaced in the 15C by a two-light, Flamboyant Gothic window.

Facing the entrance to the patio is the extension built at a right angle to the existing building in 1257. This replaced two houses which were acquired and demolished.

On its ground floor, the original gallery was continued, retaining the Romanesque style, by adding three more arches, now filled with stained glass.

Capitals of their supporting columns are foliated.

Modern frescos decorate the gallery.

•● *Exit from the patio L. First R c Santa Llúcia. Immediately R is the Santa Llúcia Chapel.*

| Location 5 | SANTA LLÚCIA CHAPEL |
|---|---|

Carrer Santa Llúcia

*Open 07.30–13.30 and 16.00–19.30.*

This small, simply designed Romanesque chapel, now apparently part of the cathedral, in fact pre-dates it by thirty years, having been constructed for Bishop Arnau de Gurb in 1268 to serve as the chapel of the Bishop's Palace. Originally, the dedication was to Mary and her saints, but later this was restricted solely to St Lucy, patron saint of those suffering from sight or mind disorders.

The portal's archivolts are heavily decorated with the usual Romanesque foliage and geometric patterns.

Depicted on the capital of the first rounded column L are the *Annunciation* and the *Visitation*.

The tympanum retains traces of a painting of St Lucy, by **Joan Llimona**, 1901.

The two-bell belfry, a 17C addition, bears the date 1681 on its upper section.

•● *Enter the chapel.*

Square in plan, the chapel is barrel vaulted.

Several recesses have been created, all with pointed arches and therefore dating from the Gothic period.

Immediately L is the mid-14C tomb chest of Canon Francesc de Santa Coloma.

Set into its base is the marble tombstone of Jauffred de Santa Coloma, dated 1319.

Opposite, behind a glass panel, is the sepulchre of Bishop Arnau de Gurb, *d.*1284, who was responsible for building this chapel and for the 13C extension to the Bishop's Palace. The recumbent figure of the Bishop, depicted in his robes, was made soon after his death.

Various tomb slabs are fitted in the pavement.

The canopied altar was installed and the wall of the apse painted in 1947, replacing earlier work destroyed in 1936.

Immediately L of the exit, a 14C marble font is supported by a twisted column.

*Exit from the chapel R (ignoring the passageway to the cathedral's cloister). Immediately L is the Archdeacon's House.*

| Location 6 | **ARCHDEACON'S HOUSE (CASA DE L'ARDIACA)** |
|---|---|

Carrer Santa Llúcia

*Patio, stairway and gallery open Monday–Saturday. Admission free.*

Although not completed in its cloister-like form until the 19C, the arcaded patio of the house is one of the most picturesque in the city.

The earliest Archdeacon's House, parts of which survive, was built in the 12C on the same site, attached to the Bishop's Gate and the Roman wall. Remodelling took place in the 15C and again *c.*1500 when the building was extended for Archbishop Lluís Desplà.

Ahead, the boundary wall is dominated by its Renaissance doorway.

Immediately R of the doorway is the letter-box, surrounded by swallows and a tortoise, possibly a reference to the eccentricity of Spain's postal service. (The many tourists who return home several weeks before their postcards arrive may consider that little has changed.) It is the work of the great Modernist architect, **Domènech i Montaner**, 1902.

*Enter the patio.*

Most of the house dates from the *c.*1500 remodelling, and combines Flamboyant Gothic forms with Italian Renaissance details. However, the patio owes much to the 1870 extension of **Josep Altamira**. Only the main wall of the house, ahead, originally possessed a colonnade; the other three, which now form an enclosed cloister, are entirely **Altamira's** 19C work.

In the centre of the patio stands an original Gothic fountain: its mushroom-top stem is modern.

The stairway L leads to the first-floor gallery, where most features date from the 15C remodelling.

Since 1919, the building has housed the archives of the Institut Municipal d'Historia de Barcelona and is open only to those engaged in research work.

*Descend the stairs and exit L. First L pl de la Seu.*

The east wall of the building, facing the square, originally belonged to the Dean's House, which was later integrated with the Archdeacon's House. Built in the 14C, the Dean's House then extended into

what is now Plaça de la Seu, but much of it was
demolished *c.*1420 when the square was created. The
present façade, incorporating the Roman watch
tower, was begun *c.*1548 for Dean Jaume Estela.

Like the Archdeacon's House, the building was
restored by **Altamira** in 1870 and again by **Josep
Goday** in 1919.

*•• Proceed to the square.*

| Location 7 | **PLAÇA DE LA SEU** |
|---|---|

*Sardana danced
Sunday from 12.00.*

Formerly known in Spanish as the Plaza de la
Catedral, the square's present Catalan name, Seu,
similarly refers to the cathedral. When it was first laid
out in 1422, the houses in Carrer de la Corribia,
which faced the cathedral, were all lost. In addition, a
long stretch of the Roman wall, at that time still
unbroken, had to be demolished, together with some
of the former canons' houses that had survived on the
east side. Nevertheless, the square was significantly
smaller until 1943, when buildings, including some
16C taverns which closed its north side, were
demolished for the construction of Avinguda
Catedral. Fortunately, the Renaissance façade of the
esparto workers' guild-house was saved and
reconstructed in Plaça Sant Felip Neri.

Every Sunday from midday, weather permitting, a
small orchestra plays in the square, passers-by place
their jackets and bags in a bundle, hold their arms
aloft, link hands and solemnly perform a stately jig,
known as the Sardana, Catalonia's national dance.
Wind instruments, mainly brass, plus a solitary cello,
make up the orchestra, which produces a wistful
sound.

From 13 December, the Feast of St Lucy, a fair is
held in the square.

*•• Cross to the east side of the square. At the south
end is the entrance to the House of Pious Alms.*

| Location 8 | **HOUSE OF PIOUS ALMS (PIA ALMOINA)** |
|---|---|

Plaça de la Seu

*Open for
exhibitions.*

A combination of mid-15C and 16C structures
provides the former headquarters of this medieval
house of charity, but over-heavy restoration in the
18C removed most original detailing.

The Pious Alms Institution was founded in 1009 to
provide a daily supply of food for 100 poor people. Its
premises were built here *c.*1450 on part of the site of
the house of the Augustinian Canons, who had been
disbanded in 1369.

The gabled section of the building, most of which
from 1991 will accommodate the Diocesan Museum,
dates from *c.*1450. This structure runs eastward along
Baixada Canonja, where it ends with a similar gable,
already described.

Below the first-floor windows are carved, from L to
R: the shield of the Catholic Chapter, attributes of
the Passion, and St Eulalia (now headless). The
building lost the remainder of its Gothic detailing in
the 18C, and restoration in 1989 was not particularly
sympathetic to its antiquity.

*•• Proceed northward.*

In 1546, the House of Pious Alms was extended northward in Catalan Gothic style, including a roof-gallery, now filled.

In the lintels of some windows, the date 1743 proudly records the building's unfortunate restoration when, once again, most Gothic details were lost.

On the Avinguda Catedral corner, between the two street names, are carved the shield of the Catholics and, below, the Holy Cross, both Gothic work.

•● *Return southward and enter L the building if an exhibition is being held.*

•● *Exit L. Immediately ahead c dels Comtes.*

•● *Alternatively, exit from the museum L and proceed to the cathedral.*

Forming the north side of Plaça de la Seu is Barcelona Cathedral. All of the building that is visible from this point was constructed in the late 19C and early 20C and the description of the cathedral begins when its genuine Gothic section is reached, immediately following the next location. However, as the cathedral closes in the afternoon and visitors are not permitted to tour the interior during Mass, it may prove more convenient to enter at this stage. The description begins on page 12.

Forming the east side L of Carrer dels Comtes are 19C houses that have been adapted to accommodate part of the Frederic Marés Museum.

These are followed by the rusticated stone façade of the former Bishop's Palace, now the core of the museum. The bishops lived here until their new palace was built further west in the late 12C. Jaume II acquired the building as an extension to the royal palace in 1316.

Four three-light Romanesque windows are original but mostly restored. At one period, a bridge, since demolished, linked the building with the cathedral at first-floor level and some of these windows were then filled.

Originally, the main entrance to the house was situated below the third window, but this has since been converted to a grilled aperture.

Fixed to the wall R, the royal arms of Philip II retain traces of gilding. Although original, they were placed here in modern times to record that the building was presented to the dreaded Tribunal of the Inquisition by Ferdinand and Isabella in 1487.

•● *First L pl Sant Iu.*

---

| Location 9 | **PLAÇA SANT IU** |

Forming the south side of this square R is the building that now houses the Archives of the Crown of Aragon. When this was built to accommodate the viceroy in the mid-16C, the section of the royal palace that stood beside it, linking the great hall (Tinell) with Carrer dels Comtes, was demolished. Although a relatively small structure, as this building immediately faced the cathedral (which is partly dedicated to Santa Eulalia) it was known as the Santa Eulalia Palace. Its removal permitted the creation of the present square in 1545.

Facing the cathedral is the gallery that was constructed in 1950 to provide public access, via steps R, to the Tinell and its exhibitions.

In 1936, the Renaissance doorway was brought to the south wall of the former Bishop's Palace L from Plaça del Rei, where it had been erected in 1542 to provide a direct entrance to the Tinell.

●● *Proceed through this doorway to the patio of the Frederic Marés Museum.*

---

Location 10

**FREDERIC MARÉS MUSEUM (MUSEU FREDERIC MARÉS)**

Plaça Sant Iu

*Open Tuesday–Sunday 09.00–14.00 and 16.00–19.00. (Closed Sunday afternoon.) Admission free. NB Upper floors are frequently closed in the afternoons and at weekends.*

The collection of wealthy Barcelona sculptor Frederic Marés was offered to the city in 1940. It is housed in the early-13C Bishop's Palace and other buildings that were specially constructed for the purpose. The museum opened in 1943. Exhibits range from Antique and Baroque sculpture to varied ephemera. Particularly outstanding are the polychromatic wooden carvings.

Immediately L, above an open, vaulted ground floor, is the former Bishop's Palace, now serving as the nucleus of the museum.

The buildings that house the museum's exhibits are modern, although some of the stonework and detailing were taken from ancient, dismantled structures.

A fountain and orange trees embellish the patio, which originally formed part of the garden of the royal palace.

Occupying the south side of the patio (the entry side) is the Tinell Hall, fronted by an arcade.

Below this structure may be glimpsed, through grilled apertures, excavated areas of Roman Barcelona, now incorporated in the City's History Museum.

●● *Descend from the patio to view remains of the Paleo-Christian cathedral (if open).*

The nave of the building straddled the north end of the present cathedral, crossing Carrer dels Comtes, and its apse lay beneath the royal palace. The 4C basilica was dedicated to St Eulalia and the Holy Cross (Santa Creu) in 559.

●● *Ascend and proceed eastward towards the steps to the second patio, which are flanked by Roman Corinthian columns.*

Three pairs of 11C Romanesque windows, separated by modern buttresses, light the Tinell.

At its east end, the large window originally served as a doorway, leading via steps to the garden.

The east extension to the Tinell is a modern replacement of the building that originally linked it with the royal chapel.

●● *Return to the first patio and enter the museum R. Cross the inner patio to the first room and descend to the basement.*

**Basement** Stone carvings from the 10C–16C include many fine capitals.

The Romanesque *Portada de Anzano*, seen immediately L, is outstanding.

**Ground floor** Roman finds in Barcelona are displayed, together with polychromatic wood carvings of religious scenes from all parts of Spain.

**First floor** Sculptures and wood carvings from the 14C to 19C include, in **Room 28**, a famous *Entombment* depicting seven figures laying Christ in his tomb.

Against the same wall is an outstanding 17C *Adoration of the Magi* by **Nalda Logrono**.

•● *Ascend to the* **second floor** *by lift from the rear of the reception desk.*

Many will find the ephemeral exhibits on this floor of greatest appeal. They include: fans, gloves, parasols, keys, irons, clocks and cameras. An exceptional collection of smokers' requisites, including pipes from Roman times, is housed in **Room 36**.

•● *Exit from the museum and return to pl de Sant Iu, immediately facing the Sant Iu portal of the cathedral.*

---

Location 11 | **BARCELONA CATHEDRAL**

*Open daily 07.30–13.30 and 16.00–19.30.*

**Cloister** *open daily 08.45–13.30 and 16.00–19.00.*

**Museum** *open Monday–Saturday 11.00–13.00 and Sunday (nominal charge). Admission charge to the museum and choir. The choir is open free for Sunday morning Mass.*

Apart from a few Romanesque touches, most of Barcelona Cathedral, begun in 1298, is an homogeneous example of early Catalan Gothic. The one important exception is its Gothic Revival façade, only started in the late 19C and inappropriately designed in northern European style. Few of Barcelona's ecclesiastical buildings escaped the arsonists in 1936, but the Generalitat ensured that the cathedral was permanently guarded, and its treasures have survived intact. Most chapels are embellished with a reredos, many of which are spectacular examples of Baroque workmanship. Other highlights include the Gothic choir, with its Renaissance screen, the crypt of Santa Eulalia, and the unique cloister, home to noisy white geese. Unfortunately, the treasury may no longer be visited, and the high altar's great 14C reredos has been controversially transferred to Sant Jaume.

**History** As recently as 1930, excavations disclosed remains of a relatively large church dating from the Roman period and these may now be visited following their restoration, as described on page 11. The Moors, led by Al Mansour, demolished much of this building in 985, and Ramon Berenger I, el Vell (the elder), commissioned a new cathedral, in Romanesque style, 1046–58. This was sited further to the north, with its apse nestling against the section of the Roman wall that then still existed, prior to the construction of Plaça de la Seu. Its ceremonial south doorway, which has been reused, is sited at the north end of the present nave.

Jaume II began the present cathedral in 1298 and work was completed by 1417, apart from the main façade, which was to remain little more than a plain wall until the late 19C. The architect of the building is unknown, but modifications to his original detailing appear to have been made at an early stage, as Romanesque features were soon abandoned.

**Exterior**

**East Transept** This arm of the transept, which does not extend from the building line, faces Plaça de Sant

Iu and appears to mark the point where construction began.

Its restrained but elegant portal, dedicated to St Iu (Ivor), combines marble with Montjuïc stone.

Carved figures decorating the capitals are still Romanesque in style.

Within a niche in the tympanum stands a figure that is believed to represent St Ivor. It is flanked by small carved heads, now rather faded.

Busts of heavenly musicians extend from the Flamboyant spandrels on either side of the portal's arch.

Panels on both sides of the portal, at low level, record the commencement of building work in 1298.

Above these are carvings of a man with a griffin and a man battling with a lion. These are believed to be 12C work, and may have been retained from the Romanesque cathedral.

Surmounting this transept is an octagonal bell-tower, more clearly seen later.

•● *Proceed southward.*

The two bays of the chancel between the east transept and the apse have round-headed Romanesque windows, a feature that does not recur on the west side, thus tending to confirm that this is earlier work.

•● *Continue southward to the polygonal apse.*

It was on this side that construction of the apse began in 1317 and the architect responsible until 1338 was **Jaume Fabre**.

All the arches of the apse are pointed.

The buttresses are external, unlike those supporting the nave, and surmounted with gargoyles.

•● *Proceed south-east of the apse to the corner of bda Santa Clara and c Freneria.*

From this point, the east transept's octagonal bell-tower, typical of Catalan Gothic work, may be seen more clearly. It was completed in 1393.

Also from here can be seen the matching bell-tower, positioned above the west transept. This was built in 1386, seven years before its twin.

•● *Follow the west side of the apse northward.*

Work was not completed on this side of the apse until 1379.

Protruding immediately ahead the sacristy and treasury conceal much of the chancel and the west transept.

The south entrance to the cloister, built in 1457, faces the street and is known as the Portal of Piety (Pietat).

The portal's tympanum is decorated with a wooden Pietà, also 15C work, believed to have been executed by the German, **Michael Lochner**, who was carving the cathedral's choir stalls during this period; only traces of the original paintwork survive.

The figure at Christ's feet represents the donor of the piece, Canon Berenguer Vila.

Little more can be seen of the west side of the body of the cathedral as it is obscured by the cloister.

*•• Return eastward to Pl de Sant Iu and follow the nave northward.*

Work was suspended on the nave in 1381 when it was two bays short of its present length, and a temporary north wall was built.

Like the chancel, the upper windows of the first building stage of the nave on this side are round headed (they are pointed on the west side).

Work recommenced in 1413 and the last two bays were completed within four years.

Both upper windows of this extension are pointed.

*•• Continue ahead to the north façade in Pl de la Seu.*

When external work on the cathedral came to a halt in 1417, the important north façade was an undecorated wall. Windows, with some Gothic tracery, were placed asymmetrically, and a portal, with carved archivolts in Catalan Gothic style, provided the entrance. Above the structure could be seen the low, pyramidal base prepared in the 15C to support a superstructure. Something eventually had to be done, but it was not until the late 19C that a wealthy industrialist, Manuel Girona, offered to provide the finance for a worthier façade. Various schemes were proposed, but eventually the design of **Josep Oriol Mestres** and **August Font** was selected. The starting point and inspiration for their work was a drawing for the portal prepared by the Rouen architect, **Charles Galtes**, known in Catalonia as Carlí, in 1408. Not surprisingly, therefore, the resulting façade imitates North European Gothic work, with its emphasis on the vertical, rather than Catalan Gothic which features a horizontal line. Many believe that a façade in the style of Santa Maria del Mar would have blended more sympathetically with the surrounding 'Gothic Quarter'. Nevertheless, the result is undeniably picturesque and the craftsmanship of a high order.

The portal and its flanking buttresses are almost exact reproductions of the design by **Carlí**.

The centrally placed north tower, with its spire, was financed by the sons of the patron of the façade and completed in 1913. Although it occupies an unusual position for a Gothic tower, there are precedents at Ulm and Freiburg in Germany.

*•• Enter the cathedral.*

Upon entering the cathedral, which is orientated south/north, almost immediately above may be seen the interior of the short tower that supports the spire. Work began on its base in 1422 but was halted after six years and a timber roof erected. Although intended to be a temporary feature, the timber roof survived for almost five hundred years, and was not removed until 1913, when the tower was at last built.

The four piers, vaulting and octagonal balustraded gallery, together with their decorative features, by the **Claperós** family (father and son), are 15C work.

*•➡ Proceed ahead towards the choir screen.*

A shallow triforium passage, at the same level as the tower's gallery, continues around the building.

Below this runs a Romanesque Lombard frieze, presumably begun at an early construction stage.

Roof bosses of the nave retain traces of their paintwork, which spreads to the vault itself.

*•➡ Proceed R towards the west aisle (ignoring the choir at this stage).*

As is usual in major Catalan churches, the aisles are remarkably high.

Bays, formed by the buttresses, are all sub-divided to provide two chapels.

A broad gallery runs above them.

*•➡ Continue to the most northerly of the west chapels.*

The Catalan and Spanish names of most chapels are displayed on plaques and there are generally multiple dedications. For the sake of brevity, however, only the first name shown is given in this book. Chapels of little interest are not described.

Iron grilles screen each chapel.

Bosses generally depict the saint to whom the chapel was initially dedicated: most have changed.

**Sant Christ de Lepant Chapel** Originally, a solid wall completely divided this chapel horizontally. In front, facing the aisle, were two small chapels separated from each other by a lateral wall. The much larger area at the rear formed the chapter house, built by **Arnau Bargués** in 1407 and then only accessible from the cloister.

To celebrate the canonization, in 1676, of Ollegarius, Bishop of Barcelona, d.1137, the chapter house became his mausoleum and the partition walls were demolished, thus opening up the present area to permit public viewing from within the cathedral.

**Joan Claperós** is believed to have carved the bosses in the star vault of the former chapter house in 1454.

Behind the altar is the recumbent figure of St Ollegarius, by **Pere Ça Anglada**, 1406.

Beneath this, the saint's Baroque sarcophagus is the late-17C work of **Francesc Grau** and **Domènec Rovira**; however, the remains of Ollegaríus now lie within a small mausoleum approached by steps on either side of the altarpiece.

In the centre of the altarpiece is the 16C *Lepanto Christ*. According to tradition, this carving of Christ on the Cross came from *La Real*, the flagship of the fleet that defeated the Turks at the battle of Lepanto in 1571.

A tombslab in the centre of the floor commemorates Bishop Manuel Irurita i Almándoz, assassinated in 1936.

*•➡ Follow the west aisle southward.*

**Sant Antoni Chapel** The mid-15C painting on the central, lower panel of the reredos, by **Bernard Martorell**, depicts Saint Cosmos and Saint Damian, both doctors.

Set within the wall niche L is the 15C sarcophagus of Sancha Ximenis de Cabrera, a patroness of the cathedral, believed to be the work of **Pere Oller**.

*•• Continue past the chapels of Sant Josep Oriol and Sant Pancraç.*

**Sepulchre de Sant Ramon de Penyafort Chapel** St Raymond, d.1234, was canonized in 1601 and lies within the 15C gilded sarcophagus that is raised on three columns above the altar: scenes from his life are illustrated on its sides. The sacrophagus, together with the figure of the saint, inset below the altar, was transferred here from the monastic church of Santa Caterina which, before its destruction in the 19C, stood where the Santa Caterina market now functions.

*•• Continue past the chapels of Sant Pau and Nostra Senyora del Pilar.*

**Sant Pacià Chapel** A huge Baroque reredos, made in 1688, covers the entire west wall. It is probably the work of **Miguel Sala**, who is known to have carved the recumbent figure of St Francis Xavier above the altar.

*•• Continue ahead to the west transept.*

From here can be seen the organ in the east gallery, on the opposite side of the cathedral. Installed in 1539, its case is original.

*•• Proceed eastward to the grille fronting the choir.*

The crossing was roofed by 1381 but work on the stone vault of the cathedral did not begin until ten years later.

*•• Descend the steps ahead to view the crypt.*

**Crypt of Saint Eulalia** At a very early stage, probably from its conception, an open crypt situated immediately below the high altar, which would house the remains of St Eulalia, patron saint of Barcelona, was planned as a major feature of the building. Jaume II may well have been influenced by the great new English church of Westminster Abbey, then being rebuilt for Henry III, primarily to accommodate the shrine of St Edward the Confessor. The crypt, which is also the cathedral's Lady Chapel, was excavated by **Jaume Fabre** and probably designed by him. It is known that the double dedication of the cathedral to the Holy Cross (Santa Creu) and St Eulalia had been continuous since 559, and the siting of St Eulalia's sarcophagus, enabling the congregation to view it simultaneously with the cross above the high altar, was an ingenious stroke.

On either side, at the foot of the steps, arches formed by carved heads indicate the former entrances to side chapels, which were blocked in 1779 when the entire flight of steps was moved forward to provide more space within the crossing.

An iron grille screens the crypt, which may not be entered by the public. A button R will illuminate the area for a token payment.

The archway to the crypt is also decorated with carved heads. They are believed to represent the most important witnesses at the ceremony in 1339, during which the Saint's remains were reburied here.

A huge boss in the star vault was carved in 1371 with the figures of St Eulalia and the Virgin holding the infant Jesus.

Although the walls of the crypt are low, a shallow gallery has been fitted.

According to tradition Eulalia, a young virgin born in Barcelona, was martyred at the stake during the 4C persecutions of Diocletian. She was canonized at some time early in the Middle Ages and what were purported to be her relics were discovered in the church of Santa Maria del Mar in 877 and reinterred in Barcelona's Roman basilica. However, some now believe that the saint never existed and was merely an adoption of a saint from Mérida named Eulalia.

The Saint's 9C sarcophagus has been fitted into the wall at the rear of the crypt.

An unknown sculptor from Pisa was responsible for the present sarcophagus. Of alabaster, it was completed in 1327 but St Eulalia's relics were not transferred to it until twelve years later. Supported by eight short columns of varying design, the sarcophagus is carved with scenes depicting the Saint's martyrdom and glorification, and the rediscovery of her relics.

●● *Return to the crossing and proceed southward to the steps of the sanctuary.*

Due to the elevated roof of the crypt on which it stands, the **sanctuary** is raised above the floor level of the remainder of the cathedral.

Since 1971, two 6C Visigothic capitals, probably from the first cathedral, have supported the high altar. They were formerly superimposed, one above the other, as a purely decorative feature of the sanctuary.

Pere III (the Ceremonious) presented the cathedral with a gilded reredos for the high altar in 1377. However, a strange and controversial decision was made in 1970. The episcopal chair was moved from one side of the sanctuary to a central position at the rear and, in order to accommodate this change, the historic reredos had to be removed. Accused of vandalism, the clergy argued that this was merely a reversion to the original situation. The reredos was transferred to Sant Jaume where it remains.

At present, a bronze *Exaltation of the Holy Cross*, by **Marés**, 1975, provides the chief decorative feature of the sanctuary; many regard this as an inadequate substitute.

The bishop's chair, of alabaster, is in the 14C Pisan style and may be the work of the sculptor responsible for St Eulalia's sarcophagus. Its wooden back is a more recent addition.

Flanking the chair are bronze reliefs by **Joan Mayne**, added to commemorate the visit to the cathedral by Pope John Paul II in 1982.

The two candelabra were made in 1674.

From this point may be seen the 14C and 15C stained glass of the apse's upper rosette windows: some have been replaced and all the others restored.

*●● Return to the west side of the cathedral. Immediately ahead is the wall of the sacristy (not open).*

Fitted in the wall are the velvet-covered wooden coffins of Ramon Berenguer 1, d.1076, and his third consort, Almodis de la Marca, who founded the Romanesque predecessor of the present cathedral in the mid 11C.

The wall behind their coffins was painted in trompe l'oeil style by **Enric Ferrandis** in 1545.

*●● Proceed to the first of the west apsidal chapels.*

**Sant Antoni Abat Chapel** The Baroque reredos was made in 1712.

**Visitació Chapel** Completed in 1475, the reredos was not composed as a triptych until 1880. Canon Nadal Garces, who commissioned the work, is depicted kneeling to the Virgin. The tomb chest of Bishop Berenguer de Palou, d.1241, set in the niche L, originally stood in the Romanesque cathedral.

**Transfiguració del Senyor Sant Benet Chapel** The reredos, **Bernat Martorell**, 1450, is regarded as the finest in the cathedral. Painted and gilded wooden panels illustrate the life of Christ.

Surmounting the piece are the arms of Bishop Simó Salvador, d.1445, who bequeathed funds for it to be made.

Recessed within the arch L is the gilded stone sarcophagus of Bishop Ponç de Gaulba, d.1334.

**Sant Josep Chapel** The reredos, made in 1570, illustrates scenes from the life of John the Baptist.

A figure of St Joseph stands in the central niche; he is the patron saint of carpenters, whose association in Barcelona has adopted this chapel.

It is not known who was responsible for the reredos, but the side wall panels were painted by the Genoan, **Joan Matas**.

**Santa Helena Chapel** Formerly sited in one of the cloister's chapels, the reredos, 1390, illustrates biblical scenes featuring the archangel Gabriel.

The modern, saccharin-sweet figure that stands above the altar depicts St Helen. It replaced the *Lepanto Christ*, which was moved from here to its present position in 1932.

**Sant Pere Chapel** St Martin of Tours and St Ambrose of Milan are depicted on the reredos, painted by **Joan Matas** in 1415.

A figure of St Peter stands on the altar and the Saint is also featured in the chapel's side wall paintings.

*●● Proceed to the west chapels.*

**Sant Lugares and Tierra Santa Chapel** Sancha Ximenis de Cabrera donated a reredos to the cathedral, intending that it should be a feature of the chapel that her sarcophagus was to occupy (Sant Antoni Chapel). Rather ungratefully, it now stands here in the cathedral, almost as far away as possible from the mortal remains of its donor.

The lower section, depicting saints, was painted by

**Miquel Nadal**, but **Pere García** completed the remainder in 1456. Work by the latter includes a Crucifixion scene and episodes from the lives of Saint Clare of Assisi and Saint Catharine of Alexandria.

**Mare de Déu la Mercè Chapel** The reredos, made in 1689, illustrates, on its central panel, the founding of the Order of Mercy. The Virgin, surveying the scene from above, wears the habit of the Order. St Raymond of Penyafort is shown presenting the habit of the Order to St Peter of Nolasco; Jaume I is seated L and Bishop Berenguer of Palou R.

St Peter and St Silvester, to whom the chapel was originally dedicated, are painted on the side walls.

*•• Pass the Sagrat Cor de Jesús Chapel and continue northward to the last of the east apsidal chapels.*

**Animes del Purgatori Chapel** The 18C reredos illustrates the *Coronation of the Virgin.*

In the wall niche R is the finest Catalan Gothic sarcophagus in the cathedral, that of Bishop Ramon d'Escales, d.1398. Carved in alabaster by **Antoni Canet** in 1409, the recumbent bishop is depicted in his pontifical robes.

Eight mourners are illustrated on the front.

*•• Proceed southward towards the east transept.*

A stone slab, set in the wall R, records the elevation of Barcelona's bishopric to archdiocese status by Pope Paul IV in 1964.

Above this slab, the blocked, round-headed aperture was inserted by Martí I in 1409 to serve as a doorway, providing a direct link with the royal palace via a bridge over Carrer dels Comtes, since demolished.

Also demolished was the flight of steps leading to it.

*•• Continue to the south-east corner of the choir.*

Integrated with the choir stalls is the pulpit, sumptuously carved by **Pere Ça Anglada** in 1403.

*•• Proceed to the east aisle.*

The pulpit's stone stairway, by **Jordi Johan**, is also early-15C work.

Its balustrade is formed by Flamboyant tracery; the iron handrail incorporates Annunciation lilies in its design.

*•• Pass the choir screen, ignoring the first two chapels of the east aisle, which are entirely modern work.*

Bishop Ramon d'Escales commissioned the stone choir screen in 1380. Coats of arms of the Bishop and the Chapter decorate five of the panels.

Old Testament figures below the tracery, many now headless, are believed to be the work of either **Jordi de Déu** or **Jordi Johan**.

*•• Proceed to the third of the east aisle's chapels.*

**P. Cor de Maria Chapel** Canon Joan Andreu Sors donated the reredos in the late 15C and he is depicted seated at the foot of St Sebastian in the upper central panel. **Rafael Vergós** and Pere Alemany were the painters.

**1**

**Santa Maria Magdalena Chapel  Guerau Gener**
painted the reredos in 1401, featuring scenes from the
lives of St Bartholomew and St Elizabeth.

The banal altar figure of Mary Magdalene is, of
course, modern.

**Mare de Déu del Roser Chapel**  The Baroque reredos
was carved by **Agustí Pujol** in 1619.

•● *Pass Santa Bernardinus Chapel.*

**Sant Marc Chapel**  St Mark and scenes from his life
are depicted on the Baroque reredos, completed in
1692 and dated above the saint's figure.

Paintings on the side walls are by **Francesc
Tramulles**, 1763.

**Sant Sever Chapel**  A local sculptor, **Francesc de
Santa Creu**, aided by **Jacint Trulls**, carved the
reredos in 1683. Scenes from the life of St Sever,
Bishop of Barcelona, are featured. In 1405, the
Bishop's remains were brought to the cathedral from
Sant Cugat del Valles: the scene is illustrated in the
bas-relief below the Saint's figure. The relics of St
Sever now repose in a reliquary kept within the
cathedral's treasury.

•● *Proceed to the north-east bay, immediately R of
the cathedral's entrance.*

**Baptistery**  Until 1420, this bay served as the sacristy
of the cathedral. **Antoni Canet** carved the stonework,
the cupboard L and doorway R in 1405.

Above the doorway, a plaque records the baptism
here of the six American natives who returned with
Columbus to Spain in 1493, an event recorded in the
first written communication received from the New
World. Two of the natives were evidently given the
names of the King (Fernando) and the heir to the
throne (Juan), who virtually adopted them.

The stained-glass window, depicting Christ and Mary
Magdalene, was made by **Gil Fontamet** to designs by
the Cordoban painter, **Bartolome Bermejo**, in 1495.

Made of Carrara marble, the font was carved by the
Florentine, **Onofre Juliá**, in 1433.

•● *Proceed to the south end of the choir.*

**Bartolomé Ordóñez** began carving the marble
section of the Renaissance choir screen (Trascoro)
*c.*1519. He planned its entire design and was
personally responsible for part of the lower frieze:
the figure of St Sever (first panel), the scenes of St
Eulalia proclaiming her faith (second panel), her
martyrdom at the stake (seventh panel) and the
figure of St Eulalia (eighth panel). **Ordóñyez** was
assisted by the Italians, **Simone de Bellana** and
**Vittorio de Cogono**, but on his death in 1520 work was
suspended. The remainder of the screen was
eventually carved, in 1564, by **Pedro Villar**.

•● *Enter the choir (admission charge except for
Sunday Mass).*

Oak side-screens, flanking both ends, were carved
with biblical scenes in Italian Renaissance style, by
**Ordóñyez**, in 1518.

Originally, only the sixty-one upper pews were

installed, the work of **Pere Ça Anglada**, completed in 1399. All are provided with decorative misericords.

**Michael Lochner** carved most of the canopies of the pews in the late 15C, his work being completed by another German, **Johann Friedrich**.

Coats of arms were painted on the backs of the pews by **Joan de Borgonya** in 1519.

The arms are those of the Knights of the Order of the Golden Fleece and commemorate their first and only convention, held at Barcelona in 1519, presided over by the Grand Master of the Order, the Emperor Charles V. Five European kings were present, but England's Henry VIII was unable to attend. The pew reserved for him is immediately R of the Emperor's.

The lower forty-eight pews were added by **Matias Bonafé**, 1456–62, to accommodate more of the cathedral's canons and curates. They are of less artistic interest.

Marble slabs in the pavement mark the tombs of the bishops and canons whose remains lie below: most inscriptions have faded.

The stone seat on the other side of the iron grille R is carved with the heron arms of Bishop Pere García, indicating that they were installed during his bishopric, *c*.1500.

In the far corner L is the pulpit, already described.

⚫ *Exit from the choir, turn L and follow the west section of the choir screen southward.*

Like the east section, already seen, this is late-14C work, carved with Old Testament figures and decorated with shields of the bishops.

⚫ *Proceed through the west transept R and enter the* **cloister**.

It is believed that most of the doorway on the cloister side has been formed from the 11C marble portal of the cathedral's Romanesque predecessor. However, that would have possessed completely rounded arches and the present slightly pointed shape indicates the removal of a central section to enable the portal to be fitted into a narrower space. This suggests that the portal's reuse may have been an afterthought.

Of paler stone, the decorated tympanum and upper cresting are in Gothic style and would have been incorporated when the doorway was installed in the 14C.

Roof bosses in the four corners of the cloister, from which lamps are suspended, depict the Evangelists; those in the passages illustrate scenes from the life of Christ.

Many tombslabs are fitted in the pavement throughout the cloister.

⚫ *Follow the east passage (running L from the door), which is attached to the west wall of the cathedral.*

Both this and the cloister's south passage were completed by the mid 14C, but work on the remaining sides was then halted for almost a century.

All, except the south passage, possess chapels, each one screened by the original iron grilles made in the 14C and 15C.

As within the cathedral, most chapels retain their original roof bosses, depicting the saints to whom they were first dedicated. Many of the cloister's chapels, particularly those adjoining the cathedral, became private chantries, their benefactors, who had the right of burial within, providing altars and altarpieces.

Some of the benefactors' coats of arms are carved within the chapels, but most of the fittings have been transferred to the cathedral's interior in order to preserve them.

An unusual feature is the linking of the capitals of the columns to form a series of friezes illustrating biblical scenes and religious legends.

The positions of the gargoyles, above the outer columns of the cloister, suggest that an upper floor was not originally planned.

•● *Continue ahead and follow the north passage.*

Construction of the last two passages of the cloister began here in 1431, financed by a legacy from Bishop Francesc Climent Sapera.

Passed R, the first doorway, with a Gothic cresting, was formerly the only access point to the original chapter house (now part of the Holy Sacrament Chapel).

The marble tomb chest of Canon Francesc Desplà, d.1453, is fitted within the recess L; its wall is decorated with a now-faded painting.

•● *Proceed to the next door and enter the* **Cathedral Museum**.

Forming the first room of the museum is the **Sala de la Cabrevación**, subdivided by a screen.

Immediately ahead, the 11C font was made for the Romanesque cathedral.

Walls display religious paintings and silk altar frontals.

A carved doorway leads to the **chapter house**.

•● *Enter the chapter house and turn L.*

Immediately L of the altar is a 16C *Calvary* painting.

The far wall is dominated by a large painting illustrating the installation of Carlos III as a canon of the cathedral.

To its R is the 15C San Lorenzo reredos.

The two remaining walls display sections of the great 15C reredos painted by **Jaume Huguet** for the Gremio de Esparters (Guild of esparto-grass workers – shoes, baskets, etc.).

Also displayed, on the entrance wall, is a Pietà, painted by **Bartolome Bermejo** *c.*1490.

•● *Exit from the museum R.*

The next door R leads directly to the chapter house but is generally closed.

Partly inset in the wall L is the bronze tomb of Antoni Tallander, d.1446. Generally known as Mossèn Borra, he served as an ambassador of the Aragon kings.

*•● Pass the rear entrance to the Santa Llúcia Chapel and follow the west passage southward.*

Inset in the third pier of the arcade is a 15C tombslab, judged the finest in the cloister. This marks the sepulchre of members of the Confreria del Senyor Rei (Association of the king).

The arms of Aragon are supported by angels. Traces of paintwork are a reminder that the preference for undecorated stonework only dates from the Renaissance.

*•● Exit from the Santa Eulalia doorway R to c del Bisbe.*

The mid-15C Santa Eulalia portal is a little more sober than the contemporary Pietat portal, although its archivolts are carved with figures and foliage, whereas the other's are undecorated.

A figure of St Eulalia stands on the lintel, flanked by the arms of the Chapter and Bishop Sapera.

*•● Return to the cloister's west passage and turn R.*

The last bay of this passage, vaulted by **Andreu Escuder** in 1448, marked the completion of the cloister.

*•● Follow the south passage eastward to the fountain.*

White geese enliven the cloister, but the reason for their existence here is unknown. Formerly, thirteen geese had to be kept, hinting perhaps at a superstitious significance, but the requirement has since been reduced to six. A rectangular basin, with a central moss-covered jet, provides the geese with swimming facilities.

In medieval times, on the feast day of St Lucy, (13 December), the blind gathered here to receive charity.

*•● Continue ahead.*

Fresh water was supplied to the cathedral from the fountain that is sheltered by a mid-15C structure designed as an open temple, and which faces the Pietat portal.

Its vault, including an outstanding St George and the Dragon boss, was carved by the **Claperós** family.

*•● Continue eastward and exit from the cathedral by the Pietat portal R to c de la Pietat R.*

| Location 12 | **CANONS' HOUSES**<br>(CASAS DELS CANONGES) |
|---|---|
| Carrer de la Pietat | Now the official residence of the President of the Provisional Council, the structure that lies between Carrer de la Pietat and Carrer del Bisbe was built in the 14C to house the canons of the cathedral. |

The house on the Carrer del Bisbe corner was decorated with sgraffiti by **Rubió i Bellver** in 1921. This was later to be known as the 'White House of Catalonia' as it was occupied, 1931–9, by successive

Catalan presidents: Francesc Macià and Lluís Companys. **Jeroni Martorell** greatly altered its interior in 1929.

A plaque commemorates Apelles Mestres, Catalan designer, writer and composer.

*Return eastward.*

**Mas i Vila** was chiefly responsible for the present appearance of the remaining canons' houses facing Carrer de la Pietat; his 19C over-restoration is a combination of pastiche and original work.

*Second R c Freneria.*

| | |
|---|---|
| Location 13 | **CARRER FRENERIA** |

The name of this street derives from the *freners* (makers of leather belts and straps), who formerly worked here.

Occupying the Baixada Santa Clara corner L, **No 14** is a medieval house, with its upper floor extending above the pavement.

A three-light Gothic window has been restored.

Forming part of the structure, and exposed above the ground floor, is what appears to be a tree trunk simply stripped of its bark.

*First R c de la Llibreteria. Cross the road.*

| | |
|---|---|
| Location 14 | **MESÓN DEL CAFÉ** |

16 Carrer de la Llibreteria

*Open Monday–Saturday 08.00–24.00.*

One of the world's most charming coffee houses, the Mesón del Café's front appears to have been inspired by Walt Disney's version of Snow White's cottage, but dates from the establishment's formation in 1909.

Painted panels decorate the front room, where the most popular stool is positioned in the corner overlooking the lively street.

On the archway between the two rooms is displayed a coffee machine of 1929.

The coffee itself is rated by habitués as the best in the city, a speciality being the capuccino, which here consists of black coffee topped with whipped cream. Food is not provided, apart from croissants and pastries. As in all Spanish coffee bars, alcoholic drinks are available.

*Exit R and continue eastward.*

| | |
|---|---|
| Location 15 | **BAIXADA DE LA LLIBRETERIA** |

The name baixada was given to streets that led directly to the Roman wall. Llibreteria refers to the booksellers who monopolized this street until the 19C. The thoroughfare follows part of the line of the Roman artery, Decumanus, that bisected the city east to west between two gateways in the wall.

Now primarily a mix of 18C and 19C houses, several possess examples of terracotta relief work.

**Xalar, No 4**, is one of Barcelona's most popular toy shops.

**Subirà Cereria, No 7**, at the far end L, retains the oldest and finest shop interior in the city. The building, with its present interior, was commissioned in 1847 by a cloth retailer. It occupied the site of a courtyard and, for a short time, was linked at upper level with the prison above the gate. The owner of the premises welcomes visitors who wish to view the little-altered interior.

All the woodwork is Classical in style and features a delicate, double staircase leading to an upper gallery. Subirà Cereria, manufacturers of wax products, was formed elsewhere in Barcelona in 1761, which explains the date inscribed above the stairs.

The two figures flanking the stairs originally held gas lamps, just four years after the installation of Barcelona's domestic supply.

A candle mould of 1762 remains in the shop's possession.

•➤ *Exit L and proceed to Pl de l'Àngel and M Jaume I.*

## Royal and Administrative Palaces

Barcelona's most important civic palaces, all dating from the Gothic period or earlier, subterranean remains of the Roman city, and the only churches of importance to escape the 1936 arsonists, are the highlights. Many picturesque streets and squares are passed en route and a visit is made to the great church of Santa Maria del Pi, which boasts the largest rose window in the world.

Although the distance covered is not great, there is much to see, and a whole day, at least, should be allocated.

*Timing:* The City's History Museum is closed Sunday afternoon and Monday morning.

An appointment, made well in advance, is necessary to enter the Generalitat Palace.

The Museum of Ancient Shoes is open 11.00–14.00 but closes Sunday.

Apart from early in the morning, Sant Felip Neri is open only 19.00–20.30.

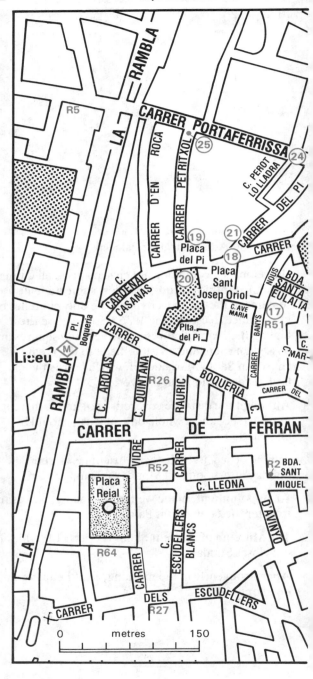

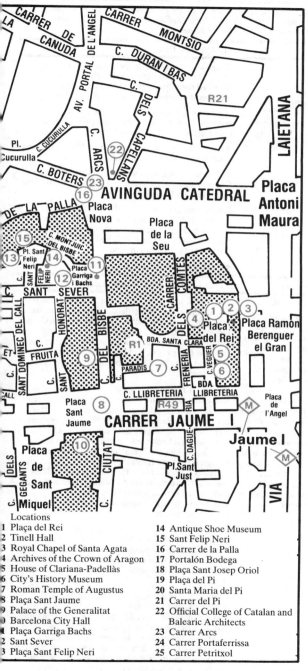

Locations

**Start** *M Jaume 1, line 4. Leave by the Pl de l'Àngel exit R. First L bda Llibreteria. First R c Veguer leads to pl del Rei passing, for the moment, the entrance to the City's History Museum.*

| Location 1 | **PLAÇA DEL REI** |

The square was formerly the courtyard of the royal palace but, in spite of this, a straw and hay market operated there for three hundred years and locksmiths offered their wares until expelled in 1387.

Immediately ahead stands the Tinell Hall, the most important part of the Palau Major (Major Palace), the residence of the Catalan kings.

Attached to its east end R, and stretching southward, is the Royal Chapel of Santa Agata.

This in turn links, at its south end, with the House of Clariana-Padellàs, which accommodates much of the City's History Museum.

Rising from the west end of the Tinell Hall is the 'Tower of Martí'. From the west end of the Tinell Hall, stretching southward, is the former Viceroy's (or Lieutenant's) Palace, that now accommodates the Archives of the Crown of Aragon.

●● *Proceed ahead to the Tinell Hall.*

| Location 2 | **TINELL HALL** (SALÓ DEL TINELL) |

Plaça del Rei

*Open Tuesday–Saturday 09.00–20.00, Sunday and holidays 09.00–13.30, for exhibitions or as part of the City's History Museum. Admission charge, or free, depending on the event. The entry point may be either from Plaça del Rei, Plaça St Iu or the City's History Museum (via the Royal Chapel), again depending on the event.*

The Tinell, which dates from the 11C, served as the Great Hall of the royal palace. Internally, a series of round-headed stone arches, typically Catalan Gothic, was added in the 14C and provides the building's dominant feature. Ferdinand and Isabella may have received Christopher Columbus in this hall on his return to Spain in 1493, following his discovery of the New World.

**History** A royal palace appears to have existed in Barcelona during the Visigothic period, but there is no evidence of an earlier, Roman equivalent. It is recorded that Ramon Borrell I (992–1017) appointed a guardian of the royal palace early in the 11C, and this is the first known reference to the residence of the Catalan kings. Its great hall, the Tinell, survives, though it has been frequently remodelled. Little of certainty is known about the other palace buildings that must have existed in the Middle Ages, although there would certainly have been domestic accommodation, and mention is made of a guard room and a library.

The original royal chapel was rebuilt in the 13C on a much larger scale, and the former Bishop's Palace incorporated in the complex in 1316. In the mid 16C the Lieutenant's Palace was added, the watch tower was erected and the small Santa Eulalia Palace was demolished.

A great deal of mystery surrounds the Tinell, the great building even being 'lost' until 1934. The hall was certainly subdivided for the king at certain times, but the functions of the separate areas are unclear. Strangely, the origin of the name Tinell is also controversial. Does it refer to the vats in which hay was kept outside, in the Plaça del Rei, or was it the sideboard on which royal treasures were displayed that gave the hall its name? Both are called 'Tinell'.

Even the most famous 'event' in the Tinell, Ferdinand and Isabella's reception of Columbus in 1493, is a matter of conjecture. Although the Tinell's official records for the year exist and appear to be complete, there is no reference to the reception of Columbus. It is learned, however, from his son's biography of the explorer, that Columbus was received by the Catholic monarchs in Barcelona and the Tinell would have been the most likely venue.

Events that certainly did take place in the Tinell include the hall's use as Parliament House in 1312 and 1377, the pleading for Catalan support by the Avignon papal legate in 1390 and the celebration of the freedom of Granada from the Moors in 1493.

Following the termination of the Catalan monarchy, notaries of the Royal Audencia (Court) took over the palace in 1542.

In 1715, Philip V began to demolish much of the Ribera district of Barcelona to make way for his citadel. One of the buildings lost was the Santa Clara Convent, including its great church. In compensation, the King presented the Tinell to the nuns of the convent, who adapted the building to a Baroque church with side chapels, making many alterations to the structure. In time, the origins of this church were forgotten and it was not until 1934 that the Tinell, then believed to have been demolished, was rediscovered. The municipality purchased the Tinell in 1940 and completed its restoration three years later.

**Exterior** Most of the wall fabric is 11C work, dating from the earliest palace recorded. Outlines of small Romanesque windows survive at upper level in the two most westerly bays L, and another example, above the entrance, has been reopened in recent years.

Three-light, round-headed windows were inserted early in the 13C.

At upper level, the rosette windows are 14C additions by **Guillem Carbonell**.

The buttresses were also the work of **Carbonell**, who added them to support the great stone vaults that he was constructing internally.

Steps lead to the entrance in the corner R, which also provides access to the royal chapel. These steps and a Renaissance doorway were installed in 1542 for the convenience of the notaries of the Royal Audencia. In 1936, the doorway was transferred to the former Bishop's Palace in Plaça Sant Iu and replaced by the present Romanesque-style portal.

The tower, known as the Mirador (or Tower) of Martí, has no connection with Martí I, who died in 1410.

•● *Enter the Tinell and proceed to the far end, if the entrance from Plaça del Rei is open. If not, continue to location 3 and return later.*

**Interior** Linking the east end of the Tinell with the royal chapel is an ante-room, designed in Gothic style in 1952 to replace the building, constructed by Pere II in 1279, that had been demolished in the 19C.

*●● Proceed ahead.*

Unfortunately, much of the interior of the Tinell is frequently obscured by exhibition displays.

The present appearance of the hall predominantly reflects the mid-14C work of **Guillem Carbonell** for Pere III.

Facing the Plaça del Rei, the fabric of the south wall is 11C, but the opposite wall was constructed in the 14C for the sake of symmetry.

Behind the latter, at a slight angle to it, runs the other external 11C wall of the Tinell, facing what is now the patio of the Frederic Marés Museum, formerly the palace garden.

Its large north window R was originally a doorway providing access, via steps, to the garden.

Against the inner north wall is a fresco, *c.*1300, depicting troops led by a king and a bishop. Originally this was painted on the inside of the external north wall, almost directly behind its present position.

It is not clear how the Tinell was subdivided when the fresco was painted, but later Pere III chose the themes for decorating various rooms created within the hall. It is said that he consulted astrologers, who also advised him on a propitious day to begin the hall's reconstruction.

Excavations of Roman remains beneath the Tinell weakened its structure and during repair work the original floor, 2 feet lower, was discovered and reverted to.

The 50-foot high timber roof is supported by six round-headed arches of stone, in typical Catalan Gothic style, the main feature of **Guillem Carbonell's** work at the palace.

Blocked Romanesque windows in the south wall L can be seen more clearly here than from the exterior.

*●● Proceed towards the west end.*

On the north side is the room's only fireplace.

The last three bays on the south side are attached to the building that houses the Archives of the Crown of Aragon. When this was built in the 16C the small Santa Eulalia Palace, which linked the Tinell with Carrer dels Comtes, was demolished.

The doorway in the north wall, at its west end, provides the entrance to the hall from Plaça de Sant Iu.

*●● Return to Plaça del Rei.*

Immediately L is the exterior of the Chapel Royal of Santa Agata.

*●● Alternatively, if more convenient, proceed through the anteroom to view the interior of the royal chapel (Location 3).*

Location 3

## ROYAL CHAPEL OF SANTA AGATA
## (CAPELLA REIAL DE SANTA AGATA)

Plaça del Rei

*Like the Tinell,
with which it links,
the former royal
chapel of Santa
Agata is open
Tuesday–Saturday
09.00–20.00,
Sunday and
holidays 09.00–
13.30, for
exhibitions or as
part of the City's
History Museum.
Admission charge,
or free, depending
on the event. The
entry point may be
from either Plaça
del Rei, Plaça de
Sant Iu (via the
Tinell) or from the
City's History
Museum, again
depending on the
event.*

The apse and subsidiary chapels of the early 14C
Santa Agata Chapel are carved with various royal
coats of arms. In the mid-15C Pere, Condestable de
Portugal (Constable of Portugal) commissioned the
painting of the roof beams and the chapel's most
prized possession, the great Epiphany retable, by
**Jaume Huguet**.

**History** The earlier royal chapel had been a small
oratory, rising no higher than the 11C Roman wall; it
accommodated holy relics of Saint Agata and was
dedicated to the Virgin in 1173. Jaume II
commissioned the present building, himself being
partly responsible for its design, based on drawings
by **Bertran Riguer**. Work began c.1302 and was
completed within ten years by **Pere d'Olivera**.

Amongst the relics housed in the chapel was the
stone on which, allegedly, the severed breasts of St
Agata had been placed following her martyrdom; for
this reason the new building was dedicated to her.
Early in the 15C, Martí I built adjacent
accommodation for the Celestines, whom he charged
with guarding the relics; they were replaced by the
Mercedarios in 1423.

The chapel was sold for industrial purposes in 1844
but became a museum in 1866. It was restored in 1936
following the recovery of the Epiphany retable.

**Exterior** The east face of the chapel, integrated with
the Roman wall, has been described on page 5. This
west façade is similar early-14C work but there are no
protruding subsidiary chapels.

The bell tower, retained from the earlier building,
was presented by Alfons I and completed in the late
12C using a Roman watch tower as its base.

*If the entrance from Plaça del Rei is open, enter
the chapel and proceed immediately ahead to the
sanctuary at the south end.*

*If entry has been made from Plaça Sant Iu, via the
Tinell, the chapel is approached from the linking ante-
room (page 31). Proceed directly to the sanctuary.*

*Alternatively, continue to location 4 and return to
the chapel later.*

**Interior** Immediately behind the high altar is the
chapel's greatest treasure, the Epiphany reredos
painted for Pere, Condestable de Portugal, by **Jaume
Huguet** in 1465. This replaced a mid-14C piece by
**Ferrer Bassa**, which has disappeared. Until 1972, the
reredos was split up, some panels being located in
Paris: all were then returned to Barcelona and
reassembled.

Carved around the apse are the royal arms of the
builders of the chapel, Jaume II (vertical bars) and
his first consort, Blanca d'Anjou (fleur-de-lis). This
Queen's funeral in 1310 was recorded as the 'first
solemn act' in the present building.

Only fragments of medieval stained glass survive in
the chapel; most of the glass was made in 1942 and
depicts royal coats of arms.

Pere, Condestable de Portugal, commissioned the decoration of the timber ceiling from **Alfonso de Córdoba** c.1465. Most of his work had been lost by the mid-19C but fragments indicated the original appearance and repainting was completed in 1857.

On the east side, the larger of the two subsidiary chapels was constructed 1338–55 by creating a structural vault between two Roman towers and building above it. The chapel was built for Pere III's first consort, María de Navarra. Her arms, incorporating small fleurs-de-lis, are carved on the wall L, accompanied by the royal arms of the King.

The central arms are those of St George.

Carved in the wall R are the arms, with two eagles, of Elionor de Sicilia, third consort of Pere III, and the arms of the King. Both Elionor and María venerated St Nicholas and the chapel was originally dedicated to him.

Tomb chests, L of Ramon Borrell and R his wife, Ermessenda, are reproductions of the originals in Gerona Cathedral.

The doorway L, at the entrance to this chapel, leads to steps that were used by the King to approach the choir in the north gallery, from where a door led directly to the royal palace.

A similar doorway on the east side of the royal chapel leads to the steps used by the Queen.

The choir, not generally accessible, retains some 15C sgraffiti on its rear wall

•► *Proceed northward.*

The smaller, subsidiary east chapel, at the north end, was built for Martí I and his first consort Maria de Luna c.1400; their carved arms, however, are believed to be late-15C work. Those of the Queen incorporate a half moon (luna).

The north doorway, built c.1400, gives access to the Tinell via the ante-room.

•► *Return to pl del Rei. Forming the west side is the Archives of the Crown of Aragon.*

•► *Alternatively, if not already seen, continue ahead to view the interior of the Tinell (page 32).*

---

| | |
|---|---|
| Location 4 | **ARCHIVES OF THE CROWN OF ARAGON** (ARXIU DE LA CORONA D'ARAGÓ) |

Plaça del Rei

*Courtyard (approached from Carrer dels Comtes) open Monday– Saturday afternoon. Admission free. Hall open for temporary exhibitions only.*

The former viceroy's palace, built in the mid-16C, incorporates a great hall similar to the Tinell's. Its patio is a rare Barcelona example of Renaissance work. Some of the finest wood-carving in the city decorates the ceiling and gallery above the staircase. Housed within are the Aragon archives, founded in 1549.

For many years, no money was spent on modernizing the Tinell, as it was intended to build a new royal palace nearer the sea. Eventually, the Spanish king's viceroy refused to live there, because of its delapidated condition, and in 1547 the Catalan administration commissioned a new palace for his use attached to the Tinell's west end. This was built by **Antoni Carbonell**, 1549–57, partly on the site of a small pavilion that had been erected for Pere, Condestable de Portugal, almost a century earlier. However, the palace building stretched beyond this, over the west side of the Plaça del Rei. The palace is contemporary with the so-called Tower or Mirador of Martí, also built by **Antoni Carbonell**.

Externally, the late-Gothic style of the façade conceals what is basically one of the few truly Renaissance buildings in the city.

Windows on the ground and first floors have Renaissance balconies, but their lintels remain Gothic, and are decorated with the cross of St George.

Typically Catalan Gothic is the undecorated stone portal.

●● *Proceed to the square's south-west corner with bda Santa Clara.*

Decorating the three corners of the building, at second-floor level, is the coat of arms of the Generalitat, supported by angels and, at roof level, a rounded Gothic corbel supports a stubby tower.

●● *Follow bda Santa Clara westward. First R c dels Comtes skirts the building's west façade. First R enter the patio.*

All is very Italian Renaissance in style, with only the gargoyles introducing a Gothic note.

The four shallow arches of the arcade support a gallery with a terrace above, both balustraded.

Ancient vines grow in the corners of the patio.

The Grotesque head, set in the side wall of the staircase L, incorporates a freshwater tap.

●● *Ascend the first flight of stairs.*

Above the staircase, the timber octagonal gallery and ceiling display some of the finest wood-carving in Barcelona.

Facing the top of the first flight of steps is a modern bronze door, the entrance to the building's great hall, now used for functions and exhibitions. Carved arches, reminiscent of the Tinell, support the roof.

●● *Return to the stairs and ascend to the gallery.*

Entered from the gallery is the reading room, open only for research. Most of the manuscripts were acquired from monasteries, the earliest dating from 844. The collection also includes several thousand royal letters.

●● *Return to the patio.*

Surviving in the basement, not generally open, are part of the foundations of the pavilion built for Pere, Condestable de Portugal.

●● *Exit L. First L bda Santa Clara leads to pl del Rei. The House of Clariana-Padellàs forms the south side R.*

| Location 5 | **HOUSE OF CLARIANA-PADELLÀS** |
| --- | --- |
| 1 Carrer Veguer | This 16C palace was built for a wealthy merchant's family at the north end of Carrer Mercaders and |

transferred here, stone by stone, in 1930. During excavations for its reconstruction, the remains of Roman Barcelona were discovered.

As was common in the 16C, basically Catalan Gothic features incorporate some Renaissance detailing. Although minor amendments were necessary, in essence the building is unchanged.

A two-light Gothic window and a roof gallery are the main features of the Plaça del Rei façade.

The Gothic lintels of the windows are carved with Renaissance figures and shields.

●● *Follow c Veguer that runs southward from the square and enter the patio of the building first L (also the entrance to the City's History Museum).*

| | |
|---|---|
| Location 6 | **CITY'S HISTORY MUSEUM** (MUSEU D'HISTORIA DE LA CIUTAT) |

Carrer Veguer

*Open Tuesday–Saturday 09.00–20.00, Sunday and holidays 09.00–13.30. Admission charge but free to minors and Spaniards.*

The museum's exhibits include paintings, tapestries, models and maps illustrating the growth of the city. Access is also provided to the Royal Chapel and the Tinell at no extra charge, when not in use. The excavated Roman city may be visited.

●● *Proceed to the ticket office and ascend the stairs L to room XVI.*

Outstanding exhibits and their locations are always subject to change and some rooms may occasionally be closed.

**XVI** The original bronze angel that surmounted an obelisk in Plaça de l' Angel was made by **Felip Ros** in 1618. It represents the archangel St Michael, who in medieval times allegedly made a miraculous appearance in the square.
**XII** Designs prepared by candidates for their examinations to join the Jewellers Guild.
**XIV** Hand-painted cotton.
**XV** Watercolours illustrating the Corpus Christi procession of 1840.

●● *Proceed directly ahead from this room to the sacristy of the Santa Agata chapel, if open.*

Situated within the bell-tower, the chamber occupies the upper stage of a Roman watch tower.

The windows are original but the vault is Gothic.

●● *Continue ahead to view the interiors of the chapel and the Tinell, if open and not already seen. They are described between pages 31 and 34.*

*Return to Room XII and continue to Room XI.*

**XI** Old plans of Barcelona, radical proposals for its extension and the plan of Llegat Cerdá that was finally adopted.
**X** Plaster cast of the Gothic doorway to the Generalitat's Room of the Council of Thirty, demolished in 1847.

Painting of the Ajuntament's Gothic façade, prior to its 19C modification in which the first floor window, R of the doorway, was lost.
**XI** On the stairway ascending from Room X is a painting of the demolished Palau Menor (Minor Palace).

**Upper floor** Paintings and drawings of the city include a copy of **Wyngarde**'s map of 1563.

Diarama of Barcelona.

*●▶ Return to the ticket office and descend the stairway ahead.*

The **Roman city** was excavated in 1943 and the route followed extends northward below the Plaça del Rei and the Tinell to the cathedral.

Passed are: baths (one flooded with blue light), huge urns that look like the broken eggs of a giant bird and a reproduced Visigothic necropolis.

Immediately beneath the Tinell, two adjoining barrel-vaulted rooms, 25 feet high, have been divided into two levels and are used for presentations and conferences.

*●▶ Exit from the museum R. First L bda Santa Clara. Second L c Paradis. Proceed to No 10.*

A beautiful garden that once bordered the street is said to have inspired the thoroughfare's name (Paradise).

Immediately outside No 10, a circular millstone, set in the pavement, marks the highest point of Mount Taber.

| | |
|---|---|
| Location 7 | **ROMAN TEMPLE OF AUGUSTUS** (TEMPLE ROMA D'AUGUST) |

| | |
|---|---|
| 10 Carrer Paradis<br><br>*Open Monday–Friday 09.00–13.00 and 16.00–19.00. Admission free.* | This corner of a Roman temple stands on the summit of the hill on which the Roman city was built. The house, within which the temple is enclosed, is one of the finest examples of medieval domestic architecture in Barcelona, but its Romanesque windows are much restored. It serves as the headquarters of the Centre Excursionista de Catalunya, founded in 1878 to promote archaeology and natural science in the province. |

*●▶ Enter the building.*

Four Corinthian columns, found *in situ*, have been re-erected in their original position R of the entrance. They represent a corner of a late-1C or early-2C Roman temple, which may have been dedicated to the worship of Hercules, legendary founder of Barcelona. The temple was demolished by invaders before the 4C defensive wall was built.
Unfortunately, the protective gates are now generally locked, due to the area's former popularity with drug addicts, and the temple is difficult to view in its entirety.

*●▶ Exit L and proceed ahead towards pl Sant Jaume.*

**No 1 bis** Carrer Paradis, facing the bend in the street, displays a carved St George and the Dragon at ground-floor level.

| | |
|---|---|
| Location 8 | **PLAÇA SANT JAUME** |

Most are surprised to learn that Plaça Sant Jaume (St James), by far the largest square within the area of the walled city and accommodating the imposing façades of the Generalitat and Ajuntament, is mainly a creation of the 19C.

Until 1823, Plaça Sant Jaume occupied only the north-east corner of the present square, covering approximately one-sixth of its area. It had been laid out at the interconnection of the two Roman roads, Decumanus and Cardo. North of the Ajuntament, the main frontage of which then faced east, stretched the great church of Sant Jaume, with its cemetery facing the Generalitat Palace. A market operated in the square and it is probable that the Roman forum had been sited here.

The south-east corner of the small square was formed by the building of the Bailia General, where bailage, the tax on goods brought into the city, was administered. Immediately east of this, at the beginning of what is now Carrer Jaume I, stood the residence of the Veguer (magistrate) followed by the rectory of Sant Jaume.

All this was swept away in 1823, together with many ancient houses, and the present dimensions of the square established. At the same time, Carrer Jaume I and Carrer Ferran were laid out and the Ajuntament given its present clinical façade, this time facing north.

On Sunday evenings, the Sardana is danced in the square and on St George's Day, 23 April, stalls are set up for selling roses – for men to give to ladies, and books – for ladies to give to men.

*•➡ Proceed to the Ajuntament, on the south side of the square, to view the façade of the Generalitat, opposite.*

| Location 9 | **PALACE OF THE GENERALITAT** |
|---|---|

Plaça St Jaume

*Open by appointment only, apart from St George's Day, 23 April, when it is open to all in the afternoon (long queues). Admission is always free.*

*One month's notice for appointments is preferred, which usually entails writing before leaving home, but on occasions it is possible to reduce this time. Letters (English understood) should be posted or delivered to Protocol, Palau de la Generalitat, Plaça Sant Jaume, 08002, Barcelona.*

The Palace of the Generalitat of Barcelona is one of Europe's most important civic buildings to survive from the Gothic period. It is now fronted by a Renaissance range, but this occupies less than a quarter of the total area and none of the ancient complex was lost when it was added. Outstanding features include medieval painted wooden ceilings, the 'Gothic' gallery, the 15C St George's Chapel and the Orange Trees Patio.

**History** The Generalitat, comprising representatives of the clergy, the army and the citizenry, was founded as an administrative council for Catalonia by Pere III in 1359, and was one of the first governing bodies in Europe empowered to moderate the absolutism of a sovereign. By the early 15C, the Generalitat had already become the foremost executive body in Catalonia and suitable premises were sought. Two houses in Carrer Sant Honorat had been taken from their wealthy Jewish owners in 1403 and eleven years later these became the nucleus of the palace which exists today. **Marc Safont** adapted and enlarged these around a central patio, which was completed *c.*1425, and the complex was then gradually extended northward until the late 16C. As a final extension, in 1603, **Pere Blai** added the Renaissance block to the south, which now provides the Plaça Sant Jaume façade.

In 1714, Philip V gained victory over Charles of Austria in the War of Succession and ruled Catalonia, which had supported the losing side, with a rod of iron. The Generalitat was abolished and its premises became law courts. Reformed in 1931, with Francesc Maciá as president, the palace again became the Generalitat's headquarters. At the termination of the Civil War, in 1939, members of the Generalitat, once more supporters of the losers, retreated into exile. The president, Lluís Companys, who had fled to France, was forcibly repatriated by the Fascist Vichy regime and shot in Montjuïc Castle.

Following the return of democracy to Spain in 1977, the Generalitat was re-established and the following year sat once more in the palace. Although remaining a Spanish province, Catalonia has obtained a large degree of autonomy which is expected to be extended further. Most of the Generalitat's administrative staff are now accommodated in the modern quarter of the city, and the palace is primarily reserved for meetings, ceremonial purposes and important functions. The Catalan parliament sits not here but at Ciutadella.

**Exterior** The Plaça Sant Jaume façade is a rare Barcelona example of the Italian Renaissance style. It was completed by **Pere Blai** in 1602, incorporating marble from Genoa for the upper floors.

Above ground-floor level, the range houses the Saló Sant Jordi, the largest hall in the complex. It was intended to be a chapel, which is why the building is surmounted by a cupola.

St George is the patron saint of the Generalitat and his cross appears above the central niche. Within this niche are carved the heads of the three deputies responsible for the building.

The figure of St George, together with the balcony, was added by **Andreu Aleu** in 1860.

From this balcony, Francesc Maciá proclaimed the Catalan Republic in 1931 and Lluís Companys the Federal Republic in 1934.

•➡ *Follow c del Bisbe , which skirts the east side of the palace.*

The first five bays of the palace mark the 16C extension, for which houses had to be demolished and a narrow street lost.

Before it was built, the main approach to the complex was from the Flamboyant Gothic entrance, which follows L, past the earliest development of the complex designed by **Marc Safont** in 1416.

Its figures, by **Pere Johan**, 1418, including St George and the dragon above the doorway, were evidently so admired that the Generalitat doubled the sculptor's agreed fee. It is daunting to contemplate the uproar that such generosity would arouse in modern times!

Gargoyles, also by **Johan**, include, immediately L of the medallion, a representation of the maiden saved by St George.

The frieze, balustrade and other ornamentation were by **Aliot de la Font**.

Immediately R are the much altered Carrer del Bisbe façades of the 14C Canons' houses, described on page 12.

Ahead is the bridge that links them with the Generalitat, picturesquely designed in Gothic Revival style and reminiscent of Venice's Bridge of Sighs.

•● *Return to pl Sant Jaume and await the guide (if an appointment has been made).*

*Alternatively, proceed to location 10.*

**Interior** Visitors will initially pass through the Renaissance extension to the early-15C buildings, which are indicated by timber ceilings and surround the patio. The two houses and their gardens, acquired in 1403, had been built here, and their adaptation and the creation of the patios and stairways took place between 1416 and 1425, under the direction of **Marc Safont**.

Cloisterlike, the first-floor gallery is one of the most delicate in Barcelona. Unusually for a Catalan secular building, its arches are pointed, a feature that recurs throughout the palace.

The upper floor, a closed gallery, is surmounted by gargoyles and pinnacles, attributed to **Pere Johan**.

Roundels, surrounding the balustrade and the walls of the gallery, are carved with medieval figures.

The Gothic entrance to the palace lies south of the patio R and is approached beneath more painted timber ceilings.

Two surprises occur at the head of the stairs: the carved bases of the two flanking columns are Renaissance in style, whereas the other columns are entirely Gothic; and there is no supporting angle column facing the Sant Jordi Chapel. It is believed that a column originally did stand here but was removed, together with a section of low wall, when the Orange Trees Patio was extended.

The timber ceilings of the gallery are carved and painted and the pavement is of Carrara marble.

**St George's Chapel** (Capella de Sant Jordi) **Marc Safont** built this chapel 1432–5, but it was partly remodelled and extended in the 18C.

Intricate Flamboyant decoration around the entrance produces a rare Gothic example of filigree work.

•● *Enter the chapel.*

Immediately R of the entrance hangs a cloth altar frontal by **Antoni Sadurni**, 1450. Trimmed with gold, this illustrates the St George legend, surrounded by heads and the Generalitat's shield.

The central boss of the rib vault also features St George and the dragon.

Corbels depict the Evangelists.

A rose window L lights the chapel.

In the 18C, the chapel was extended eastward and the cupola constructed.

Allegorical paintings were added to the cupola in 1928.

The silver altar frontal reproduces the design of the cloth original.

Baroque silver candlestick holders flank the altar.

Behind the altar stands a copy of the 15C silver figure of St George, an early depiction of the Saint dismounted: the original is now kept in the chapel's treasury.

Three 16C Flemish tapestries decorate the walls of the sanctuary; two illustrate the life of Noah and the other displays a fleur-de-lis pattern.

**Patio of the Orange Trees** (Pati dels Tarongers) This upper-level patio, in two sections, was begun by **Pau Mateu** in 1500; **Tomàs Barsa** took over in 1536 and completed the first section within eleven years. The Gothic style of **Safont**'s earlier patio, including gargoyles and pinnacles, was maintained.

**Gil de Medina** carved the pink Tortosa marble columns which, together with their capitals, introduce the only Renaissance element in the patio.

A pavement of ceramic tiles was laid to the arcade (and the gallery above) by **Pere Mata** in 1526, but this was replaced by the present Carrara marble slabs in 1545.

From the east side of this section of the patio a vestibule, carved by **Subirachs** in 1976, leads to the bridge of 1928 (not open to visitors) which crosses Carrer del Bisbe to the president's official quarters in the former canons' houses.

**Pere Ferrer** extended the patio northward, 1570–91, around the belfry that he had completed two years earlier.

A new carillon, erected above the Renaissance range in 1977, plays traditional Catalan songs on the hour.

**Gilded Hall** (Saló Daurat) **Pere Ferrer** was responsible for this building, but its main façade was remodelled in the 17C.

St George, in the centre, was carved by **Aleu** in the mid 19C.

The gilded coffered ceiling, by **Ramon Puig**, 1578, is the most opulent in the palace.

Floor tiles are of Carrara marble.

Allegorical tapestries illustrate Petrarch's *Life and Death* L and *Triumph of Good over Evil* R.

The Diputació, which administers the four Barcelona provinces, sits in this room.

Traditionally, portraits of kings and queens position the king to the left, but the painting of Juan Carlos and Sofia, exhibited here, was originally two separate works and, when combined, it would not have been acceptable for the King to be facing away from his consort.

**Torres-García Hall** (Saló Torres-García) The paintings in this hall are the work of the Uruguayan-born artist of Catalan parentage, **Torres-García**. They originally decorated St George's Hall and the figures were completely naked. However, the prudish dictator, Primo de Rivera, insisted that the painter should add clothes and, in addition, delete the Catalan coat of arms. Eventually, it was decreed that the paintings should be removed from St George's

Hall and they were kept in storage until hung in this hall in 1974. An original Gothic door survives R.

**St George's Hall** (Saló de Sant Jordi) Major functions take place in this hall, which overlooks Plaça Sant Jaume and forms the most important area within the late-16C extension, by **Pere Blai**.

The Renaissance entrance, with its bronze grille, is fitted into what was the Generalitat's 15C external wall, built by **Marc Safont**.

Its iron door is modern.

A Gothic window survives R.

Within, allegorical paintings of historical Spanish themes were added in 1928 as a replacement for the **Torres-García** works.

The Bohemian crystal chandelier weighs in excess of one ton and incorporates 236 light bulbs.

On 6 April 1914 the Mancomunitat, the first Catalan administrative body in modern times, that united the assemblies of the four Catalan provinces, was constituted in this hall.

At the foot of the Stairway of Honour R is the bronze figure of a mastiff, and a bronze lion stands L of the vestibule. Both are modern works by **Vallmitjana Abarca** and match similar sculptures in Madrid's Parliament House.

*•● Exit from the Generalitat and view the exterior of the Ajuntament, opposite.*

---

Location 10

# BARCELONA CITY HALL
(AJUNTAMENT BARCELONA)

---

Plaça Sant Jaume

*Open only for guided tours Monday–Friday. Admission free, by application to the Ajuntament's Service Protocol. Proof of identity, preferably a passport, will be required.*

Whereas the Generalitat is responsible for administering the province of Catalonia, the Ajuntament wields authority only over the city of Barcelona itself. Its headquarters, once again, is basically a Gothic complex and although, like the Generalitat, it has been given a Classical main façade, most of the earlier Gothic façade remains, but facing another direction. Rare medieval ceilings and a Renaissance arcade survive at ground-floor level, but the Gothic Hall of the Council of One Hundred is the Ajuntament's greatest attraction.

**History** Barcelona citizens' rights were established in written constitutional form in the 13C and a municipal council created. Meetings were held in convents until 1372, when the house of Simó Oller was purchased as headquarters. Early in the 15C, a patio was created in front of the original house, formed by buildings accommodating the Hall of the Council of One Hundred, the Trentenari and the Carrer de la Ciutat façade. The Plaça Sant Jaume façade was built in the mid 19C. Remodelling of the Ajuntament in the 1920s drastically altered its internal appearance, particularly at ground-floor level, and recent extensions, overlooking Plaça Sant Miquel, have greatly increased its size.

**Exterior** Following the demolition of Sant Jaume church, **Josep Mas i Vila** built the Plaça Sant Jaume façade in Classical style to complement the Generalitat which it faces. Begun in 1845, the structure was ready to receive its heraldic roof sculpture, by **Filippo Casoni**, in 1853.

Ground-floor rustication and a balconied Ionic loggia are the only notable features of this façade, the aridity of which is compounded by the omission of architraves.

Standing in niches flanking the entrances are marble figures L of Jaume I and R of Joan Fiveller, 15C royal councillor, both by **Josep Bover**.

●● *Follow c Ciutat L, which skirts the east façade of the building.*

Until the 19C the Carrer Ciutat frontage provided the main façade of the Ajuntament. It was built by **Arnau Bargués**, 1399–1402, in Flamboyant Gothic style, assisted in the carving by **Jordi de Deú** and **Jordi Johan**.

Originally, the façade extended slightly further northward, to the apse of Sant Jaume church, since demolished. When the Plaça Sant Jaume façade was built in the 19C, the section of the doorway's Flamboyant cornice, that would otherwise have been lost, was transferred to the new wall.

Figures of St Eulalia, on the corner L, and St Sever R, were positioned on the façade in 1550, but that of St Sever disappeared *c.*1825 and was replaced with a copy by **Puigjaner**.

Pointed arches throughout, as at the Generalitat, make a rare secular appearance in Barcelona; however, the simple round-headed entrances, together with cornices, maintain the horizontal lines of Catalan Gothic architecture.

Flamboyant first-floor windows incorporate cusping in their tracery, another Catalan rarity. An additional window towards the north was lost to the 19C extension.

Heraldic devices relating to the City's administration are carved above the doorway.

The winged figure of St Raphael is by **Pere Ça Anglada**, 1400.

●● *Return to pl Sant Jaume and enter the building.*

●● *Alternatively, continue to location 11.*

**Interior** The ground floor of the Gothic section of the Ajuntament was remodelled, 1926–9, and both stairways were built at that time.

Originally, when the Renaissance arcade R was built in 1559, it enclosed the Patio of the Orange Trees, now lost. Approached from this was the Hall of the Council of Thirty (Trentenari), only a doorway and one original window of which remain (fronting the offices of the Protocol Department).

Wooden ceilings, some dating from the early 15C, have survived at this level, but all decoration is restoration work.

Facing the stairs is a large figure of St Michael, a modern work by **Josep Llimona**.

Walls of the gallery are decorated with historical Catalan themes by **Josep Maria Sert**.

Approached from the gallery is a sumptuous

Renaissance doorway, originally made in 1580 for the Hall of the Council of Thirty. It is now the ceremonial entrance to the **Hall of the Council of One Hundred** (Saló del Consell de Cent).

This hall was created 1369–1407 by **Pere Llobet** and its original three-light windows survive.

Now forming the side entrance to the hall, but originally its principal, is the Classical doorway designed by **Jaume Granger** in 1648. Carved by **Jaume Rates** and **Pere Serra**, it was moved to its present position in 1926.

The original vaulted and painted wooden ceilings survive within the hall.

Both end bays, L of the entrance, were built as an extension by **Mas i Vila** in 1860, following restoration of the roof, much of which had been destroyed during Barcelona's bombardment of 1842.

Furniture dates from 1914, but the Gothic Revival decor, president's podium and alabaster reredos were added in 1925.

**Hall of the Regent Queen** (Saló de la Reina Regente) Built in the late 19C for public meetings, by **Francesc Daniel Molina**, the room gains its name from the occasion when it was used as a dining hall for the visit to Barcelona of the Regent, Maria Cristina de Borbón, for the Universal Exhibition of 1888.

Paintings are displayed of the Queen with her son, Alfonso XIII, by **Josep Masriera**.

**Hall of the Chronicles** (Saló de les Cròniques)  Shades of brown and gold dominate this rare example of unaltered 1920s decor, the work of **Josep Maria Sert**, 1928.

Murals depict Catalan expeditions to Greece and Byzantium in the 14C.

The **black marble stairway** was built in 1926.

Murals illustrating a Catalan poem are by **Miquel Viladrich**.

A newel-post at the foot of the stairs is carved with the early arms of Barcelona, supported by a lion.

Modern sculptures by **Frederic Marés** and **Joan Miró** stand in the vestibule.

Dating from 1401 is the vestibule's painted timber ceiling, much restored, by **Pere Arcagna**.

•➡ *Exit from the Ajuntament L and cross to the north-west corner of pl Sant Jaume. Follow c Sant Honorat northward.*

The entire east side of the street comprises the west façade of the Generalitat. After the five Renaissance bays have been passed, the elegant trimmed-stone Gothic façade of **Marc Safont**'s original palace is reached. This work represents part of the remodelling of the two houses belonging to wealthy Jews that were confiscated in 1403.

Upper floors retain two- and three-light Gothic windows.

Above the door is the Generalitat's arms, supported by angels.

*● Continue northward.*

A further Gothic range, with same original windows, follows. At the north end of the street R is the rather grim façade added to this part of the Generalitat by **Pere Pau Ferrer**, 1610–30.

*● First R c Sant Sever leads to pl Garriga Bachs.*

The north façade of the Generalitat is also the fortress-like work of **Ferrer**.

*● First R c del Bisbe.*

This façade of the Generalitat, more of **Ferrer**'s work, is his most extensive, but apart from small shields above the windows of the upper floors, the only decorative element is the Baroque coat of arms carved above the doorway.

*● Return northward to pl Garriga Bachs.*

| Location 11 | **PLAÇA GARRIGA BACHS** |
|---|---|

Ancient houses between the Bishop's palace and the Generalitat were demolished to form this small square in 1929.

The monument to Barcelona's victims of the Napoleonic wars dates from the same year. Its bronze is by **Josep Llimona** and the Baroque-style stone carving of angels cavorting in the clouds by **Vicente Navarro**.

Ceramic tiles depict early-19C events in the city: the third panel illustrates an execution that appears to be upsetting all present.

*● Follow c Sant Sever westward from the south-west corner of the square.*

| Location 12 | **SANT SEVER** *Arnaudies 1705* |
|---|---|

**Carrer Sant Sever**
(Tel. 318 16 81)

*Apart from weddings, the church is rarely open, but entrance may generally be gained via No 9 (ring the bell beside the second door L of the church).*

Protected from the 1936 arsonists by its proximity to the heavily guarded Generalitat, Sant Sever possesses the finest original Baroque interior in Barcelona.

In the 15C, benefactors of the cathedral formed a community and, in 1698, commissioned this church, dedicated to their patron, from **Jaume Arnaudies**.

Above the doorway, in a niche, the figure of St Sever is by **Jeroni Escarabatxeres**, 1703.

*● Enter the church.*

St Sever retains a perfectly preserved Baroque interior, made even more startling by its uniqueness in the city. Most of the carving is the early-18C work of **Escarabatxeres**; the gilder was **Francesc Mas**.

Apparently, this interior, although much smaller, is reminiscent of Betlem church in the Rambla before it was burnt.

Sgraffito decoration throughout is original.

The chapels on either side, in the manner of transepts, give the building a cruciform plan.

Within the semicircular apse stands the high altar's reredos, the most sumptuous of its type in Barcelona.

At upper level are the organ and carved private pews.

*●● Exit R and proceed ahead to the junction of c Sant Sever and bda Santa Eulalia.*

Against the wall immediately ahead, at first-floor level, is a shrine to St Eulalia. By tradition, she was rolled in a barrel of broken glass down this street during her martyrdom.

*●● Return eastward. First L c Sant Felip Neri. Proceed ahead to pl Sant Felip Neri.*

| | |
|---|---|
| Location 13 | **PLAÇA SANT FELIP NERI** |

The square, much of which now comprises façades of buildings brought from elsewhere, or built in pastiche style, was created on the site of the cemetery of Montjuïc del Bisbe. It is still dominated by the façade of Sant Felip Neri immediately ahead (location 14).

Forming the west side L is the austere façade of the residence of the Secular Priests of the Oratory, known as the Filipenses. Their convent was built in 1673 over existing houses erected against the Roman wall. It was remodelled early in the 18C and retains a Baroque cloister (not open). In the 19C the complex became a university, but has now reverted to a monastery.

Immediately R of this church is the **St Felip Neri School**. Its façade originally stood in Carrer de la Boria, part of which was demolished for the construction of Via Laietana. The façade was then rebuilt in Plaça de Lesseps before being moved once more, this time to its present site.

Renaissance-style details were added by the Gremi dels Calderers (Coppersmiths' Guild) when they acquired the building in the 16C.

Occupying the south-east corner of the square, where it joins Carrer Sant Felip Neri, is a house with a façade designed in Catalan Gothic style; it is, however, of recent construction.

*●● Proceed to the east side of the square.*

| | |
|---|---|
| Location 14 | **ANTIQUE SHOE MUSEUM**<br>(MUSEU DEL CALÇAT ANTIC) |

Plaça Sant Felip Neri

*Open Monday–Saturday 11.00–14.00. Admission charge.*

The museum occupies a building that has been given the Renaissance façade of the Gremi dels Sabaters (Shoemakers' Guild) founded in 1202. Originally, this fronted the guild's premises, built in 1565 in Carrer de la Carriba. When the street was demolished for the laying out of Avinguda Catedral in 1943 the façade was dismantled and re-erected here.

Between the first-floor windows is carved the lion of St Mark.

The museum displays shoes discovered in Barcelona from the medieval period to the 19C, together with shoes worn by famous people.

*●● Proceed to the church.*

| | |
|---|---|
| Location 15 | **SANT FELIP NERI** *1752* |

Plaça Sant Felip Neri

*Open daily 19.00–20.30*

Like Sant Sever, this church was also protected by the Generalitat, thus escaping the 1936 arsonists. It boasts no fewer than nine altarpieces, four of which are Baroque works.

An oratory, constructed in 1673, was rebuilt in 1677 and again in 1752, to form the present building.

The façade follows the usual Jesuit style of Il Gesù in Rome. Damage to the external stonework was caused by a bomb dropped in the square during the Civil War.

●● *Enter the church.*

Carved private pews at upper level are partly gilded.

At the north end, the high altar's Calvary reredos is late-18C work.

The reredos in the west transept, a Baroque piece by the Valencian, **Ignasi Vergara**, is dedicated to St Felip Neri.

A chapel and late-18C reredos occupy every bay of the church.

●● *Exit L and follow c Montjuïc del Bisbe eastward from the north-east corner of the square (beneath the arch) to pl Garriga Bachs. L c del Bisbe leads to pl Nova. First L c de la Palla.*

| | |
|---|---|
| Location 16 | **CARRER DE LA PALLA** |

This curved road follows the route of the north-west section of the Roman wall, part of which L (facing Nos 31–25) has been revealed. Above the Roman section is evidence of Romanesque windows and towers.

St Philip Neri lodged at **No 10 bis** in the 16C during his visit to Barcelona.

Baroque architraves surmount the three entrances.

On the corner, facing the portal of No 21, a niche contains a life-size figure of the Saint.

**No 21** This early example of Renaissance work in Barcelona was built in 1462, the date carved above the doorway's lintel. The building originated as the hospital of Sant Sever, founded elsewhere by Mossèn Alomat in 1412 to care for priests.

Within (not open), is a small chapel that once accommodated the famous Nunyes reredos.

●● *Proceed ahead and follow the fork L, c Banys Nous.*

The line of Carrer Banys Nous continues to follow that of the Roman wall, the west section of which was demolished from this point in the 19C, apart from fragments. There are many antique shops.

●● *Continue southward.*

| | |
|---|---|
| Location 17 | **PORTALÓN BODEGA** |

20 Carrer Banys Nous

*Closed Sunday*

Now the most impressive 'cave' bodega to survive in Barcelona, Portalón's ancient, decayed charm is unfortunately in danger of succumbing to the misguided whims of the Ajuntament's clean-up brigade, as has its formerly even more spectacular sister establishment in Carrer Regomir.

The front bar is barrel vaulted and always has a good selection of reasonably priced (for Barcelona) tapas.

Ancient bottles and photographs decorate the room at the rear, in which some of the best value meals in the city are served. A great place for a party in an 'old Barcelona' atmosphere.

●● *Exit L. First R c Ave Maria leads to pl Sant Josep Oriol.*

| Location 18 | **PLAÇA SANT JOSEP ORIOL** |
|---|---|

Undoubtedly, this is one of the most charming squares in the city, an excellent place to take refreshment beneath the trees, served from Bar del Pi on the north side. The square, which is in two sections and interconnected with two other squares, Plaça del Pi and Placeta del Pi, commemorates a late-17C Barcelona priest. It was laid out in the 19C, and like most central Barcelona squares occupies the site of an ancient cemetery.

On the east side, immediately north of Carrer Ave Maria, is its most notable building, the **Palau Fiveller**, **No 4**, constructed in 1571 and occupied during the Napoleonic period by the French general, Duhesme. It is now the premises of the Catalonian Agricultural Institute.

The small 18C–style courtyard may generally be viewed.

**Coses de Casa, No 5**, forming the opposite corner with Carrer Ave Maria, is renowned for luxurious fabrics.

●● *Proceed northward, following the east wall of the church, to Pl del Pi.*

| Location 19 | **PLAÇA DEL PI** |
|---|---|

*Artisans' market held in the square, the first Friday in the month.*

A pine (pi) standing in the square commemorates the great trees that grew nearby in medieval times, giving the quarter its name. On Saturday and Sunday mornings paintings and sketches are sold in the square; there is a monthly artisans' market where produce from the surrounding countryside, particularly cheeses and jams, may be purchased.

**No 1**, on the west side, forming the corner with Carrer Cardenal Casañas, was built in 1542 for the Congregation of the Pure Blood, an association formed to offer consolation to those under sentence of death. Remodelling of the building took place in 1613 and 1789, but the roof-gallery survives, although now blocked, and a carved Renaissance shield remains above the doorway R. A postcard shop has occupied the premises since 1789.

**No 3**, built in 1683, possesses what may be the oldest, although completely restored, sgraffiti in Barcelona. Originally, this was the premises of the Guild of Retailers.

In the centre of its second floor, within a Baroque niche dated 1683, stands a figure of St Michael.

The neighbouring house, **No 4**, retains only traces of its sgraffiti.

| Location 20 | **SANTA MARIA DEL PI** |
|---|---|

Plaça del Pi

*Open 08.00–13.00
and 17.00–20.30*

This rather barn-like church, dedicated to St Mary of the Pine Tree, is one of the best examples of the Catalan Gothic style. Its rose window is said to be the largest in the world. Although burnt by the 1936 arsonists, an exceptionally dramatic Baroque reredos and a carved Gothic sarcophagus, both in mint condition, have survived.

A church on the site was recorded in the 10C. It was rebuilt between c.1320 and 1453 and the architect is unknown, but both **Guillem Abiell** and **Francesc Bassett** worked on the building in the 15C.

**Exterior** A Flamboyant rose window, allegedly the largest in the world, is the major feature of the typically early-14C Plaça del Pi façade.

The flanking towers are unfinished, as is usual in Catalan Gothic churches (with the unique exception of Santa Maria del Mar).

Of the portal's original figures, only the Virgin and Child in the centre of the tympanum survive. Both side figures have been lost.

•• *Proceed southward to the pl Sant Josep Oriol façade.*

The Transitional style of the portal (note its Romanesque capitals) and the simplicity of the buttresses are typical of the early 13C. This is somewhat mysterious, as work on the present building is not believed to have started before 1320. It therefore seems probable that the portal's capitals, at least, originated elsewhere, possibly in the first church on the site.

The nave was completed by the mid 14C.

•• *Continue southward to Pla del Pi.*

West of the sanctuary's polygonal apse, **Bartomeu Mas** added the chapter house, 1468–85, now the sacristy.

It is also believed that **Mas** completed the octagonal belfry that rises behind it.

•• *Return to pla del Pi and enter the church.*

**Interior** The rib-vaulted building possesses side chapels but no aisles. Fire damage in 1936 was repaired three years later, but most of the ancient stained glass was lost. An exception was the 18C Adoration window, in the third bay L, by **Antoni Viladomat**, the well-known Catalan painter (1678–1755) who is buried in the church.

The penultimate chapel on the east side L is dedicated to Nostra Senyora de Montserrat. Beneath its pavement lies St Josep Oriol, a local healer, d.1702, who was canonized in 1907.

Decoration of the **choir** is mid-19C work.

The nave's rose window, at the west end but best viewed from here, lost its stained glass in 1936; the present glass is a copy based on records.

Glass in the apse is entirely modern.

Immediately R of the high altar, within a niche in the

wall of the sacristy's vestibule, lies an outstanding well-preserved Gothic sarcophagus.

A star-vaulted **crypt**, beneath the sanctuary, was excavated in 1573 and this later housed a reliquary containing what was alleged to be a 'holy thorn'. The crypt was abandoned in 1763 and later flooded. Restored in 1968, it may be visited on request, when convenient.

The penultimate west chapel possesses a Baroque reredos dedicated to St Michael; made in the 18C it is exceptionally dramatic.

*● Exit R and proceed to the south-east corner of pl del Pi, which leads to the north side of pl Sant Josep Oriol. Directly ahead follow c del Pi northward.*

| | |
|---|---|
| Location 21 | **CARRER DEL PI** |

A cinema and a modern shopping gallery with multiple entrances have greatly altered the character of this ancient street in recent years.

**Casa Barnola No 1** is early 18C but the Rococo sgraffiti have faded.

The keystone of its fourth portal is carved in Louis XIV style; the others, which would have been similar, have been lost to accommodate the shops.

**No 5**, on the south corner with Carrer Perot Lo Lladre, now pierced by shopping galleries, was built in the 17C for the Cortada family. When Jaume Cortada received the title of Baron Maldà i Maldanell in 1766 the building was henceforth called the Maldà Palace.

During a heated meeting in the late 19C of the right-wing Fomento del Trabajo, whose headquarters the building had become, a bomb exploded: the first example of terrorist bombing in Barcelona. The Basque government operated their church from this building during the Civil War, the only venue where Mass was held in Barcelona between 1936 and 1939.

Galerias Maldà, the shopping arcade, revives the name of the palace.

Immediately L, **Carrer Perot Lo Lladre** (Peter the Thief) commemorates a robber who was caught, but pardoned by a sympathetic bishop. He later became a renowned soldier, fighting heroically in Italy. Perot is believed to have inspired one of the episodes in *Don Quixote*.

**No 12**, opposite, retains its 'Romantic' façade with terracotta medallions.

*● First R pl Cucurulla.*

**Fargas**, one of Barcelona's best-known confectioners, displays huge chocolates in the corner building R at **No 16** Carrer del Pí.

In the same building, but at **No 2** Plaça Cucurulla, **Monge**, philatelists and numismatists, occupies an exceptional shop, fitted throughout with Gothic-Revival woodwork in 1904.

**No 4**, formerly the Castanyer Palace, possesses a dressed-stone façade but its patio has for long accommodated a market where 'popular' paintings are sold.

*•● Follow pl Cucurulla ahead to c dels Boters. First L c Arcs.*

| | |
|---|---|
| Location 22 | **OFFICIAL COLLEGE OF CATALAN AND BALEARIC ARCHITECTS** (COL·LEGI OFICIAL D'ARQUITECTES DE CATALUNYA I BALEARS) |
| 2–4 Carrer Arcs and 5 Plaça Nova | Occupying the prominent corner site facing Plaça Nova, this building was designed by **Xavier Busquets Sindreu**, who won the architectural competition for it in 1962. However, of greater interest is the frieze, based on designs by **Picasso**, 1960, and executed in cement by the Norwegian **Carl Nesjar**. The frieze, facing three separate thoroughfares, is laid out as follows: Carrer Arcs: *Joy of Life*, Plaça Nova: *Fiesta*, Carrer Capellaris: *Procession*. |

Within the building, on the first floor, are two murals, also designed by **Picasso**: *Vision of the City* and *Poem of the Sardana*.

Architectural exhibitions are held and there is a comprehensive arts book shop in the basement.

*•● Leave by the c Arcs exit R.*

| | |
|---|---|
| Location 23 | **CARRER ARCS** |

The street's name refers to the arches (arcs) of the Roman aqueduct, the line of which it follows.

**Palacio del Juguetes, No 8**, a toy shop, is decorated round its windows with an unusual 19C plaster frieze.

Above, the building retains traces of the original roof-gallery, now filled.

**Casa Bassols, No 5**, immediately opposite, is occupied by the Reial Circle and the Instituto Barcelones de Arte. Some windows are Gothic but most of the building has been heavily restored.

*•● Enter the patio.*

Within the patio, an original doorway R possesses unusual carvings of dogs in its spandrels.

*•● Exit L.*

Caixa de Barcelona's art gallery, **Sala Arcs**, follows. Exhibitions are open, free, on weekdays (closed 14.00–17.00) and the building incorporates a vaulted Gothic vestibule.

*•● Continue ahead to the corner L with c Cucurulla.*

Fronting the corner is a **Gothic fountain** erected in 1356. Baroque urns were added early in the 19C and ceramic tiles, by **Josep Aragay**, in 1918.

Behind the fountain the Gothic pastiche building, also owned by Caixa de Barcelona, was built in 1968, incorporating some genuine windows from other sources.

*•● First L c Cucurulla.*

**Casa Soler, No 4**, is a 16C building. Above its first-floor windows Renaissance medallions depict the tasks of Hercules.

A second-floor Gothic window survives.

The roof level cornice is original.

*•➤ Continue ahead to pl Cucurulla. First R c
Portaferrissa.*

| Location 24 | **CARRER PORTAFERRISSA** |

Shops in this ancient street now specialize in clothing.
A great gate in the 13C wall stood at the Rambla end
until the 19C. To this were attached plates of iron
(ferriss), hence the name given to the thoroughfare.
A few earlier properties survive, but most of the
buildings are late 19C.

Immediately R, **Nos 25–27** were built in 1857 as an
imposing mansion for the Jover banking family.

*•➤ Proceed to No 13. Open the gate and enter the
passage.*

**No 13** This house was built in the 15C for the Procura
de Montserrat, the Barcelona representative of
Montserrat monastery. Immediately R is its
Renaissance doorway, added in the 16C to the Carrer
Portaferrissa frontage, but later transferred here.

In its tympanum is portrayed the Virgin in the
mountains of Montserrat.

**No 7**, facing Carrer Petritxol, is the oldest house to
survive in the street. Although built *c.*1600 as a
mansion for a wealthy family, its façade was
remodelled in the 18C.

Within, the small patio is well preserved, retaining its
open stairway.

*•➤ Exit ahead and follow c Petritxol southward.*

| Location 25 | **CARRER PETRITXOL** |

With its profusion of plants suspended from
balconies, and varied shops, this narrow street is one
of the prettiest in Barcelona. It was named after the
owner of the land when the thoroughfare was opened
in 1465. Establishments of greatest general interest
are located at the south end.

**Granja La Pallaresa, No 11**, is a survivor of the many
cafés that once stood in the street. It is renowned for
hot chocolate and Catalan desserts.

**Beardsley, No. 12**, will delight lovers of kitsch.
Chunky glassware is outstanding.

**Sala Parés, No 5** Parés, the art dealer, opened his first
gallery in this street in 1840 and it is the oldest to have
been founded in Barcelona. The present building was
constructed in 1884. It was here that a painting by the
twenty-year-old Pablo Picasso was displayed for sale,
for the first time, in 1901: the critics were
unimpressed!

**No 4** A plaque commemorates the Catalan poet and
dramatist, Àngel Guimerà, 1847–1924, who lived
here.

*•➤ Continue to pl del Pi. R c Cardenal Casanyas.*

**No 16**, which faces Carrer d'en Roca, is the Parish
Office of Santa Maria del Pi. Its façade incorporates
three Catalan Gothic portals.

*•➤ Continue ahead to pl Boqueria. R La Rambla and
M Liceu.*

# 3

## Plaça Reial and the Medieval Jewish Quarter

Streets and squares are explored on either side of
Carrer de Ferran and Carrer de Jaume I, both laid
out in the 19C to form the main artery of the city.
Resonances of Italy are found in Plaça Reial,
Barcelona's grandest Classical square, and some of
the finest examples of Romanesque and Gothic
domestic architecture in the city are seen,
particularly in the former Jewish Quarter.
Shopfronts preserved from the 19C are the feature
of Carrer Ferran and the streets that link it with
Plaça Reial.

*Timing:* The Museum of Illustrious Catalans, within
the outstanding Palace of the Countess of Palamós,
is only open the third Sunday of each month 10.30–
14.00.

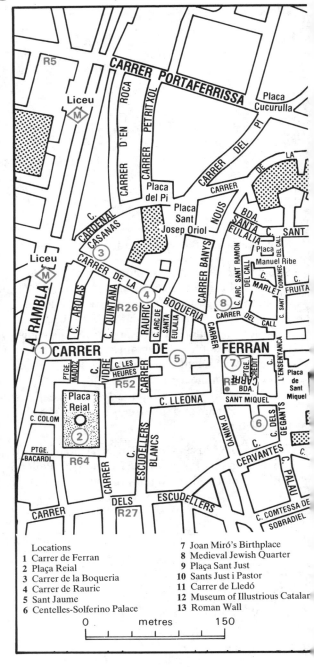

Locations

1 Carrer de Ferran
2 Plaça Reial
3 Carrer de la Boqueria
4 Carrer de Rauric
5 Sant Jaume
6 Centelles-Solferino Palace
7 Joan Miró's Birthplace
8 Medieval Jewish Quarter
9 Plaça Sant Just
10 Sants Just i Pastor
11 Carrer de Lledó
12 Museum of Illustrious Catalan
13 Roman Wall

0          metres          150

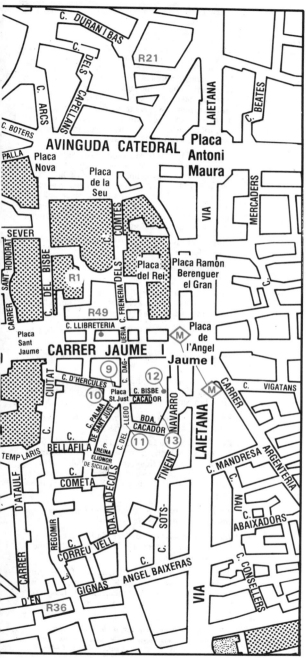

**Start** *M Liceu, line 3. Leave by the Boqueria exit and follow La Rambla southward. Second L c de Ferran.*

| Location 1 | **CARRER DE FERRAN** |
| --- | --- |

Shops of various types, many with original frontages, line this 19C street, which acts as the northern border to a rectangular area of a rather sleazy nature, where clip-joints, ladies of the night, unemployed North Africans and drop-outs abound. There are also, however, some excellent restaurants. Although the district is well policed, care must be taken when venturing southward at night, particularly in the narrow streets around **Plaça Reial**.

**Josep i Mas Vila**, who was also responsible for the present façade of the Ajuntament, began to lay out this street in 1824 as an important part of the extension to Plaça Sant Jaume. Work began at the Rambla end and the western section was completed by 1826. Buildings were given little decoration and the shopfronts were originally identical; within thirty years, however, variations were occurring.

During Corpus Christi, the street is decorated with flowers for the procession.

The delicate suspended street lamps were installed in 1905.

**Farmàcia de la Estrella**, **No 7**, retains its 19C wood and ceramic tile interior, ancient bottles and a brass till adding to the sense of longevity.

Also at **No 7**, **Wolf's** is decorated with Art-Nouveau work.

•● *Cross immediately to the west corner with ptge de Madoz.*

**Clausolles**, **No 2**, an orthopaedic shop, preserves an exceptional Gothic Revival interior, with intricately carved tracery to the woodwork.

•● *Follow c de Ferran eastward towards the west corner with* **c del Vidre** *(first R).*

**Casa Massane**, **No 14**, founded here in 1835, are confectioners, with a coffee lounge at the rear of their premises. Original signs remain externally, while delicate Ionic columns and a marble counter present a cool interior. The brass till, still used, was made in 1879.

•● *Proceed southward along c del Vidre to the north-east corner with c Les Heures (first L).*

**Antiqua Herboristeria Ballart**, **No 1**, retains on its window the inscription 'Herboristeria del Rei (the King's herbalist).

The mid-19C interior survives, dark and apparently undecorated since it was built. Venerable ladies, who serve all manner of herbal medicines and teas, give the impression of having been part of the original fixtures.

•● *Continue beneath the arch ahead to pl Reial.*

| Location 2 | **PLAÇA REIAL** *Francesc Daniel Molina 1848–59* |
| --- | --- |

One of the most Italian squares outside Italy, with an additional touch of North Africa provided by tall

palm trees, the spacious Plaça Reial comes as a
surprise, situated as it is in the heart of the old city's
maze of narrow streets. Cafés with terraces dominate
all but the south (sunless) side.

**History**  Plaça Reial (King's Square) was laid out on
the site of the Capuchin monastery, which had been
built against the Rambla wall in 1718. The monastic
complex was given to the municipality by the Spanish
parliament (Cortes) in 1822 and partly demolished
for the creation of a square dedicated to Spanish
heroes. Although political change led to its
restoration three years later, the possessions of the
monasteries were once more appropriated by the
state in 1835 and this time the buildings were
completely demolished. At first, a theatre and
shopping galleries were planned, but in 1838 it was
agreed that a grand square would be laid out. The
architectural competition for this was won by
**Francesc Daniel Molina**, who completed the Plaça
Reial in 1859, the only square in Barcelona to be built
in the 19C exactly as envisaged.

Closing of the roads to traffic has permitted the cafés
to extend their terraces and, in theory, this should be
a sophisticated spot in which to eat and drink.
Unhappily, however, the reverse is true; junkies,
alcoholics, beggars and petty criminals from the
cheap hostels and tenements in the area home in on
the free benches like bedraggled pigeons returning to
roost and, whilst rarely bothering the al fresco diners
unduly, impose a seedy, dilapidated ambience. In
spite of this, the cafés still feel justified in charging
almost double the normal price for any kind of
beverage taken on 'the terrace'.

The design of the square as a homogeneous unit
disguises the fact that although it appears to be
rectangular, the north and south sides are both set at
a slight angle.

Above colonnade level, the rich ochre of the painted
plaster is highlighted by the white stone pilasters.

A Baroque balustrade crowns the roofline.

Immediately L, two large street lamps, early works
by **Gaudí**, flank the central *Three Graces* fountain.

•● *Follow the square's colonnade clockwise.*

**Museum of Natural Sciences** (Museu Pedagogic de
Ciencias Naturals), **No 8**, at the north end of the east
side, is a delight to children. Not strictly a museum,
as everything is for sale, items include stuffed
animals, primitive carvings, shells and semi-precious
stones. Open Monday to Saturday afternoon, closing
13.30–16.00, admission is free.

A plaque that faces the square, fixed to a column in
front of No 10, commemorates the Catalan
philosopher Francesc Pujols, who was born in the
house in 1883.

•● *Proceed to the south-west corner.*

From here, **Passatge de Bacardí** runs westward to La
Rambla. Opened in 1856, both sides are linked by a
decorative iron bridge. Intrinsically pretty, the
passage is in need of renovation.

•● *Continue northward.*

The west side of the square is bisected by Carrer Colom, which is its main direct link with La Rambla. At this point, but best seen from the centre of the square, the upper floors are decorated with terracotta medallions of explorers. Crestings continue the theme of nautical discoveries.

•● *Follow the north side of the square eastward.*

Cervesseries (ale houses) dominate the north side, and their huge 'tancs' of lager are a tourist attraction.

•● *First L ptge Madoz. First R c de Ferran. First L c Quintana.*

The fact that mercenary ladies haunt Carrer Quintana day and night should not deter one from visiting **Can Culleretes** at **Nos 5–7**. Founded in 1786, this claims to be the city's oldest surviving restaurant. Catalan dishes are authentic and reasonably priced (see page 212).

•● *First L, c de la Boqueria.*

| Location 3 | **CARRER DE LA BOQUERIA** |
|---|---|

When laid out, this street linked the gateway of Castell Nou in the Roman wall with that of Boqueria in the 13C wall facing La Rambla. Its name referred to the many butchers who had premises in the street.

Immediately L, **Pension Dalí, No 12**, was built in the 18C, but its chief interest is the outstanding doorway added *c*.1900. The capitals of the doorway's columns are charmingly carved to depict a lady and a monocled gentleman. One wonders who they were – the owners of the property, perhaps?

**Nos 11–15** form a building that is a good example of Modernism, incorporating iron, stone and mosaic. Its roofline of three curved gables appears to be · influenced by **Gaudí**.

•● *Return eastward to c Arc de Sta Eulalia (third R).*

By tradition St Eulalia, immediately prior to her martyrdom, was imprisoned in a building that once stood in this street.

•● *Continue eastward to the junction with c dels Banys Nous (first L).*

**No 47** is dated 1716 above its first-floor window in the Carrer dels Banys Nous façade. Sgraffiti on this side are better preserved than in Carrer de la Boqueria.

•● *Return following c de la Boqueria westward. Third L, c de Rauric.*

| Location 4 | **CARRER DE RAURIC** |
|---|---|

This is a street of many bars, all of which attract pimps, alcoholics, transvestites and whores of either sex – plus those seeking their company.

Others, however, should still make a brief expedition to the irresistible **Ingenio** at **No 6** (and No 8c). This delightful shop sells masks, toys, novelties and festive costumes (which may also be hired). Its 19C wooden front, partly gilded, serves as an endearing framework to the contents.

•● *First L, c de Ferran. Cross the road.*

| Location 5 | **SANT JAUME** |
|---|---|
| 28 Carrer de Ferran | Little original Gothic detailing has survived, apart from the doorway. Within stands the great 14C reredos, initially presented to the cathedral. |

**History** Originally built in the 14C as a synagogue, Jews converted to Christianity remodelled the building to serve as their church in 1394. The Barefoot Trinitarians acquired the property in 1529, dedicating the church to the Trinity and carrying out various extensions. In 1823, the dedication of this church was altered to Sant Jaume (James) to perpetuate the name of the nearby church of Sant Jaume which had just been demolished. The building became the parish church in 1835 when the Trinitarians were dissolved, and drastic remodelling soon took place.

**Exterior** Although apparently Gothic, most external detailing is 19C Gothic Revival work, dating from the restoration of **Josep Oriol Mestres**, 1866–80.

Surviving, however, from the Jewish converts period is the doorway of 1398, the work of **Ramon de la Porta** and **Bartomeu Gual**.

The doorway's tympanum was carved by **Josep Santigosa** in 1879.

Built of brick with stone trims, the belfry was added in 1722.

Attached to the east side of the church is the Classical **Sant Blas Chapel**, fitted into the end-of-terrace house at No 30.

●● *Enter the church.*

**Interior** Immediately R, in the north-west corner, stands a Baroque marble font.

Little of interest survived the 1936 fire, but in 1970 the cathedral presented St Jaume with its masterly Gothic reredos, that now stands behind the high altar (see page 17). The piece was commissioned for the cathedral by Pere III in 1357 and completed twenty years later. Restoration took place in 1596, when the present base was made.

●● *Exit from the church R. First R c d'Avinyó. Proceed to the bda de Sant Miquel corner (first L).*

On the south corner, **No 11** is an extraordinary Colossal style building, a nightmare in stone, with a brick upper storey.

●● *Follow bda de Sant Miquel eastward towards pl de Sant Miquel.*

| Location 6 | **CENTELLES-SOLFERINO PALACE** |
|---|---|
| 8 Baixada de Sant Miquel<br><br>*Patio open free.* | This early-16C palace is a typical Barcelona example of the period in that it combines Gothic form with Renaissance detail. The patio possesses two outstanding Renaissance doorways. |

Lluís de Centelles commissioned the palace, which was completed in 1514. One of his descendants, Bernat Llanza, married Maria Pignatelli, Duchess of Solferino, in the mid 19C and the palace has retained her family name since then.

The building now belongs to the Department of the President of the Generalitat (Presidencia) and only its patio may be entered.

**Exterior** All façades are of Montjuïc stone. The main façade fronts the street, not the square, which was only created in the 19C.

Typical Catalan Gothic features include the round-headed entrance and first-floor windows with segmented late-Gothic arches supported by figure corbels.

Carved above the doorway, within a Renaissance border, are the arms of the Centelles family.

*Enter the patio.*

The open stairway has a Gothic arcade, which was extended in front of the main entrance wall with slender wrought-iron columns in the 19C.

Two Renaissance doorways are approached from the stairs. Atlantes and angels, respectively, support the family crest above each door.

*Exit from the patio R and continue to **pl Sant Miquel**.*

**Plaça Sant Miquel** was laid out in the 19C on the site of Sant Miquel church, which was demolished for it.

The east façade of the Centelles Palace continues the basic Gothic theme. When built, it overlooked a narrow street.

Opposite, to the east, is the modern extension to the Ajuntament, only distinguished by the frieze sculpted above its Information Office by **Josep Maria Subirachs** in 1969: Barcelona emblems are depicted.

*Return westward, following bda Sant Miquel to No 7. First R ptge del Crèdit. Above the entrance arch is displayed the name of the passage in Spanish: Pasaje del Crédito.*

| Location 7 | **JOAN MIRÓ'S BIRTHPLACE** |
|---|---|
| 4 Passatge del Crèdit | A plaque above **No 4**, at the north end L, records the birth here, in 1893, of Joan Miró, the internationally renowned abstract artist. |

Another plaque, R of its entrance, commemorates his ninetieth birthday.

A wide range of Miró's works is displayed at the Miró Foundation on Montjuïc. The artist died in Majorca on Christmas Day, 1983, but his body was returned to Barcelona and buried in the Montjuïc cemetery.

This short passageway was built in 1879, when iron structures were at their most fashionable. Its completion predated that of the Eiffel Tower by ten years.

Iron columns and girders are exposed on both lower floors, reminiscent of contemporary arcades in Paris.

*L c de Ferran. First R c d'Avinyó.*

Proceed to the junction of c del Call (first R), c de la Boqueria and c dels Banys Nous.

Location 8        **MEDIEVAL JEWISH QUARTER**

Barcelona's Jewish Quarter survived for almost four hundred years, with Carrer del Call as its 'high street', but only an inscribed stone survives to record directly the Jews' presence in the area. Nevertheless, many of their houses and practically all the narrow winding streets have survived.

**History** The north-west quarter of the Roman city became the Jewish area 'El Call' from the 11C, Carrer del Call, Carrer dels Banys Nous, Carrer de la Palla and Carrer del Bisbe marking its limits. Philosophers, astronomers, doctors and writers lived here and the Call soon became Catalonia's most important centre of culture: baths, hospitals and what was virtually a university were built. In 1243, as was usual in the 13C, a wall was built segregating the Call from the rest of the city, its only access point being from a gateway in Plaça Sant Jaume. The Jews were not allowed to leave this ghetto between dusk and dawn without express permission, and they were forced to wear distinctive clothing. However, successive kings protected them against ill-treatment, partly because Saint Augustine had proclaimed that they were royal serfs, who could therefore be taxed indiscriminately. Additionally, the usefulness of such highly educated and financially adroit people was recognized. Many who persecuted the Jews were therefore executed but, when in 1348 the Jews were accused of introducing the Black Death to Spain, three hundred were massacred. As anti-Semitism mounted, based on jealousy, the religion of the Jews was suppressed and their synagogues and cemeteries demolished. In 1424 they were expelled from the Call and in 1492 all unconverted Jews were evicted from Spain.

Just north of the Carrer de la Boqueria and Carrer dels Banys Nous junction stood the Jewish baths that gave the street Banys Nous (New Baths) its name. The establishment survived from 1160 until 1834.

👁️‍🗨️ *Follow c del Call eastward.*

**Carrer del Call** marks part of the route of the Roman street, Decumanus.

**Pulpos, No 1**, displays a sign 'Muralla Romana', and welcomes visitors to inspect, within the shop, a rare fragment of the western stretch of the Roman wall. A round-headed arch and a section of a fluted column are incorporated.

👁️‍🗨️ *Continue eastward.*

**No 5**, built for a wealthy Jewish usurer in the 13C, retains its elegant two-light Gothic windows at upper-floor level.

Embedded in a wall is part of the Roman archway of the Porta del Castell Nou (New Castle Gate) that marked the western entrance in the wall.

**No 8**, opposite, from the 'Romantic' period, is decorated with terracotta reliefs and fanciful ironwork.

**No 14**, built in 1591, retains some of Barcelona's finest 18C sgraffiti; restored as recently as 1966, they already require further attention.

**3**

●● *First L, c Domènec del Call.*

No 5 is entered by a doorway designed in 1899 by **Antoni Gallissà**, the 'William Morris of Catalonia'.

Press the bell indicated for Pensió Sant Domènec del Call. The friendly English-speaking proprietor welcomes visitors to view the patio, to which much-needed renovation is projected. The building is early 13C, and part of a Romanesque window and all of a later, Gothic, window survive.

**Gallissà** decorated the patio with a blend of old and new ceramic tiles in 1900.

No 6, opposite, one of the oldest houses in Barcelona, is believed to be of late-12C origin. Two Romanesque windows survive at second-floor level and two three-light Gothic windows on the first floor.

No 8, a Gothic house, retains from its original period a round-headed entrance and, at upper level R, a two-light window.

●● *Continue to follow c Domènec del Call northward, passing L plta de Manuel Ribé.*

No 15 displays a panel of ceramic tiles at first-floor level. Designed in 1944, this records that St Domingo de Guzmán, who is depicted, founded the Convent of the Order of Preachers here in 1219. This Dominican Order gave the street its name, which formerly had referred to the main synagogue nearby.

●● *Return southward. First R, plta de Manuel Ribé leads to c de l'Arc de St Ramon del Call L. First L **c de Marlet***.

No 1 Inserted in the wall is a 14C stone inscribed in Hebrew, known as the **lápida de Hassareri**. The stone, which was found almost *in situ*, came from the synagogue and commemorates the holy rabbi, Samuel Hassareri, who 'never parted this life'. It suggests that although Hassareri died in 1314 his goodness was immortal. A Spanish translation was added beneath the Hebrew text in 1820.

●● *Follow c de Marlet eastward. First R c Domènec del Call which leads to c de l'Ensenyança. First L, c de Ferran leads to pl Sant Jaume. Follow the north façade of the Ajuntament R eastward. First R, c de la Ciutat. First L c d'Hercules leads to pl Sant Just.*

| Location 9 | **PLAÇA SANT JUST** |
|---|---|

The square was laid out in 1820 on the site of the ancient cemetery of Sant Just which, like other parish cemeteries in the city, was abolished that year. By tradition, some of the earliest of the city's Christian martyrs had been buried there. Early-18C houses surrounding the square make it one of the most picturesque in Barcelona, even though cars parked here during the day are obtrusive.

On the south corner, between Carrer Palma de Sant Just and Carrer Lledó, is the **Gothic fountain**, erected on the instructions of Joan Fiveller in 1367.

The terracotta balustrade was a Classical addition.

Below this, flanking the figure of St Just, are the royal arms and the arms of Barcelona, partly obscured by plants.

On the Carrer dels Lledó side, above the rosette window, the falcon is a reference to Fiveller's love of hunting.

In the north-east corner, between Carrer Daqueria and Carrer Bisbe Caçador, stands **No 4**, the **Moixó Palace**, built in the 18C on the site of the medieval Caçador House for the Marquess of Sant Mori.

The building, decorated with Rococo sgraffiti, combines the Louis XV style with Louis XVI detail.

| Location 10 | **SANTS JUST I PASTOR** |
|---|---|
| Plaça Sant Just | A mid-Gothic church, built in typical Catalan style, Sants Just i Pastor was formerly the royal parish church, and for a brief period served as Barcelona's cathedral. Internally, in spite of the 1936 fire, some outstanding carving and a 16C reredos survive. |

**History** By tradition this church, situated within the south-east quarter of the Roman city, was founded in the 4C thus making it the oldest in Barcelona. It was rebuilt in 801 by **Lluís el Piadoso** and became the direct responsibility of the cathedral in 965. Until the Catalan dynasty ended, Sants Just i Pastor was the royal parish church and its priest automatically became the archdeacon of the see, a privilege that survived until the 15C.

During much of the construction period of the Romanesque cathedral, Sants Just i Pastor took over its mantle.

The present church was begun in 1342 and it appears that the first four bays of the nave were completed in twenty years. However, work on the fifth bay did not begin until the 15C.

**Exterior** A doorway and a large window, both surrounded by 15C crestings, are the features of the austere façade, believed to be the mid-14C work of **Bernat Roca**.

Between 1750 and 1884, a building that accommodated the parish archives obscured this façade. After its removal, restoration was completed by **Josep Oriol Mestres** in 1887. Catalan church façades were usually flanked by two bell towers (which were seldom finished at upper level). The polygonal north tower of Sants Just i Pastor was completed by **Pere Blai** and **Joan Safont** in 1567, but it appears that its twin was never finished.

●● *Enter the church.*

**Interior** Bosses of the nave's vault bear traces of decoration. They are 14C work, carved with scenes from the lives of Christ and the Virgin.

The first west bay L is occupied by the **Chapel of the Daguerias** (swordmakers). In its central altarpiece, a figure represents St Maria de Cervelló who, by tradition, was born in the Dalmases Palace in Carrer Montcada.

Occupying the third north bay is the **Sant Paciano Chapel**. The lower figure of its altarpiece, the Virgin of the Snows, is 17C. Formerly, on the Saints' feast day, the church was decorated with imitation snow.

Immediately L of the high altar, before the sacristy is

reached, is the **Sant Feliú Chapel** (request its illumination from the sacristy). In 1525, Jaume Joan de Requesens was given permission to be buried here on condition that he paid for the chapel to be decorated. Work included the reredos, which was created by the Flemish carver **Joan de Bruseles** and the Portuguese painter **Pero Nunyes**.

A marble tombslab towards the front of the pavement marks the vault of the Requesens family.

It was in front of the altar in this chapel that witnesses to a Barcelona citizen's will, made anywhere in the world, in verbal or written form, had to verify its content within six months of returning to the city. First recorded in 1082, this 'Right of Sacramental Wills' was incorporated in Barcelona law in 1283 and is still valid.

Between the 11C and 15C, citizens' disputes could be settled by duel, it being believed that providence would grant victory to the righteous party. In front of the Sant Feliú Chapel's altar, contestants pledged that they would only duel with the arms specified and that they would carry no talismans or precious stones, then thought to guarantee invulnerability.

*◆▶ Proceed to the* **sanctuary**.

The Annunciation boss in the apse is believed to have been carved by one of the **Claperós** family.

Until the 19C the sanctuary, now in the apse, was sited in the centre of the nave.

Medieval stained glass survives in the apsidal windows.

A 16C reredos to the high altar was replaced in 1832 by the present Classical piece, supported by six columns of Tarragona marble. Its chief feature is a copy of the black Virgin of Montserrat, who is highly venerated in this church.

St Just and St Pastor, on pedestals, flank the carving.

*◆▶ Exit R. First R* **c de la Palma de Sant Just**.

The **Esperança Church, No 2**, displays on its façade some Baroque features: the portal, carved with a figure, and sgraffiti above the entrance.

**No 4**, a Gothic building, is decorated with 18C sgraffiti, most of which above first-floor level have been lost.

The central first-floor window retains its original cresting.

Below this, a plaque records the canonization of St Josep Oriol.

The other first-floor windows, with corbelled architraves, are also Gothic, but later work.

Renaissance stone brackets support the balconies.

**No 6** also has preserved corbels to the first-floor windows and Renaissance brackets to the balcony.

There are sgraffiti on the first floor.

**No 5** Figure corbels, rather decayed, support the lower Gothic window R of the portal.

*◆▶ First L* **c del Cometa**. *L* **c de Lledó**.

Location 11     **CARRER DE LLEDÓ**

From the 14C until the 19C this was one of the most aristocratic streets in Barcelona, and although it is no longer a fashionable address, several palaces and mansions survive. Unfortunately, most have been greatly altered, particularly by the addition, in the 18C, of balconied windows and carriage entrances.

**No 13**, formerly the Casa Lledó, now the social club of the **Caixa de Barcelona**, is decorated between its first floor windows with Renaissance medallions in the form of female busts.

The ground-floor interior, divided into aisles by Ionic columns, may be viewed.

**No 11**, a college of Carmelite nuns, preserves an 18C carriage entrance and is decorated with sgraffiti from the same period.

Within the tiny patio, two of the stairway's columns are broken but do not align – apparently an alarming case of settlement.

**No 6**, formerly the Casa de la Reina Elionor de Sicilia, is a 14C building, retaining its round-headed portal and remains of a two-light window L at first-floor level.

On the Carrer de la Reina Elionor de Sicilia façade, figure corbels support the architrave of the square ground-floor window.

**No 7**, a 14C palace, possesses a large carriage entrance, probably added in the 18C. The ground-floor window, L of the carriage entrance, is decorated with carved figures.

A plaque records the birth here of the founder of the Caja de Ahorras, Francesc Moragas Barret, in 1869.

First-floor windows were altered in the 18C, when balconies were added.

The short tower is lit by an original lobed window.

The open roof-gallery survives.

**No 4** Formerly the Fiveller Palace, Joan Fiveller, the famous Catalan statesman and adviser to the King, lived here in the 14C.

Although intrinsically a Gothic building, the palace has been greatly altered and little original detail survives.

The lintel of the carriage gateway is supported by Classical corbels.

Gothic first-floor windows were replaced in the 18C and balconies added.

The neglected patio has a three-flight open staircase and some 15C carving at first-floor level. Note the corbel busts of a man and a woman to the window facing the second flight of stairs.

●● *Continue northward. Second R* **c del Bisbe Caçador** (**Cassador** *on the name plate). Proceed to the end of the street and enter the patio ahead.*

Location 12

**MUSEUM OF ILLUSTRIOUS CATALANS
(MUSEU GALERIA CATALANS ILLUSTRES)**

Palau del Condessa
de Palamós
3 Carrer del Bisbe
Caçador
(Tel. 315 00 01 or
315 11 11)

*Museum open the
third Sunday in
each month 10.30–
14.00.*

*Admission, by
prior arrangement
only, is free.*

This Romanesque palace is the finest private
medieval residence in Barcelona. Unfortunately, its
outstanding 17C interiors are rarely open, due to
their occupation by the Royal Academy of Fine
Letters.

**History** The building was constructed early in the
13C, originally as a fortress. During the late 15C the
palace, as it had by then become, was occupied by
Galceran de Requesens, Count of Palamós and
Governor of Catalonia. His widow lived here for
many years and the palace still bears her name,
although it is also known as the Requesens Palace.

•● *Enter the patio.*

**Exterior** The building was constructed in the
Romanesque style early in the 13C, above the
Roman wall and between two of its watch-towers that
had been heightened in the 12C.

Ahead L, the tower retains its Romanesque
windows.

The roof-gallery and three-light window were added
during the Gothic period.

All windows in the wall R are Gothic.

Two blocked Romanesque arches survive at ground-
floor level.

In the 17C, the palace was remodelled internally and
the main windows of the entrance wall were altered
and given balconies. However, a three-light
Romanesque window survives beside the stairs.

Arches of the first-floor gallery and the windows in
the tower R are pointed, possibly indicative of the
importance of the building.

A series of stepped-pyramid buttresses decorates
much of the roof line. This is a typical feature of
medieval buildings in the city and would appear to
have been influenced by Moorish architecture.

•● *Enter the museum.*

•● *Alternatively, proceed to location 13.*

Some of the finest 17C interiors in Barcelona survive
within the palace, now partly occupied by the Reial
Academia de Bones Lletres (Royal Academy of Fine
Letters), and it is unfortunate that access to the
museum is so limited.

Paintings depict famous Catalans.

•● *Exit ahead. First L c dels Lledó. First L bda de
Caçador.*

Immediately ahead, **No 9**, **Carrer del Sots-Tinent
Navarro**, is a large Gothic Revival building, dated
1921, a late example of Modernism, incorporating
outstanding ceramic work and twisted brick columns.

•● *L c del Sots-Tinent Navarro.*

Location 13

**ROMAN WALL**

On entering Carrer del Sots-Tinent Navarro, which
was laid out early in the 19C, a further major stretch

of the Roman wall is reached. (See page 4 for general details of the wall.)

●➤ *Continue northward.*

Immediately L, a Corinthian column from Roman Barcelona stands in the garden.

The first of the two watch-towers that flank the Palace of the Countess of Palamós has been rebuilt almost entirely in brick.

The Roman section of the stone tower retains its original symmetrically placed windows: four in front and two on each side.

Part of the roof gallery of the palace is visible above the linking arch.

●➤ *Continue ahead to pl de l'Àngel and M Jaume 1.*

## Picasso Museum and Palace of Catalan Music

The northern and eastern sections of the old city that lie between the Roman and the 13C wall are explored. A visit is made to the cloistered monastic church of Santa Anna, the 4 Gats Bar and the Palace of Catalan Music, Domènech i Montaner's masterpiece, considered by many to be the quintessential Modernist building. Carrer de Montcada includes the world-famous Picasso Museum.

*Timing:* Carrer Montcada, where all the museums on this route are located, is best visited Tuesday–Friday, when everything is open; Monday should definitely be avoided.

A return visit at 19.30 will be necessary to view the interior of Sant Pere de les Puelles (of specialized interest).

The Picasso Museum and the Textile and Costume Museum close Monday and the latter also closes Sunday at 14.00.

The Maeght Gallery is closed 13.30–16.30 and Sunday and Monday.

Omnium Cultural is closed weekends.

Casa Esteban bar is closed Monday.

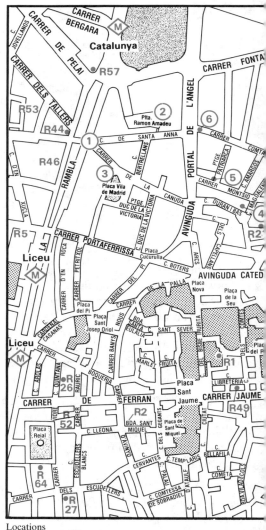

Locations

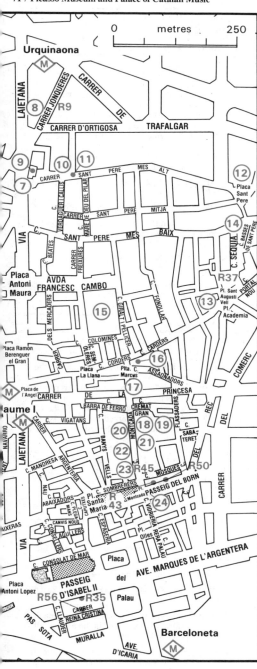

**Start** *M Catalunya, lines 1, 3 and FF.CC. Generalitat. Exit and proceed to the east side of La Rambla. First L c de Santa Anna.*

| Location 1 | **CARRER DE SANTA ANNA** |
| --- | --- |

Although an ancient street, little medieval work survives, apart from the church of the former monastery of Santa Anna that gave the throughfare its name (location 2). Carrer de Santa Anna runs from the western extremity of the Pine Tree Quarter (Barri del Pi), which was originally built as a new township outside the Roman wall. Apparently, many tall pine trees formerly grew in the area, not just one in what is now the Plaça del Pi, as is generally believed. In the 13C the new wall enclosed the quarter and the pine trees began to disappear.

**No 10** possesses freshly restored Louis XV period sgraffiti.

**No 19** is decorated with geometric sgraffiti.

**No 21**, a Modernist building with copious floral decoration, follows the style of Domènech i Montaner.

**No 27** retains elaborate sgraffiti, in need of repainting.

•● *Proceed through the passage L to plta de Ramon Amadeu. Immediately R of the archway is a carved figure corbel.*

| Location 2 | **SANTA ANNA** |
| --- | --- |
| Placeta de Ramon Amadeu | A mid-12C monastic church, Santa Anna retains much of its simple, Romanesque appearance. |

**History** The Knights Templar commissioned the church on their arrival in Barcelona in 1141, and it was completed in five years by **Carfilius** as part of a monastic complex. At that time Santa Anna stood in open country, outside the Roman wall. In the 15C, the Montsió monastery merged with Santa Anna and, to increase accommodation, chapels and a chapter house were added and the cloister begun. Spain's parliament (the Cortes), met in the monastic hall in 1493, with Ferdinand the Catholic presiding. While the cloister and chapter house survive, the other domestic buildings were demolished in 1835.

**Exterior** The main doorway to the church, set in the south transept, was built in 1300.

This transept's side chapel L was added in the 13C and its side chapel R in the 15C.

Eastward from the transept runs the chancel, mostly concealed by houses.

Above the crossing rises a small belfry.

West of the transept is the buttressed nave, extended in the 13C.

Through the gate, L of the church, can be seen the two-storey cloister, constructed in the first half of the 15C. It is not generally open.

**Interior** Santa Anna's simple cruciform interior is dimly lit by small Romanesque windows, augmented by modern skylights above the crossing.

Until the 14C the church was entirely barrel vaulted,

but the nave was then given its present rib vault.

The transepts and chancel retain their original vaults.

Immediately L of the entrance is the All Saints Chapel, added in the 13C. Its decoration is now entirely modern. Incorporated in the paving of the nave are many tombslabs.

The gate to the north-east chapel of Sant Roc, the rail to the high altar and the pulpit's balustrade display outstanding ironwork.

Sculptures of the high altar's reredos are the 20C work of **Esteve Monegal**.

Above the crossing, the modern structure replaced 16C work lost in the 1936 fire.

Request permission to view the **cloister** and former chapter house (sala capitular), now the **Capella de Poblet**.

The two-storey cloister is entered from the end of the western extension to the nave. It was completed c.1590 and restoration has been sympathetic.

Square columns of Gerona stone, supporting the bracketed wooden roof, possess capitals carved with an abacus and rosettes.

Approached from the north-west corner of the church, the former chapter house was converted to a chapel in 1835. It was built in the 15C to provide additional accommodation when the Montsió monastery merged with Santa Anna.

Two high windows were incorporated to enable non-monastic worshippers to observe religious ceremonies within.

Carved on the 15C boss of the apse's vault is the figure of the priest responsible for constructing the chapter house; he is depicted kneeling to St Augustine.

●● *Exit and return via the passage to c de Santa Anna R. First L c de Bertrellans. First R c de la Canuda. Pass pl de la Vila de Madrid (first L).*

| Location 3 | **ATENEU BARCELONI** |
|---|---|
| 6 Carrer de la Canuda | The 19C Classical façade, by **Josep Font i Goma**, disguises an earlier building incorporating a salon and library, with ceilings painted in the 18C by **Francesc Pla**. |

Early occupants included the Baron de Savassona and, later, the Parellada family, but since the 19C the building has accommodated the Athenaeum Library of Barcelona, founded as a cultural club in 1836. The library is regarded as the most important private collection in Spain.

Public concerts are occasionally given, but visitors are no longer permitted to view any part of the interior or the charming rear garden.

●● *Return eastward. First R pl de la Vila de Madrid.*

Remains of a Roman way outside the city's 4C wall have been excavated in the square's sunken garden. It is flanked by a series of funeral stones, approximately *in situ*.

*●● From the south-east corner of the square follow ptge del Duc de la Victoria eastward. L c del Duc de la Victoria. R c de la Canuda. Second L av del Portal de l'Àngel. Cross the road and follow c de Duran i Bas directly ahead.*

**No 9, Avinguda del Portal de l'Àngel**, on the north corner with c de la Canuda, was built in the 17C for the Sarriera family, one of Catalonia's oldest established. The patio has been remodelled and retains little original work. Judged the most splendid in Barcelona, the interior is not, unfortunately, open to the public.

*●● Cross av del Portal de l'Àngel and follow c de Duran i Bas immediately ahead.*

| Location 4 | **BALMES LIBRARY** (LLIBRERIA BALMES) |
|---|---|

9–11 Carrer de Duran i Bas

*Library open Monday–Friday 10.00–13.00.*

This extraordinary, Neo-Medieval building, known as 'Balmesiana', was constructed in 1923 using, as foundations, the remains of early-13C houses. Some Gothic details from the houses were also incorporated. The name commemorates the 19C philosopher Jaume Balmes.

Displayed in the second-floor library are important murals from the walls of the original houses that stood on the site. Their style marks the transition from Romanesque to Gothic.

*●● Exit L. First L c Magdalenes. First L c Montsió.*

Immediately L, at **No 10**, is the rear façade of 'Balmesiana'.

*●● Continue westward.*

**No 5** is a 19C Modernist building with high-quality Gothic Revival work to the ground floor, where bricks, ceramics and ironwork are incorporated. Decorative themes throughout are based on plant life, in the manner of Domènech i Montaner.

A roof gallery continues the Catalan Gothic theme.

The building's sgraffiti are better preserved on the side facing Passatge del Patriarca.

*●● Proceed to the opposite side of the passage.*

| Location 5 | **ELS 4 GATS** *Puig i Cadafalch 1900* |
|---|---|

3 bis Carrer Montsió

The 4 Gats (cats) bar/restaurant occupies much of the ground floor of the Casa Martí, built by the Modernist **Puig i Cadafalch** in Gothic Revival style.

Features on the passage façade include a great oriel window and a large St George and the Dragon at the corner.

*●● Continue to the c Montsió façade.*

The roof line incorporates stepped-pyramid battlements and a gallery.

Fanciful railings and rich stone carvings decorate the building.

*●● Enter the 4 Gats by the doorway R.*

The 4 Gats ale bar became a meeting place for avant-garde artists and writers shortly after it opened. Picasso was an early habitué and it is said that his work was shown publicly here for the first time. Later, the bar became the headquarters of the Cercle Artiste de Sant Lluc, of which Gaudí was a member.

Although the front room is greatly altered, a photograph that it displays of the bar, taken in 1919, shows that many original features survive: ceramics, the beamed ceiling, the tiled floor and one of the doorways. A restaurant is now situated behind the bar.

•➤ *Exit R. First R av del Portal de l'Àngel.*

**Avinguda del Portal de l'Àngel** follows the route of the street that led northward from the gate in the 13C wall, originally called Portal dels Cecs; its name was changed to Portal de l'Àngel in 1466. The thoroughfare is now a major shopping street with the emphasis, particularly on the east side, on clothing.

**Catalana de Gas i Electricitat, No 22**, was designed by one of the leading Modernists, **Josep Domènech i Estapà**, in 1895; the building displays the architect's eclectic tendencies.

•➤ *First R c Comtal.*

| Location 6 | **CARRER COMTAL** |

Carrer Comtal, where a wide variety of goods is displayed, is a refreshing change from the numerous Barcelona shopping thoroughfares that are now dominated by boutiques offering similar clothes at similar (high) prices.

**La Casa del Bacalao, No 8**, might well be described as a boutique, but what it is selling are various cuts of salted and dried North Sea cod, beautifully displayed as if they were Swiss watches.

**No 14**, (second section), retains first-floor window lintels carved in the 18C with the Virgin of the Rosary and St Christopher.

Its upper-floor sgraffiti are now much faded.

**Raima, No 27**, decorated with sgraffiti, retains a three-light 15C window on the first floor R.

Its lower floor is pastiche Gothic.

•➤ *Continue ahead to Via Laietana.*

Immediately ahead, **No 50**, on the east side of Via Laietana, is decorated with 18C sgraffiti featuring giant figures. It has been judged the finest example of such work in Barcelona.

•➤ *Turn L and follow Via Laietana northward to the junction with c dels Jonqueres (first R).*

| Location 7 | **VIA LAIETANA** |

Of the many 19C plans to modernize the old city, only this wide north-south avenue came to fruition. It cut through a warren of ancient streets, and in spite of conservationist protests some historic buildings, notably the Jonqueres monastery, were lost. First projected in 1869, work eventually began, at the north end, in 1907 and the thoroughfare was then called Carrer Bilbao. It is this early section that holds the greatest architectural interest, as banal commercial buildings dominate to the south.

| | |
|---|---|
| Location 8 | **CAIXA DE PENSIONS** *Sagnier i Villavecchia 1917* |

| | |
|---|---|
| 56–58 Via Laietana | This Modernist building is a late work of **Sagnier**, who built so much in Barcelona that he might be compared, for industry, with Britain's George Gilbert Scott. Beginning as a Modernist, then moving to Baroque, **Sagnier** returned here once more to his original style – if eclecticism run riot can be called a style. Gothic predominates, incorporating some Nordic themes – even contemporary Glaswegian influences have been noted. However, for **Sagnier** the work is remarkably sober. |

Another Modernist work by **Sagnier** faces this building, at No 2 Carrer de las Jonqueres, now also owned by *Caixa de Pensions*.

*•• Return southward towards the junction with Sant Pere Mès Alt (second L).*

| | |
|---|---|
| Location 9 | **HOUSE OF THE SAILMAKERS** *Joan Garrido 1763* |

| | |
|---|---|
| 50 Via Laietana | The Via Laietana façade of this building, seen earlier from the west side of the street, is notable for its sgraffiti, the early 19C work of **Soler i Rovirosa**, restored in 1930 by **Ferran Romeu**. |

*•• Proceed to the corner with c Sant Pere Mès Alt (first L).*

In the corner niche the figure of *Purity* was carved by **Joan Enrich**.

*•• First L c Sant Pere Mès Alt.*

The completion date of the building, 1763, is carved above the doorway.

*•• Continue to the east façade of the building, facing pl de Lluís Millet.*

Sgraffiti on this side were entirely the 1930 pastiche work of **Romeu**.

*•• Follow c Sant Pere Mès Alt eastward.*

Immediately L, the church of **Sant Francesc de Paula** was almost completely rebuilt in shortened form in 1989. Its predecessor, originally the church of the Minimos convent, was damaged by fire in 1854 and 1909, finally being destroyed internally in 1936. Construction of the building has proceeded under the direction of **Oscar Tusquets**, as a combined project with the extensions to the adjoining Palace of Catalan Music.

The rectory and a narrow block of flats separate the façades of the church and the concert hall.

| | |
|---|---|
| Location 10 | **PALACE OF CATALAN MUSIC** (PALAU DE LA MÚSICA CATALANA) *Domènech i Montaner 1908* |

| | |
|---|---|
| 13 Carrer Sant Pere Mès Alt (Tel. 3011104) | This, Barcelona's foremost concert hall, has been judged the most representative architectural example of Catalan Modernist work. |
| *Open only for concerts.* | It was commissioned as the headquarters and performance hall of the Orfeó Català, a choral society formed by Lluís Millet to revive Catalan music. The building's site had been occupied by the cloister of the Minimos convent until this was lost in |

1835. **Domènech i Montaner**'s otherwise open brief was to design a 'Temple of Catalan art, a palace to celebrate its renaissance'.

Between the ground-floor arches are carved the arms of Barcelona and the Orfeó Català.

On the corner R, the sculpture between the two lower floors is by **Miguel Blay**, who has signed his work.

Busts of Palestrina, Bach and Beethoven are by **Pau Gargallo**.

Allegorical mosaics at upper-floor level were designed by **Lluís Bru**.

A short tower and a cupola crown the building.

•● *Enter the vestibule.*

A mural by **Massot** (regarded by many as unsympathetic) decorates the vestibule.

The amphitheatre, one of the most delightful in the world, can accommodate an audience of up to two thousand and is the only major concert hall in existence lit by daylight.

Floral themes throughout incorporate stone, mosaic and stained glass in a typical Modernist manner.

**Pau Gargallo** was responsible for much of the carving including, L of the stage, the leaf pattern and the bust of Clavé, representing popular Catalan music and, R of the stage, the Valkyries and a bust of Beethoven, representing international music .

•● *Exit L.*

| Location 11 | **CARRER SANT PERE MÈS ALT** |
|---|---|

Three ancient streets, named to commemorate St Peter, converge at their east end in Plaça Sant Pere: Mès Alt (the uppermost), Mitjà (middle) and Mès Baix (lowest).

This street is probably the most elegant of the three, but none of its Gothic mansions escaped complete remodelling in the 18C and 19C.

**Nos 17** and **25** are restrained Classical examples, with elegant ironwork.

**No 18**, the early-19C **Dou Palace**, retains faded sgraffiti, the theme of which gave the building its local name 'The House of Four Seasons'. **Antoni Celles**, a leading Catalan exponent of Classical purity, was the architect.

**No 27**, also Classical in style, preserves unusual decoration above its first-floor windows.

•● *Continue eastward to pl Sant Pere.*

| Location 12 | **SANT PERE DE LES PUELLES** |
|---|---|

Plaça Sant Pere

*Open daily at 19.30 (preceding Mass at 20.00).*

Only limited medieval features have survived in this ancient church, due to insensitive 'restoration'.

**History** Romanesque fragments tend to confirm the tradition that the church was first built in 801. Formerly dedicated to St Saturnino, it was incorporated in a Benedictine nunnery in 945 and rededicated to Sant Pere de les Puelles. The Moors destroyed the church twice and although rebuilding took place between the 10C and 12C a few original features were incorporated. It was decided to rebuild the church completely in 1816, but the state's anti-monastic measures prevented this, the nuns being expelled in 1835. Sant Pere de les Puelles became the parish church in 1854 and the former domestic buildings of the nunnery were demolished twenty years later. Fires in 1909 and 1936 caused some damage to the structure, but not as much as resulted from the disastrous over-restoration that followed both events.

**Exterior**  Fortress-like, the almost entirely pastiche façade is the work of **Eduard Mercader**, 1911.

The doorway alone survives from the 15C.

*➤ Enter the building.*

**Interior**  Internally, the church owes most of its appearance to the post-1936 fire restoration, although the Greek Cross plan, with a 12C structure above the crossing, is maintained.

Originally, the building had a wooden roof but this was replaced in the 14C by a rib vault.

Monolithic, crude Corinthian columns that support the first arch at the west end were reused from the 9C church.

A similar reused column (with iron band) forms the south-west pier of the crossing R.

The apse, a 15C addition, has been needlessly remodelled in Romanesque style.

*➤ Proceed immediately north of the sanctuary, to the square north-east chapel.*

Restoration demolished this chapel's original vault but its walls are believed to have originally formed the porch of the 9C chapel.

A Romanesque arch on the south side and a Romanesque frieze on the north side survive.

The north transept retains its 14C rib vault.

Further sections of a Romanesque frieze decorate the north-west corner of the crossing.

A Gothic doorway, preserved in the north wall of the north arch, originally led to the two-storey 11C and 14C cloister, which was demolished in 1873. A section of this has been preserved in the Museum of Catalan Art.

*➤ Exit from the church ahead and follow the short street that forms part of pl Sant Pere, southward. Cross immediately to **c de les Basses de Sant Pere**.*

At **No 22**, a bar, apparently nameless, specializes in black beer and a rarely served shellfish, 'Escupinyas', which is excellent accompanied by piquant sauce.

**No 4**, still awaiting long-promised restoration, preserves Gothic features: round-headed portal, roof gallery and tower with a two-light window at upper level.

*➤ Continue ahead to pl Sant Agustí Vell. First L c del Portal Nou.*

On the opposite side, houses preserve their Gothic shopping arcade.

*●● Return to pl Sant Agustí Vell and proceed southward.*

| Location 13 | **PLAÇA SANT AGUSTÍ VELL** |

Little altered in modern times, this village-like square is one of the most characterful in Barcelona.

Three 19C street lamps dominate, that in the centre surmounting a fountain.

*●● Second L pl de l'Acadèmia.*

Inserted in the wall ahead, the Renaissance doorway originally formed the entrance to the 15C church of the convent of Sant Agustí, from which the main square is named. Abandoned in 1716, only a small part of the church, lying behind the doorway, survives. It has been converted to accommodate a military academy (hence the name of this small square) and is not open to the public.

*●● Return to pl Sant Agustí Vell. Ahead (at upper level) follow c de la Sèquia. L c Sant Pere Mès Baix.*

| Location 14 | **CARRER SANT PERE MÈS BAIX** |

A mix of Gothic and Baroque buildings lines this lively shopping street.

**No 48** retains on its upper floor L a Flamboyant Gothic canopied window.

**No 46**, a 15C house, was decorated with sgraffiti in 1779, each floor depicting a landscape: only traces now remain.

**No 37** preserves a 16C portal and tower, but the original windows and roof gallery have been lost.

**No 42**, a simple Baroque house, has a surprise in its small patio – a flourishing palm tree.

Its rear façade, with Romanesque Revival windows and cast-iron columns (rusting), was built in 1860.

The **Camilos Chapel, No 33**, although completed in 1827, is Napoleonic in style, displaying a fanlight above the door that is typical of the Empire period. The building is generally open and it can then be seen that there is a cupola.

**No 29 bis**, a 13C building, retains its original portal and on the first floor, the outline of a two-light Gothic window, now filled.

**Santuari de la Mare de Déu de l'Ajuda, No 18**, is an oratory chapel created in 1808.

*●● Enter by the side door.*

Frescos in the apse were painted by **Montserrat Casanova** in 1949.

**No 16** is decorated with sgraffiti, dated 1783, above the door.

The **Institut del Teatre, No 7**, a 15C building, retains its patio's original stairway.

*●● Return eastward. First R c de les Beates. Continue southward to the south-east corner of pl de les Beates with c dels Mercaders.*

**Casal de Joves Palau Mercaders, No 42**, is a 17C
mansion with a carriage entrance.

Tuscan columns form the arcade of the patio, which
has been partly filled L with modern additions.

The open staircase has a particularly delicate iron
balustrade.

Carrer dels Mercaders was broken into just south of
this point by the construction, in 1943, of Avinguda
Francesc Cambó. Fortunately, the street's most
important building, the House of Clariana–Padellàs,
had been transferred stone by stone to Plaça del Rei in
1930, and now accommodates the City's History
Museum.

●● *First L av Francesc Cambó. Cross the road and
continue ahead to the Santa Caterina Market.*

| Location 15 | **SANTA CATERINA MARKET**<br>(MERCAT SANTA CATERINA), *Buixareu 1848.* |
| --- | --- |

Formerly, at this point, stood the church of the 13C
Dominican monastery of Santa Caterina. Demolition
and fire had removed all traces by 1837 and the present
food market was completed eleven years later in
Classical style.

Great wooden trusses cover the open passageways.

●● *Exit from the market at its south-west corner and
follow c de les Semoleres southward to pl de la Llana.*

As its name suggests, **Plaça de la Llana** was formerly a
wool market. Leading eastward from it are Carrer dels
Corders (cordmakers) and Carrer dels Carders
(spinners), both names recording the members of fibre-
processing trades who formerly lived in the locality. The
area was well watered by streams in the Middle Ages,
making it particularly suitable for these industries.

**No 11**, on the east side L, is a late-19C chemist's shop
retaining its original front. Internally, the décor is
Art-Nouveau, *c.*1900.

●● *Leave the square from its north-east corner and
follow c dels Corders to c dels Carders. At their junction
is plta d'en Marcus and the Marcus Chapel (location 16).*

The east gate in the 13C wall, Portal Nou (New
Gateway), formerly stood at this point and Carrer dels
Carders led eastward from it towards France. The
thoroughfare soon became a centre for businesses
connected with international trading and was lined
with warehouses and inns, many existing until the 19C
when stage-coaches were replaced by the railways.

**Farmàcia Josep Divi, No 3**, facing the Marcus Chapel,
retains its 19C interior with fine woodwork and a
painted ceiling.

●● *Continue eastward.*

**Bar Bon Sort, No 10**, is a unique survivor of the street's
once numerous coaching inns. Its former name,
Hostal Bon Sort, may still be deciphered on the
façade. Immediately to its east stands the inn's original
coachyard, arcaded and galleried. All is very
picturesque, but rarely visible as the portal is kept
locked.

●● *Return westward to the Marcus Chapel.*

| Location 16 | **MARCUS CHAPEL** (CAPELLA MARCUS) *1166* |

Carrer Carders

This tiny Romanesque chapel retains much of its original form.

**History** Originally the chapel served a small hospital for the poor, constructed by means of a legacy from Bernat Marcus in 1166. An ancillary cemetery stood on what is now the Placeta d'en Marcus, the whole complex occupying what had been the donor's vegetable garden. At the adjacent Portal Nou, mail between Spain and the rest of Europe was exchanged, and during the medieval period members of the Postmen's Guild lived in the area for convenience. Their guild adopted the chapel, dedicating it to Our Lady of the Guide. The hospital and cemetery have long since disappeared but the chapel survives, little altered externally. In the 19C a second storey was added to the building, but this was later demolished during restoration.

**Exterior** The belfry and the porch, facing Carrer dels Carders, both 19C additions, have been retained.

Above the porch is the only Romanesque window to remain unblocked.

•● *Proceed to the plta d'en Marcus façade.*

At upper level runs the building's original Lombard frieze.

All Romanesque windows and the Gothic portal have been blocked.

Originally, the chapel possessed a shallow apse at its east end, but this was demolished in 1787 when the house which now adjoins it was built.

Internally, the chapel was remodelled in Classical style in the 19C, but fires in 1909 and 1936 destroyed this work. There is now little of interest to be seen and the chapel is rarely open.

•● *Continue southward.*

**No 7**, adjoining the chapel, was built in 1787, after the apse had been removed.

A small corner niche supports the figure of St John the Evangelist.

**No 3**, on the opposite side of the square, possesses a lintel carved with a Baroque relief of a child who, by embracing Christianity, has triumphed over death (the skull).

•● *Continue southward to the c de Montcada corner with c Assaonadors.*

**No 1, Carrer de Montcada**, forming the corner, was constructed in the 18C but remodelled on its Carrer Assaonadors façade in Gothic style c.1840: four 16C windows from an ancient building being inserted at first-floor level.

The house retains original sgraffiti and displays its construction date, 1723, on the bevelled corner.

•● *Enter the vestibule from Carrer de Montcada (not always open).*

A stone records the great storm which struck Barcelona on the day of the 1723 Corpus Christi procession and during which the Custodian of the city took shelter in this house. The building was henceforth known as the House of the Custodian (Casa de la Custodia).

*•● Follow c de Montcada southward to the c Princesa crossing.*

| Location 17 | **CARRER DE MONTCADA** |

A street of aristocratic palaces, dating from the 12C but much altered, many of its buildingsa have been adapted to museums, including the world-famous Picasso Museum.

Guillem Ramon de Montcada owned the land on which this street was laid out in the mid 12C, but its earliest name commemorated the Catalan soldiers killed in the battle for Majorca. By the 14C, Carrer de Montcada was entirely urbanized and extremely fashionable, particularly with merchants, as it formed a major route from the walled city to the sea. The wealth of the property owners permitted recurrent modernization of practically all the buildings, particularly during the 17C, and most of the original Gothic detailing on the street façades has been lost. However, much of architectural interest survives, particularly within the patios.

By 1930, the thoroughfare had become run down and a conservationist group was formed. Although no funds were available, sufficient public interest was aroused to prevent further despoliation, and in 1953 the municipality purchased two adjacent palaces which, ten years later, were to form the Picasso Museum. Gradually the other major buildings in the street were renovated, many of them also destined to house museums.

**Carrer Princesa**, which bisected the north section of Carrer de Montcada in 1853, possesses little of interest. A few 17C buildings survive at its west end, towards Plaça de l'Àngel, but are not worth a detour.

*•● Continue southward following c de Montcada to c Cremat Gran (first L). It is this southern section that contains the buildings of greatest interest.*

| Location 18 | **AGUILAR PALACE** (PALAU AGUILAR) |

15 Carrer de Montcada

Now forming the entrance to the Picasso Museum (Location 19), the palace was commissioned by Joan Berenguer d'Aguílar in the 15C. However, 13C murals have been discovered and the building must, therefore, have incorporated an earlier structure.

Although some Gothic features are preserved, a roof gallery and tower were lost during 18C remodelling.

**Exterior** On the street façade, lower-floor windows are basically 15C but heavily restored.

At the south end, one first-floor and one second-floor window in Gothic style survive.

*•● Enter the patio.*

Tickets for the Picasso Museum, part of which occupies the interior of the palace, are sold immediately L of the entrance.

Similarities with the Generalitat Palace suggest that

**Marc Safont** may also have been the architect of this building.

Immediately ahead is the museum's shop.

☛ *Ascend the first flight of stairs.*

The first level's doorway is notably carved in a filigree manner, reminiscent of the Sant Jordi Chapel's doorway in the Generalitat Palace and possibly by the same hand.

Angel heads decorate its tympanum.

Immediately R of the door is a carved St Christopher.

☛ *Ascend the second flight.*

The lower of the two Flamboyant windows incorporates a shield supported by angels and surmounted by fantastic dragons.

Gargoyles, a gallery with pointed arches and canopies are again reminiscent of the Generalitat Palace.

☛ *Enter the museum.*

---

| Location 19 | **PICASSO MUSEUM** (MUSEU PICASSO) |
|---|---|

15–19 Carrer Montcada

*Open Tuesday–Sunday 10.00–20.00. Admission charge, but free to minors and Spaniards.*

Pablo Picasso, 1881–1973, spent much of his youth in Barcelona and the museum is particularly rich in examples from his formative years. Pride of place, however, must be given to the later *Las Meninas* series. Since 1963, when the museum opened, examples of Picasso's art have been acquired from many sources, chiefly by means of donations, and now total almost 3,000.

It was Jaume Sabartés i Gual, the artist's secretary, who suggested that the works presented to him by Picasso during the many years of their friendship should form the basis of a museum. Picasso agreed and suggested as its venue Barcelona, a city for which he always retained great affection. Examples, then in the Modern Art Museum, were added and painter Salvador Dalí supplemented them with his own collection.

Sabartés died in 1968 and, in his honour, Picasso presented the fifty-eight Las Meninas variations, based on the great work by Velázquez in the Prado, Madrid. The Castellet Palace was incorporated in the museum in 1970 and that year the painter donated a further 900 works, many of them youthful examples that had been kept by his family. Eight years later, the two upper floors of the Meca Palace were presented to the museum, and in 1981, to mark the centenary of Picasso's birth, its ground floor was added to house temporary exhibitions. (The history and exterior of the two buildings are described on pages 82 and 84.)

Works are exhibited basically in chronological order.

The surname of the artist's father was Ruíz and his mother Picasso, and it is interesting to note that early signatures vary from Pablo Ruíz to Pablo Ruíz y Picasso, before finally becoming established as Pablo Picasso, presumably because the latter was more memorable and therefore more commercial.

**Room 5** retains its 13C painted ceiling. It was here

that the 13C Majorca battle scene mural, now in the Museum of Catalan Art, was discovered.

**Anteroom to Room 7** This, the sumptuous Baroque ballroom of the Castellet Palace, was created early in the 19C, occupying two storeys.

All the doors and windows are flanked by gilded urns and surmounted by putti.

**Room 19** Picasso returned to Barcelona in 1917 for the entire summer. The horrific disembowelled horse that he painted offers a foretaste of *Guernica*.

**Rooms 20–32** display the *Las Meninas* series.

From **Room 29** is approached the strategically placed stairway down which the young and those of a delicate nature are hastily led. This is because **Room 30** (in three sections) exhibits works of a sexually explicit and, to some, titillating, nature. You have been warned!

If a temporary exhibition is being held on the ground floor of the Meca Palace it will be possible to see its painted ceiling, believed to be late-12C work.

•● *Exit L and cross the street.*

| Location 20 | **TEXTILE AND COSTUME MUSEUM** (MUSEU TÈXTIL I DE LA INDUMENTÀRIA) |
|---|---|

12–14 Carrer de Montcada

*Open Tuesday– Saturday 09.00– 14.00 and 16.30– 19.00. Sunday and holidays 09.00– 14.00. Admission charge.*

The museum exhibits fabrics, costumes and dolls in its permanent collection, displayed on the upper floor. Temporary exhibitions are held on the ground floor.

**No 12**, formerly the Palace of the Marques de Llió, was restored in the 16C but retains some earlier features, including the tower, with one three-light window, two three-light 14C windows at first-floor level and a roof gallery.

In the 16C the house was extended northward, square ground-floor windows inserted, balconies added and the present square portal formed.

•● *Enter the patio.*

The patio was remodelled in the 18C for the Marquès de Llió but one Gothic window survives immediately R in the entrance wall.

•● *Enter the ground floor to view temporary exhibitions.*

The permanent Rocamora collection is displayed on the first floor.

•● *Ascend the stairs and enter the Baroque doorway.*

Costumes and dolls date from the 18C and are displayed chronologically. The museum possesses more than 4,000 exhibits.

Many of the timber ceilings are painted.

•● *Exit R and cross the road.*

**Castellet Palace, No 17**, apparently with 13C origins, the palace was almost completely remodelled in the 18C for Baron de Castellet, and its ashlar stone façade dates from this period.

Above the first-floor window a figure of Christ is surrounded by cherubs.

Occupying the first and second storeys is the ballroom, already described within the Picasso Museum.

•• *Continue southward.*

**Meca Palace, No 19,** begun in the 12C, construction seems to have been almost continuous until the early 15C. Formerly known as the Desplá Palace, the building was renamed by its owner Josep Meca i Caçador in the 16C.

All external features date from remodelling in the 17C and 18C.

•• *Exit and cross the road.*

**No 14** (which houses part of the Textile and Costume Museum), retains its 14C façade, including a ground-floor window R with corbels depicting an old man and a young woman.

The Tuscan portal was added in the 19C.

•• *Proceed to the adjacent building (also No 14).*

**Fundació Caixa de Pensions, No 14,** is the patron of this art gallery. Admission is always free to the exhibitions, which are temporary.

**No 16,** built in 1851 expressly for rental income, is the sole interruption in this part of the street to the sequence of private mansions.

**No 21,** basically Gothic, was remodelled in Baroque style in the 17C. Its windows are fitted with venetian blinds, some dating from the 18C when virtually all the buildings in the street possessed them.

**No 18** retains its roof gallery, probably 15C work, but restored.

**No 23,** in need of restoration, possesses the oldest external features in the street. Built partly in the 13C, its portal, roof gallery and tower with a three-light Romanesque window survive.

All the first-floor windows were altered in the 18C and balconies added.

---

| | |
|---|---|
| Location 21 | **MAEGHT GALLERY** (GALERIA MAEGHT) |
| 25 Carrer de Montcada<br><br>*Open Tuesday–Saturday 10.00–13.30 and 16.30–20.00. Admission free.* | Temporary exhibitions are held in this late-Gothic building. Constructed in the 15C as the Cervellós Palace for the noble Catalan family of that name, some remodelling took place in the 16C, but the street façade is less altered than any other example in Carrer de Montcada.<br><br>The round-arched portal, ground-floor window R and roof gallery are all 15C features.<br><br>Balconies were added to the first-floor windows in the 17C.<br><br>•• *Enter the patio.*<br><br>Although the stairway is Gothic, much remodelling took place in the 17C.<br><br>The lower two bays of the staircase have been blocked to form a room, but the capitals of their arcade were kept and have been exposed.<br><br>•• *Ascend the staircase.* |

At the landing level, a 16C doorway and window are preserved.

•● *Enter the gallery.*

Although the Gothic structure survives, much detail was lost in 1625 when a revolt against the owner of the palace, Giudice, a Genoese merchant, resulted in the burning of the interior.

Exhibits continue on the ground floor.

•● *Exit from the gallery L and cross the street.*

---

| Location 22 | **OMNIUM CULTURAL** |
| --- | --- |

20 Carrer de Montcada

*Patio open Monday–Friday. Chapel and salon open Monday–Friday when convenient. Admission free.*

An exquisite 15C chapel and a painted 17C salon are two of Barcelona's best-kept secrets. The patio's Baroque staircase is the finest in the city.

A combination of Gothic and Baroque, the building has been known as the Dalmases Palace since the 18C, when its owner was Pau Ignasi de Dalmases, Catalonia's ambassador to England.

Carved corbels to the architraves of the first-floor windows survive.

Large gargoyles dominate the roof line.

•● *Enter the patio.*

The roof gallery's structure remains, but has been filled.

Ahead, the twisted column Baroque staircase is richly carved on the patio side to depict the Rape of Europe and, separated by minstrels, Neptune in his chariot.

•● *Ascend the stairs.*

On this side, the balustrade is carved with cherubs playing round a vine.

•● *At the head of the stairs ring the bell R.*

The Omnium Cultural are responsible for promoting Catalan culture. Staff are most friendly and, if convenient, will show visitors the 17C salon and 15C chapel. English may not be spoken: indicate your requirement by 'saló i capella?'

The **salon** was painted in trompe l'oeil style in the 17C, obviously influenced by work discovered at Pompeii. Unfortunately, Barcelona's notorious humidity has severely damaged the walls, but the ceiling is in a reasonable shape.

During the War of Succession, the War Commission held their meetings in this room.

From Baroque to Gothic splendour: the adjacent 15C **chapel** is a delight. Its low ceiling, in the form of a star vault, is carved with a central Epiphany boss, round which a heavenly orchestra plays musical instruments. The style and high quality of the work suggest that it may be from the studio of the **Claperós** family.

Allegedly, Santa Maria de Cervelló was born in this room.

| Location 23 | **CASA ESTEBAN BAR** |
|---|---|

22 Carrer de
Montcada

*Open Tuesday–
Saturday 12.00–
16.00 and 18.30–
23.30. Sunday
12.00–16.00.*

This bar, one of the most attractive and fashionable in the old city, refuses to display its official name on the facia, preferring to be known simply as the Xampanyet. Unfortunately, its popular semi-sweet 'xampanye' is not even genuine cava. Draft cider (sidra) is better.

A low ceiling and cream paintwork are enlivened by delightful ceramic tiles and ancient bottles. Tapas prices are high.

*Exit R and proceed to* **Plaça de Montcada** *ahead.*

Formed in 1425, few Gothic details survive in this, the north section of the square due to the adaptation of most buildings to apartment houses in the 18C.

**No 8** retains original windows at first- and second-floor levels.

**No 10** preserves a figure corbel supporting its first-floor window L.

*Return northward. First R c de les Mosques.*

Carrer de les Mosques is reputedly the narrowest street in Barcelona and even the most determined Catalan motorist won't try to get through this one.

*Second L c dels Flassaders.*

At **No 40**, the Bourbon coat of arms indicates the former entrance to the mint that functioned here in the 18C.

*First R c del Sabateret. First R c del Rec. Proceed southward across the pas del Born intersection.*

South of Passeig del Born **Carrer del Rec**, on its west side, preserves late-Gothic shopping arcades. Stone columns support the terraces, where some gardens colourfully obscure the general dilapidation.

Opposite, on the east side of the street, the uniform houses were built in 1797 by General Lancaster (not an Englishman although of English ancestry).

*Return northward. First L pas del Born.*

| Location 24 | **PASSEIG DEL BORN** |
|---|---|

Stretching eastward from the apse of Santa Maria del Mar to its former covered market, this street, due to its unusual width, was a popular medieval venue for carnivals, fairs and tournaments.

In 1706, during the War of Succession, a bronze statue was erected in the centre, commemorating a success by the followers of Charles of Austria. Following Philip V's eventual victory, the statue was replaced by a dais bearing an anti-clerical proclamation. Some Gothic details survive but few buildings now pre-date the 18C.

**No 17** A tower, roof gallery and three-light windows give the appearance of a genuine 14C mansion. All, however, is modern.

**No 20**, opposite, displays two iron dragons at first-floor level, supported by posts.

**No 13** is embellished with a figure of St Anthony, inset in a first-floor niche.

Simple sgraffiti around the windows are in good condition.

**No 16**, opposite, retains a section of a Flamboyant 15C window at upper-floor level L.

Fashionable late-night bars (**Nos 15**, **17** and **19**) occupy the north side of this section of the street.

•➡ *Continue westward to Plaça de Montcada. First L c de la Vidrieria becomes c Rera Palau. R av Marquès de l'Argentera. First L Plaça del Palau (described on page 96). First L av d'Icària and M Barceloneta.*

## Santa Maria del Mar, Columbus Monument and Maritime Museum

Barcelona's most picturesque medieval streets are explored and visits made to Santa Maria del Mar, the only completely finished church in the Catalan Gothic style, and La Verge de la Mercè, with its sumptuous Neo-Baroque interior. The Columbus Monument is ascended; Catalan naval exhibits, which form the Maritime Museum, are housed in the medieval shipyards, dating from the 13C.

*Timing:* Santa Maria del Mar is open 10.00–12.30 and 17.00–19.30 (from 18.00 Saturday and Sunday).

The Xampanyeria is closed Sunday.

Barcelona Stock Exchange's Great Hall is open Monday–Friday 09.00–15.00.

The Maritime Museum closes at 14.00 on Sunday and all day Monday.

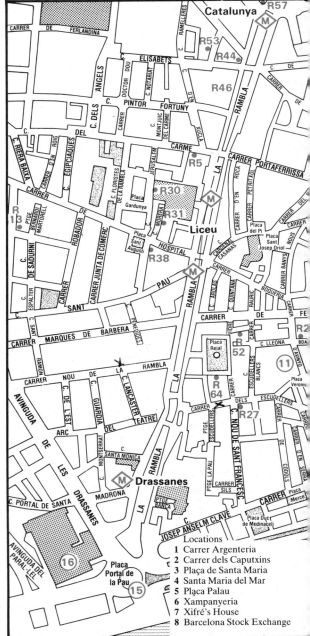

Locations
1 Carrer Argenteria
2 Carrer dels Caputxins
3 Plaça de Santa Maria
4 Santa Maria del Mar
5 Plaça Palau
6 Xampanyeria
7 Xifré's House
8 Barcelona Stock Exchange

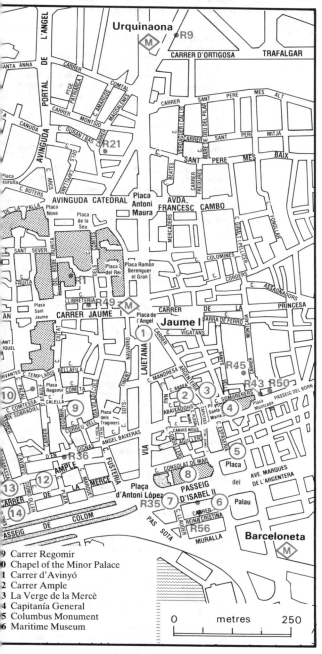

9 Carrer Regomir
0 Chapel of the Minor Palace
1 Carrer d'Avinyó
2 Carrer Ample
3 La Verge de la Mercè
4 Capitanía General
5 Columbus Monument
6 Maritime Museum

**Start** *M Jaume 1, line 4. Leave by the Via Laietana exit R. First R c Argenteria.*

| Location 1 | **CARRER ARGENTERIA** |
|---|---|

Carrer Argenteria was originally called Carrer del Mar (of the sea) as it led directly to the waterfront. Its present name, meaning silversmith, reflects that members of this trade formerly operated in the street between Plaça de l'Àngel and Plaça de Santa Maria. Window displays of silverware and jewellery were described as recently as 1850 as the most splendid in Barcelona, but the silversmiths moved to the newly-built Carrer de Ferran in the last years of the 19C. Most shop-fronts were protected by wooden porches until, in 1823, the Ajuntament decided they were a fire hazard and ordered their removal. While the street now presents little of exceptional interest, a picturesque quality remains, particularly on the east side where narrow arches give access to mysterious-looking alleyways. Closing the vista southward are the medieval bell towers of Santa Maria del Mar.

*Second R c Basea.*

Most of the properties on the north side of Carrer Basea have been demolished and a temporary car park occupies their site. However, on the south side 15C features include round-headed portals and a filled roof gallery to **Nos 2, 4** and **6.**

Only two upper windows of **No 6** preserve their Gothic appearance.

The last house in the terrace retains its tower.

Rising behind the buildings is the highest medieval domestic tower in the city to survive.

*Return to c Argenteria R. Second R c dels Abaixadors. First L c dels Caputxes.*

| Location 2 | **CARRER DELS CAPUTXINS** |
|---|---|

Built in the 15C, this is recognized as the most picturesque of Barcelona's medieval streets, due to its projecting floors, archways and timber beams. However, almost all Gothic details were lost during 18C remodelling.

**No 2** The upper three floors project over the street, resting on beams that are supported by great timber corbels fixed to square stone pillars.

Remodelling took place in 1735, the date inscribed on the house.

**Restaurante Castaneira, No 4** Wine is served at the bar, Galician fashion, in a *cunca de vino*, a shallow ceramic bowl.

**No 3** The first floor, supported by pillars, and the three floors above it, project; their eaves are beamed.

**No 6** An octagonal column partly supports the three upper levels.

A double arch, with a timber roof, gives additional support and also links the house with the building opposite (No 5 Plaça de Santa Maria).

*Proceed through the arch.*

**No 8** Both upper floors extend with beamed eaves.

**No 10**  Restored in 1989 this building, the ground floor of which accommodates a florist's shop, is dated 1764 on a wooden girder, presumably to commemorate its remodelling.

•● *First R c dels Canvis Nous*.

**No 15** occupies the same corner building as No 10 Carrer dels Caputxes. Timber upper storeys are supported by a rounded pillar of stone, combined with one corbel of stone and another of stone.

A small carved St George and the dragon is inserted on the corner with Carrer dels Plegamans.

•● *First R c dels Plegamans*.

At the rear of **No 10**, the first floor partially projects.

•● *Return southward. First L c dels Canvis Nous. First L c dels Canvis Vells. First R c Anisadeta. First L pl de Santa Maria. Proceed to its north-west corner.*

| Location 3 | **PLAÇA DE SANTA MARIA** |
|---|---|

As with most Barcelona squares that face churches, this was laid out on the site of a parish cemetery, in this case the Fossar Major (main cemetery).

At the north end of the square's west side a **Gothic fountain** is preserved.

Above the spouts, facing the church, the rosette window is original.

On the north side, immediately facing Carrer Argenteria, two shields have been carved.

Gargoyles project above.

•● *Return southward.*

**No 7**, adjacent to the fountain, preserves, albeit somewhat faded, an 18C sgraffiti façade.

| Location 4 | **SANTA MARIA DEL MAR** |
|---|---|
| | *Berenguer de Montagut, 1329–84* |

**1 Passeig del Born**

*Open Monday–Friday 10.00–12.00 and 17.00–19.30. Saturday\* 09.00–12.30 and 18.00–19.30. Sunday\* 09.30–12.30 and 18.00–19.30.*

*\*May not be toured during Mass (Saturday 09.30, 17.00 and 19.30. Sunday 10.00, 11.00, 13.00 and 18.00).*

*The church is floodlit internally and externally from dusk.*

This is the only church in the Catalan Gothic style to have been completed externally. Although outstanding fittings, mostly Baroque, were destroyed in the 1936 fire, the purity and spaciousness of the interior remain unaffected and, to a degree, have been emphasized by the loss. Surprisingly, this outstanding church is open less than five hours a day to visitors, apart from weekends, and even then tours are not permitted during services – there are lots of weddings.

**History**  A church on the site is first mentioned in 998. It was then surrounded by marshland and the parishioners were practically all fishermen. The marsh was drained in the 13C and a new defensive wall enclosed the area, which was called the Vilanova (new town) de la Ribera (shore). Soon tradesmen moved to the quarter, and its increasing importance led to pressure for a new, more splendid edifice of arch-diocese status to be built. Following his victory in Majorca, Jaume I (1213–76) had vowed to construct a splendid church dedicated to the Virgin, and veterans of that campaign agreed to sponsor the new building. **Berenguer de Montagut** was commissioned to design the church in 1329, receiving assistance from **Guillem Metge**.

**Exterior** Pere III organized the operation with such fervour that this great church was completed in just fifty-five years, a speed rarely equalled in the Middle Ages for such a building. This speed resulted in a unity of style throughout. The façade of Santa María del Mar is the only Catalan Gothic example to be flanked by completed bell towers, the north tower, L, being finished in 1495 and the south tower in 1902.

The external emphasis is horizontal, typical of Catalan Gothic, with a broad portal and little wall decoration apart from cornices. Many regret that this style was not followed when the north façade of Barcelona Cathedral was built in the late 19C.

Flanking the portal are the figures of St Peter and St Paul.

Figures of the Virgin, Christ and John the Evangelist stand on lintels.

The original rose window was destroyed by an earthquake in 1428; its replacement, mid-15C work, is believed to be an exact copy.

Emphasizing the roof line is a cornice, another rare finishing touch to a Catalan church.

Iron torch-holders extend from both west corners. Formerly, pine was burned in them to illuminate the square.

•● *Follow c dels Sombrerers, which skirts the north façade.*

A figure of the Virgin and Child decorates the tympanum of the north door, which also retains original Flamboyant tracery and fragments of a painting.

•● *Proceed to the c dels Banys Vells junction (second L).*

Most clearly observed from here is the belfry, rising above the north transept.

Houses are built against the church at its east end, concealing the apse from this side.

•● *First R pl de Montcada. First R pas del Born.*

Ahead, the doorway of the apse, frequently the only point of access to the church, was added by **Bernat Salvador** in 1542. It appears to be modelled on the portal of Sant Agustí Vel, part of which survives in the Barri Xinès.

•● *Continue westward to the south door of the nave.*

Until recently houses clustered picturesquely against this side of the nave, forming part of Carrer de Santa Maria del Mar, but they and other houses opposite them have since been demolished. Also demolished on this side was a passageway, in the form of a bridge, that linked the palace of the Capitanía General, on the south side of the street, with his private pew in the church.

Stone plaques in Latin and Catalan flank the south doorway, commemorating the laying of the foundation stone of the church by Alfons III 'The Benign' in 1329; an act that gave thanks for the conquest of Sardinia.

The south door, surrounded by a figure of the Virgin, originally led directly to a small cemetery, the Fossar de les Moreres (cemetery of the mulberries).

*●▶ Return to the west front and enter the building. Frequently entry is restricted to the doorway in the apse at the east end; if so, enter from there and proceed directly to the west end of the church.*

**Interior** As opposed to the exterior, the internal emphasis is on the vertical, as if to indicate the contrast between the earthly and the heavenly worlds.

Unlike most northern European churches, the aisles are almost as high as the nave, and the eight octagonal columns that form their arcades are sited no fewer than thirteen metres from each other in each direction. This creates a spaciousness exceeded in no other medieval church.

The large, gilded reredos in the eighth north bay was designed in the 19C.

*●▶ Proceed to the sanctuary.*

The rose window of the west front may best be appreciated from this point. Its mid-15C stained glass depicts the *Coronation of the Virgin*.

Flanking the steps to the **sanctuary** are slabs, carved in the 14C to commemorate the cutting and transportation of stone from Montjuïc for the construction of the church.

Ten unusually high octagonal columns surround the sanctuary, which was given its present form in 1967, following the destruction caused by the 1936 arsonists. During the fire, the church lost not only its magnificent Baroque reredos but also an outstanding organ and carved choir stalls.

Buried beneath the pavement of the sanctuary is Pere IV, Constable of Portugal.

Just below the vault of the apse, the stained glass is the 18C work of various Catalan designers.

*●▶ Proceed to the apsidal* **Santísimo Chapel** *(behind the postcard stall).*

**Francesc Vila** remodelled this chapel in Classical style in 1835.

*●▶ Proceed to the south aisle and continue westward to the sixth chapel from the east door.*

**Chapel of Nostra Senyora dels Desemparats de València** This is the only chapel to retain its screen, which is dated 1851. Fixed to the wall L, within a wooden frame, is the tombstone of Pere IV, Constable of Portugal, elected King of Catalonia in 1464. The tombstone, bearing the much-faded effigy of the King, was recently transferred here from the sanctuary, where he is buried.

*●▶ Exit from the church and proceed directly south of its south-west corner following c Espaseria.*

Carrer Espaseria is a continuation of Carrer Argenteria towards the sea; its name commemorates the sword-makers that formerly occupied premises here.

*●▶ Continue ahead to pl Palau L. First R Nos 12 and 13.*

| Location 5 | **PLAÇA PALAU** |
|---|---|

The name of this square commemorates the royal palace (Palau Reial) that once formed its north-east range, where Nos 12 and 13 now stand. Rather pompous Classical and Neo-Classical official buildings surround the square.

In the late 14C the Wheat Hall (Alla del Blat) was built, in Gothic style, facing the Stock Exchange that was then being reconstructed. It became the City Arsenal in 1554, and a century later was converted to the viceroy's palace. The ancient building was put at the disposal of the King in 1846, but fire completely destroyed it twenty-nine years later.

*••* *Proceed southward.*

In the centre of the square the marble **fountain**, dedicated to *Catalan Genius*, was erected by **Francesc Daniel** in 1825; sculptures are by the Belgian, **Baratta.** This work replaced a Temple of Liberation, built by **Genesi** in 1822 but soon demolished.

*••* *Proceed to the south-east corner with av Marquès de l'Argentera.*

**Govern Civil de Barcelona**, **No 2**, was designed as the Customs House by **Count Miguel de Roncali**, building minister of Carlos IV, in 1792. In 1902 it became the Civil Government's headquarters (as it is now), and during the period of Catalan autonomy, 1931–9, the Conselleria de Governació.

Its Classical façade of marble was restored when the building was partly remodelled by **Adolf Florensa** *c.* 1930.

*••* *Proceed to the south side of the square.*

Closing the south side of the square is the **Nautical School** *Florensa*, 1932. This was built on the site of the Portal del Mar, the mid-19C monumental gateway in the defensive wall. At that time, the sea lay immediately behind the wall, land not yet having been reclaimed.

*••* *Continue westward to the south-west corner block between pas Sota Muralla and c Reina Cristina.*

**Casa Carbonell-Collasso**, the 19C Classical work of **Rovira i Riera**, retains its Doric colonnade.

*••* *Proceed northward. First L c Reina Cristina. Cross to the north side.*

**Carrer Reina Cristina** has become the 'electronics centre' of Barcelona, practically every bazaar offering electronic equipment for sale, from watches and cameras to the latest hi-fi and television equipment.

| Location 6 | **XAMPANYERIA** |
|---|---|

7 Carrer Reina Cristina

Open Monday–Saturday 10.00–22.00

A Barcelona landmark, this anonymous cave-like bodega is the cheapest cava bar in the city. Cava, once known as Spanish Champagne, is the only drink sold, although there are rumours that water can be obtained if demanded firmly. Similarly, charcuterie or Roquefort cheese, in various sandwich combinations, is the only food available. Four varieties of cava are offered, but most are too sweet for foreign tastes; however, the Brut, the most expensive at 55 pesetas a glass, is dry and most acceptable. One glass will bring refreshment, but more may well lead to a complete abandonment of further sightseeing for the day.

There are no seats or bar stalls and the crowd that gathers between 14.00 and 16.00 can be daunting. Better to come early or late. At the rear, food is sold to take away, again at bargain prices. Cabrales, a strong blue cheese from Asturias, is a particularly good buy.

•• *Exit R.*

At **No 3**, Pablo Picasso and his family occupied a second-floor apartment for a month on their arrival in Barcelona from La Coruña in 1895.

•• *Return eastward. First L c Llauder leads to pas d'Isabel II. Cross immediately to the north side to view Xifré's Houses.*

| Location 7 | **XIFRÉ'S HOUSE** (CASA DE 'N XIFRÉ) *Buixareu* and *Vila 1840* and *1852* |
|---|---|
| Passeig D'Isabel II | These two blocks of colonnaded buildings form the entire south side of the thoroughfare. They were commissioned as a development by Josep Xifré i Cases, a wealthy merchant, to provide ground-floor shops and a restaurant, with apartments above. |

**East block** Built 1836–40, this building, the larger of the two, is embellished on its corners with allegorical reliefs relating to the sea and the import/export trades (through which Xifré had made his fortune). These are the work of **Tomàs Padró** and **Domènec Talarn.**

Medallions, set in the spandrels of the arches, refer to the sea and Spain's American discoveries.

Lintels of the first-floor windows are decorated with swans of wrought iron, the earliest use of this material in Barcelona.

Surmounting the centre of the building is a terracotta allegorical relief of Chronos, god of time, designed by **Damiá Compeny**, Spain's best-known Classical sculptor, who worked in Rome with Canova.

**Set Portes**, **No 14**, the renowned restaurant founded in 1836, is one of the oldest in the city. Catalan specialities are served daily, non-stop from 13.00–01.00 (See page 214).

**West block** Much smaller and plainer, the building's only feature of note is the date of its completion, 1852, carved in Latin at roof level.

•• *Proceed eastward, following the south façade of the Llotja. First L pl del Palau.*

A Tuscan portico, immediately L, indicates the main façade of the Llotja, although its public entrance is from c del Consolat de Mar (see Location 8).

•• *First L c del Consolat de Mar. Cross to the north side.*

**Nos 37, 35** and **33** date from the 15C. Their Gothic colonnade links at an angle with the 17C colonnade of **No 31** to form a picturesque corner.

The south side of the street is entirely occupied by the north façade of the Llotja.

| Location 8 | **BARCELONA STOCK EXCHANGE** |
|---|---|
| | (BORSA DE BARCELONA) *Pere Arvey 1380–92* |

*La Llotja*
*42 Carrer Del*
*Consolat de Mar*

Incarcerated within its Classical outer skin, the Gothic hall of the Llotja continues to serve as Barcelona's Stock Exchange.

*Gothic Hall open*
*Monday–Friday*
*09.00–15.00.*
*Admission charge*
*(nominal).*

**History** Since the mid 13C, the Barcelona Stock Exchange has occupied a building known as La Llotja. The first structure was erected in 1357, on the shore of the Ribera quarter, to provide basic weather protection for merchants and their wares. Storms, and the Castilian raid two years later, caused considerable damage and Pere III commissioned **Pere Arvey** to construct the enclosed hall that survives. In the 15C, a floor was added to provide accommodation for the Consulate of the Sea and an extension on the waterfront side provided a Customs House. During the occupation of the city by Charles V's troops in 1714, much of the Llotja was despoiled and it was decided to rebuild the entire complex apart from the medieval hall. **Fran Soler i Faneca** designed the Louis XVI style building, work beginning in 1774, and Charles V presided over its inauguration ceremony in 1802.

*Passports are*
*required and*
*gentlemen must*
*wear a jacket and*
*tie.*

*Rooms of the Junte*
*de Comerç and the*
*Museum of the*
*School of Fine Arts*
*are open, when*
*convenient, 09.00–*
*13.00.*

•● *Enter the courtyard from the west end of the complex.*

Now serving primarily as a car park, the courtyard occupies the site of the Garden of the Six Orange Trees.

To the west, on the site of the chapel, the *Neptune fountain* is a 19C work by **Nicolau Travé.**

Classical sculptures in the corners, by **Bover i Oliver**, represent the four major continents.

•● *Enter the doorway in the east range.*

Typically Mediterranean Gothic, the **Gothic Hall** (Saló Gòtic) or Trading Hall (Saló de Contractacioneś), as the hall is officially known, was built 1380–92, its proportions being identical to those of the Loggia dei Lanzi that had been completed in Florence nineteen years earlier.

Three great rounded arches support the flat timber roof, and these in turn are supported by extremely thick external walls, thus obviating the need for buttresses.

A clock indicates the year, hour, day and temperature.

•● *Exit L and ascend the stairs ahead.*

Late-18C rooms of the **Junte de Comerç** may be viewed if convenient, but only in the morning.

Painted ceilings are by **Pere Pau Montanya** and the furnishings are mostly contemporary.

•● *Descend to the courtyard and proceed to the north range.*

The School of Fine Arts (Belles Artes) occupied this part of the building in the 19C. Picasso studied here, his father, Jose Ruíz Blasco, being a teacher. Joan Miró also attended lectures in the building.

Although the school has been transferred elsewhere, its museum, **Museu de la Reial Academia Belles Arts Sant Jordi**, may be visited.

*•• Exit L and proceed ahead to pl d'Antoni López (first L). Continue ahead to the Post Office building (Correus Telegrafs), on the north side of the square.*

The **Post Office**, built by **Torres** and **Goday** in 1927, dominates the square, which was created in 1910 on the sites of Plaça de Sant Sebastia and the Sant Sebastia convent.

*•• Proceed southward to the junction of the square with pas de Colom R.*

**No 1**, on the corner, is the only building to survive from the former Plaça de Sant Sebastia; its 18C Rococo sgraffiti have been faithfully restored.

**Cervantes House, No 2**, was where, according to tradition, the great writer lived during his visit to Barcelona, a city that he loved and praised. Window mouldings from the 16C survive at third- and fourth-floor levels, but the remainder was refaced in the present century.

**No 6**, a Renaissance palace, comprises two linked pavilions. The austere façade has little decoration, apart from its solid cornice and heavy corbels.

*•• Return eastward. First L c Fusteria leads to c de l'Hostal d'en Sol and pl dels Traginers.*

On the north side of **Plaça dels Traginers** stands the remains of the south-east corner of the Roman wall. Part of the cylindrical tower and other fragments have been revealed.

*•• First L c del Correu Vell.*

Immediately L, **Café la Torre, No 14**, apparently late 12C, preserves two-light Romanesque upper windows. It is possibly the oldest building in Barcelona to incorporate a bar.

*•• Follow c del Correu Vell westward.*

**Correu Vell Palau, No 5**, basically a 15C building, probably received its sgraffiti in the 18C. These were restored in 1989 together with the Gothic patio.

*•• R c Regomir.*

| Location 9 | **CARRER REGOMIR** |
|---|---|

A picturesque street, Carrer Regomir boasts numerous ancient and reasonably priced bodegas. In the 10C, the Count of Rego Mir constructed a canal through the quarter, bringing a fresh water supply from the mountains; the name of this street commemorates his generosity.

**No 13**, a 14C building, is entered through a 17C Baroque doorway that is more Castilian than Catalan in style, and also more exuberantly sculpted than usual in Barcelona.

*•• Proceed to the patio.*

The blocked two-light Gothic window, ahead R, possesses a central lobe that is pointed; a rare secular example in the city.

**Bodega, No 11** A Barcelona tragedy. Until 1989 this bodega (unnamed) was the most characteristic of Barcelona's 'cave' bars. The serving area stood immediately L of the entrance and, from the opposite side, Catalan food was cooked on ancient equipment. Undeniably, the state of the walls could not have been tolerated in a hospital ward but it gave harmless character and a sense of time-past to this establishment. Then, in 1988, the Ajuntament's health department struck. A clean-up was ordered and, needlessly, Barcelona lost one of its showpieces. It is not clear who is to blame for the dreary tiles, balustrade in Neo-Classical(!) style or other tasteless 'improvements', but it is to be hoped that the same fate does not await 'Portalón', the bodega's sister establishment in Carrer Banys Nous (page 216).

*➣ Exit R.*

**Sant Cristòfol Chapel, No 5**, was built in 1503, the date inscribed on the door's lintel in Roman numerals. **Joan Martorell** remodelled the interior in Gothic Revival style in 1899, retaining the original rib vault. As St Christopher is the patron of travellers, on his feast day, 10 July, motorists pull up in this narrow street, which is decorated with paper chains and flowers, to receive a speedy blessing at the doorway.

*➣ Exit R.*

Adjacent to the building are the remnants of a **Roman portal** in the 4C wall, restored in 1989.

*➣ Continue northward to pl Regomir. First L c de Calella. First R c d'Ataülf.*

| Location 10 | **CHAPEL OF THE 'MINOR' PALACE** |
|---|---|
| Carrer d'Ataülf | This small chapel is all that survives of the Minor Palace (Palau Menor) of the Catalan kings. |

Built for the Knights Templar in the 13C, beside a gate in the Roman wall, the palace was occupied by members of the Order until their dissolution in 1317. It then passed to the Knights of St John, who promptly sold it to the Bishop of Vic for his town house.

Pere III, who owned the adjacent Dominican convent, purchased the property and remodelled both buildings to form a palace for his consort Elionor de Sicília. Its botanical and zoological gardens were amongst the earliest in Europe. Various extensions were built until, in the 15C, Joan II presented the property to the Requesens family. A descendant of theirs, the Countess of Sobradiel, committed one of the greatest acts of vandalism that the city has known by demolishing the venerable complex and selling its site for property development. Only the chapel was spared.

The present façade of the chapel, the work of **Rogent**, 1868, incorporates a 12C portal which originally stood at the west end of the chapel's south wall, now blocked by adjoining houses.

A bas-relief figure, with raised arms, forms the corbel L, an outstanding example of Romanesque carving.

At upper-floor level R, a 14C two-light window has been preserved.

Jesuits now occupy the late-Gothic interior, which is not open to the public.

●● *Continue northward. L c dels Templaris leads to c de Cervantes ahead. First R c d'Avinyó.*

| | |
|---|---|
| Location 11 | **CARRER D'AVINYO** |

Until the 19C, most of this street was skirted on its east side by the western section of the Roman wall. Gradually, however, the wall was demolished and no fragments appear to have survived. Carrer d'Avinyó was built up in the medieval period, but most buildings are now early 19C, many of them occupied by bars and restaurants. Once fashionable, the street declined in the late 19C and prostitutes moved in, plying for trade from the doorways. Picasso remembered them when, in Paris, he painted *Les Desmoiselles d'Avignon* in 1907, the first truly Cubist work: Avignon refers to the name of this street, not the city in Provence as most surmise.

**No 26** retains an 18C Baroque carving above its doorway. Contemporary sgraffiti are faded.

**The House of Hercules, No 17**, was built in the 16C in late-Gothic style but with the usual Renaissance detailing.

In the ground-floor window's lintel R, two eagles support a laurel wreath.

Above, Hercules fights with the lion of Nemea.

Corbels to the architraves of the first floor windows take the form of bats, the ancient symbol of Barcelona.

●● *Return southward and cross to the north side of the street.*

**The House of the Four Rivers, No 30**, is named from the allegorical illustrations, on its façade, of the Danube, Nile, Ganges and River Plate – now almost lost.

●● *Cross to the south side of pl de la Verònica opposite.*

*Since 1939 the* **Fine Arts School**, founded in 1775 in La Llotja, has occupied **No. 2**, which was built by **Tiberí Sabatér** in 1883 for the Casino Mercantil. The Casino, formed in Madrid fifty years earlier, operated as a stock exchange, but the exchange situated in La Llotja was given official status in 1915 and the Casino's importance declined.

●● *Continue southward.*

**No 42**, dated 1859, retains Tuscan columns in its vestibule.

●● *Continue ahead. Third L c Ample.*

| | |
|---|---|
| Location 12 | **CARRER AMPLE** |

Now a thoroughfare of many restaurants and bars, from the 16C to the late-19C this was the residential street most favoured by Barcelona's aristocracy.

Carrer Ample was laid out to link La Rambla with the Stock Exchange. Much of the southern section, from Plaça Duc de Medinaceli to La Rambla, was occupied by the 13C Sant Francesc monastery until its buildings were demolished in 1835.

Throughout the 16C, many members of the nobility

settled in the street. They included the viceroys, Charles V and his consort, the Kings of Hungary and Bohemia, the Infant Don Federico of Portugal and the Duchess of Alençon, sister of the King of France. Residents during the 18C included Isabel Cristina of Brunswick, the wife of Archduke Charles (later Charles VI of Germany) and Elizabeth of France, sister of Louis XVI. Deterioration set in during the 19C and the houses were taken over by the middle classes.

**No 24**, built in Romantic style, has almost lost the late example of sgraffiti on its first floor's façade.

**No 28**, formerly the Sessa-Larrard Palace, now the **Col-legi Calassanci**, was built for the Duke of Sessa by **Josep Ribes Margarit** in 1778. The building became the residence of the Captain General in 1832.

The Corinthian portal and decorative iron balcony above are in the Louis XIV style.

*First R c de la Plata.*

At **No 15**, Picasso had his first studio in Barcelona. It is now an art gallery, **Cambra Picasso**.

*Return to c Ample L. Second R c d'en Carabassa.*

**Carrer d'en Carabassa**, although set in the heart of a seedy area, is one of the most picturesque streets in Barcelona and typical of the surprises that the city keeps up its sleeve.

Both sides are linked by two bridges, and palm trees grow in the upper-level gardens.

*Return southward.*

Immediately ahead, fitted into the north side of the Baroque church of La Verge de la Mercè, is the original 15C Gothic façade of Sant Miguel, the remainder of which was demolished in 1832 for the extension of the Ajuntament.

Its doorway, with Renaissance features, was the work of **René Ducloux**, 1561.

*Continue westward to pl de la Mercè.*

This square was created by demolishing properties in the streets that surround it. Among those lost was, on the south side, No 3 Carrer de la Mercè, where the Picasso family occupied a third-floor apartment from 1896, their main house in Barcelona.

| Location 13 | **LA VERGE DE LA MERCÈ** *Jaume Mas 1765–75* |
| --- | --- |
| Plaça de la Mercè | Architecturally, this church is a rare Barcelona example of late-Baroque work. Its interior was beautifully restored after the 1936 fire and remains one of the finest in the city. |

**History** Muslim pirates discovered, in the 13C, that there were advantages in taking hostages rather than killing their victims – how history repeats itself – and a large number of Christians were incarcerated in North African prisons until their ransom was paid. By tradition, the Virgin appeared in a dream, apparently simultaneously, to Saint Peter of Nolasco, Saint Raymond of Penyafort and the King, Jaume I, exhorting them to create a monastic Order to secure the release of the captives. Thus was born the Order of Our Lady of Mercy (or of Ransom). The first church of the Order was completed on the present site in 1267. Remodelling took place in 1336 and 1408 and the Virgin of Mercy was adopted as patron saint of Barcelona. In the 17C, domestic buildings were built south of the church for the monastery (Location 14).

The present Baroque church was commissioned from **Jaume Mas** in 1765 and completed within ten years, a remarkable achievement considering its sumptuous interior.

With the expulsion of the monastic Order in 1835 the Verge de la Mercè became the parish church.

*➥ Proceed to the north-west corner of the square.*

**Exterior** With its colourful roof tiles, the dome, best viewed from this point, was completed by **Joan Martorell** in 1888. It is surmounted by a huge figure of the Virgin, by **Miguel Oslè**, 1940.

**Jaume Mas**, the architect, was a follower of Borromini, and the curved sides of the façade are a unique example of this late-Baroque feature in Barcelona.

Below the most northerly urn of the curved north section, the date, 1768, records the completion of the façade.

Sculptural embellishments, both externally and internally, were by **Carles Crau.**

*➥ Enter the church by the façade's most northerly door.*

**Interior** Due to the importance of this church, which emanates from its dedication to the patroness of the city, damage caused by the 1936 arsonists has been meticulously repaired and the Baroque/Neo Baroque interior is the richest in Barcelona (Sant Sever, which escaped the fires, is equally sumptuous, but on a much smaller scale).

Carved woodwork and intricate plasterwork, all heavily gilded, are apparently reminiscent of Betlem church before its fire, particularly in the upper, heavily screened pews.

Superb marble work lines the sanctuary.

*➥ Exit to pl de la Mercè L and continue to c de la Mercè (first L).*

Two bridges cross the street, linking the church directly with the former domestic buildings of the convent, now the Capitanía General.

*➥ Continue southward following c de Boltres. L pas de Colom.*

| Location 14 | **CAPITANÍA GENERAL** |
|---|---|
| Passeig de Colom | Pompous modern stonework provides the façade to the former monastery of the Order of Mercy, built in the 17C. The cloister, which can occasionally be glimpsed, is the finest Classical example in Barcelona. |

**History** Domestic buildings for the monastery, stretching from the church to the sea wall, were constructed in 1642, on the site of an orchard, by the

Santacana nuns. Shortly after the dissolution of the Order, the complex was acquired by the Capitanía General, Barcelona's military establishment, in 1846.

The present façade, in a heavy Neo-Classical style, was built in 1928 by order of Primo de Rivera; it has been suggested that the Spanish dictator was influenced by contemporary work in Rome, commissioned by Mussolini. Formerly, the building was entered directly from the sea wall at first-floor level, where the central balcony is now sited.

As the army now occupies the complex, entry for viewing is impossible; this is particularly unfortunate because its courtyard, the former monastic cloister, is the most lavish Classical example in Barcelona. Uniquely in the city, all its decorative work is of marble. Occasionally, the first doorway L is open and the courtyard's riches may be glimpsed. However, the Spanish soldiers look as if they might assemble an instant firing squad if excessive interest is shown – be prudent!

Internally, the rooms were sumptuously redecorated by **Adolf Florensa** in 1928.

•• *Cross pas de Colom to the central pedestrian strip.*

Most of **Passeig de Colom** has been constructed on land reclaimed from the sea. Until recently this was an unattractive area of warehouses called Moll de la Fusta, but a waterfront promenade lined with palm trees and an upper promenade with bars and restaurants have now been laid out. A sunken road bisects them, but two brightly painted 'Dutch' bridges link the promenades. This must be one of the most outstanding environmental improvements to a European city in recent years: a delightful place from which to observe the marine activities and take the sun; or – more important in Barcelona's humid summer months – the air. Surprisingly, the promenade only appears to be popular with the locals at weekends.

•• *Cross either bridge to the waterfront promenade and proceed westward.*

**Plaça Portal de la Pau** (portal of peace) is named to commemorate the former gateway in the 13C wall that was opened at the south end of La Rambla in 1849. Comprehensive remodelling of the old port of Barcelona will involve wholesale alterations to the south side of the Plaça by 1992, incorporating the International Trade Centre, an entertainments complex and a completely new square on the site of Barcelona Quay.

On its south-east corner, the modern administrative centre of the port, **Puerto Autónomo de Barcelona**, imitates the French Renaissance style.

On the south-west corner of the square is the **Customs House** (Duanes), built over the canal that formerly linked the sea with the shipyards. It was designed, in Colossal style, by the ubiquitous **Sagnier** in 1902.

Giant winged griffins surmount the building.

Opposite, on the north-west corner, occupying the medieval shipyards (drassanes), is the Maritime Museum (Location 16).

The north-east corner is occupied by the army headquarters of the **Gobern Militar**, built in the style of the 18C Llotja.

Rising from the centre of the square is the Columbus Monument.

| Location 15 | **COLUMBUS MONUMENT** (MONUMENT A COLOM) *Gaietà Buigas Monrarà 1886* |

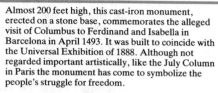

Plaça Portal de la Pau

*Lift operates: Summer, daily 09.00–21.00; winter, Tuesday– Saturday 10.00– 14.00 and 15.30– 18.30. Sunday 10.00–19.00. Admission charge (nominal).*

Almost 200 feet high, this cast-iron monument, erected on a stone base, commemorates the alleged visit of Columbus to Ferdinand and Isabella in Barcelona in April 1493. It was built to coincide with the Universal Exhibition of 1888. Although not regarded important artistically, like the July Column in Paris the monument has come to symbolize the people's struggle for freedom.

The bronze figure of *Columbus*, by **Rafael Arché**, is approximately 23 feet high.

•• *Proceed to the south side of the monument, descend the steps to the lift and ascend to the top of the monument.*

Views, whilst extensive, are somewhat obscured by the decorative ironwork.

•• *Descend and proceed to the north-west side of the square.*

| Location 16 | **MARITIME MUSEUM** (MUSEU MARÍTIM) |

Plaça Portal de la Pau

Open Tuesday– Saturday 09.30– 13.00 and 16.00– 19.00, Sunday and holidays 10.00– 14.00, admission charge.

Dating from the 13C, the former shipyards that accommodate this museum are the largest and most complete medieval example in the world and, in truth, of greater interest to most visitors than the exhibits.

**History** Barcelona's former shipyards (drassanes), first recorded in 1243, were situated much further east and approached directly from Carrer del Regomir. It was decided to replace them in 1255 and work on the present complex, to accommodate the construction, repair and dry-docking of naval vessels, was commissioned by Pere II (the Great). A large fortified courtyard with four corner towers, but little weather protection, was built.

The construction of eight covered aisles was begun by **Arnau Ferrer** for Pere III (the Ceremonious) in 1378, immediately north of the earlier complex. By the 17C, however, the original courtyard was almost entirely covered by the roofs of additional aisles, and a further three aisles were built by the Generalitat to its east. The shipyard was closed in 1663 and converted to a military storehouse. In the 18C the two central naves were combined and the façade facing the sea was remodelled. The artillery took over the buildings in 1792. Wholesale redevelopment of the area to form a new district threatened to demolish the former shipyard in 1876, but preservationists defeated the attempt. The army presented the buildings to the city in 1936, restoration began three years later and Spain's most important Maritime Museum opened in 1941.

**Exterior** First seen, running at a right angle to the short entrance tower, are the three aisles added by the Generalitat, 1612–18.

Gargoyles surmount the buttresses of the east façade.

The entrance to the museum is situated in the south-east corner tower, one of the four built by Pere II in the 13C. Pyramidal crenellations originally formed a battlement to its roof.

Carved above the window are the arms of Pere II, an unrestored and exceptional example of Gothic work.

The cross of St George, above the arms, commemorates the period of the Generalitat's stewardship from the late 16C.

**••** *Proceed clockwise following pas de Josep Carner. Originally, the south façade consisted of eight bays, but when the two central aisles were combined in the 18C it was remodelled.*

Classical urns decorate the apexes of the three central bays.

A canal originally linked the sea with the shipyard, but this has been filled and the entrances to the bays glazed.

**••** *First R av de Paral-lel.*

A south-west corner tower has been demolished.

The 13C wall of the shipyards is fronted by a dry moat.

Pyramidal crenellations have been restored to the north-west corner tower.

Immediately following this tower is the unique surviving stretch of the city's 14C–15C wall, the last Barcelona enclosure to be constructed.

Its square tower, the Porta de Santa Madrona, is the only example of the wall's original three gateways to remain. This lost its battlement in the 16C but it has been rebuilt.

An access bridge crosses the moat.

**••** *Return to the south-east tower and enter the museum.*

**Interior** Great curved arches of stone form the aisles and support the timber roof. Although internal work spans five centuries, all is harmonious, with little to distinguish the different periods.

Complete reorganization of the museum began in 1989.

**••** *Proceed ahead from the ticket office and pass through the glass door.*

Of greatest architectural interest internally is the 13C north-east tower of Pere II and, adjoining it L, the two-storey 14C structure of Pere III: the upper floors of both may be visited.

**••** *Proceed to the north-east garden. Towards the end*

*L is the 14C façade of Pere III's aisled extension.*

The collection of exhibits is based on that of the Barcelona Naval College, its emphasis being on the maritime history of Catalonia.

Most impressive is a full-size reproduction of *La Real*, Don Juan of Austria's flagship at the battle of Lepanto, 1571, during which the combined Hispano–Venetian fleets defeated the Turks. The original ship was built here and the present full-size replica was made in 1971, to celebrate the four-hundredth anniversary of the battle.

Also of interest is a chart of 1439 that belonged to Amerigo Vespucci, the discoverer after whom America was named.

Documents include a report by the curator of the shipyards in 1357.

➥ *Exit from the museum L. Second L La Rambla and M Drassanes.*

## La Rambla, Santa Creu Hospital and Sant Pau del Camp

The entire length of La Rambla, one of the world's most famous thoroughfares, is explored, together with its most interesting side streets. Visits are made to the 'Boqueria' food market, the great medieval complex of the former Hospital de la Santa Creu and the Romanesque church of Sant Pau del Camp, with its gem-like cloister.

*Timing:* The Vicereine's Palace is closed Monday.

The former Hospital de la Santa Creu is closed Sunday.

Tours of the Liceu Theatre do not take place Saturday and Sunday.

Generally Sant Pau del Camp is open only 19.30 weekdays and 18.30 Sunday.

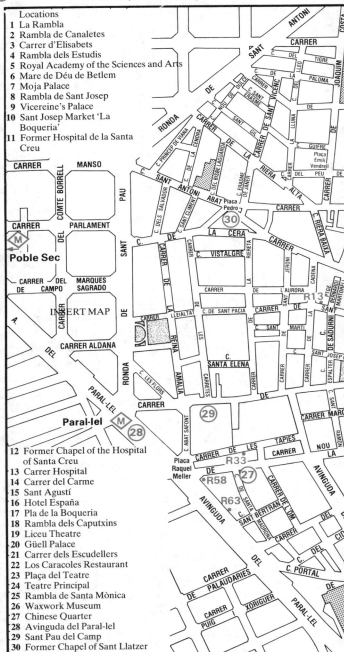

**Locations**

1 La Rambla
2 Rambla de Canaletes
3 Carrer d'Elisabets
4 Rambla dels Estudis
5 Royal Academy of the Sciences and Arts
6 Mare de Déu de Betlem
7 Moja Palace
8 Rambla de Sant Josep
9 Vicereine's Palace
10 Sant Josep Market 'La Boqueria'
11 Former Hospital de la Santa Creu

12 Former Chapel of the Hospital of Santa Creu
13 Carrer Hospital
14 Carrer del Carme
15 Sant Agustí
16 Hotel España
17 Pla de la Boqueria
18 Rambla dels Caputxins
19 Liceu Theatre
20 Güell Palace
21 Carrer dels Escudellers
22 Los Caracoles Restaurant
23 Plaça del Teatre
24 Teatre Principal
25 Rambla de Santa Mònica
26 Waxwork Museum
27 Chinese Quarter
28 Avinguda del Paral·lel
29 Sant Pau del Camp
30 Former Chapel of Sant Llatzer

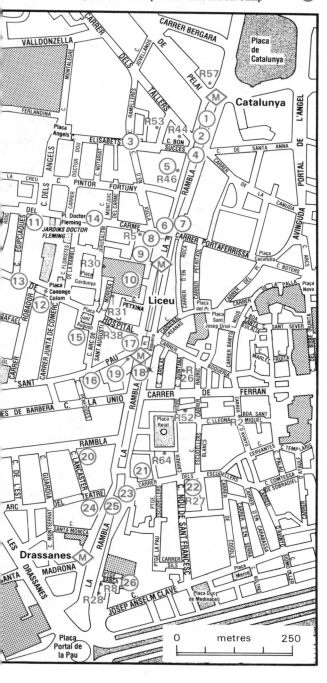

**Start** *M Catalunya, lines 1, 3 and FF. CC. Generalitat. Leave by the La Rambla exit and proceed to the fountain, immediately ahead R, in the central promenade.*

| Location 1 | **LA RAMBLA** |

One of the world's best-known thoroughfares, this tree-lined promenade, almost one mile long, maintains a lively ambience throughout all seasons and virtually twenty-four hours a day.

Rambla has no connection with the English verb to ramble, its origins being the Arab word, pronounced ram-la, meaning the sandy bed of a dry stream. Until the early 18C, an open river ran along the entire length of the present street, its source lying in hills to the north-west of the city. When this dried up in the summer months, its bed was used as a promenade. La Rambla lies well outside the area of the Roman city but only just outside the site of the 13C wall, which skirted its east bank; four gates in the wall led directly to bridges across the stream. Monastic institutions were built on the west bank from the mid 16C and, within a hundred years, so many were established that La Rambla was known as Convent Way. When dissolved in 1835, there were nine monasteries on the west bank and two on the east bank.

In 1704, the stream was enclosed in a conduit and trees planted; at the same time demolition of the wall began, buildings gradually taking its place. Street lamps and chairs for hire were provided in 1781, and in 1843 the former University (Estudis General) that had straddled La Rambla, blocking its north end, was demolished, permitting the extension of the street towards what is now Plaça de Catalunya.

To aid identification, La Rambla has been, for many years, unofficially broken down into five distinct stretches, from north to south: Canaletes, Estudis, Sant Josep, Caputxins and Santa Monica. However, one numbering system now applies to the entire stretch and it is incorrect to refer to the street in the plural as either Les Rambles (Catalan) or Las Ramblas (Spanish).

| Location 2 | **RAMBLA DE CANALETES** |

A fresh water spring, the Canaletes, provides the water for the cast-iron fountain and gave this stretch of La Rambla its name. The expression 'A drinker of the Canaletes water' came to define a citizen of Barcelona. For many years, the enthusiastic supporters of 'Barça' (Barcelona Football Club) have gathered around this fountain, discussing the day's match animatedly.

Chairs may be hired from concessionaires in Rambla de Canaletes (also further south round Liceu), but after 23.00 the attendants leave and no charge is then made. Free public seating is not available until the sea-end is reached, at Plaça Portal de la Pau, which is technically past the southern limit of La Rambla. Other chairs are leased to the nearby cafés, and only their customers may use them.

**Modelo, No 131**, opposite the fountain, is a clothes shop with striking external lighting.

**Cerveceria, No 127**, far from being a humble beer

house as its name implies, is a luxurious tapas bar, possessing the city's most outstanding shellfish display – almost up to Paris standards.

**Boadas**, No 123 (entered from Carrer Tallers first R), is one of Barcelona's most popular cocktail bars.

**Farmàcia Antiga Dr Maso Arumi**, No 121, is decorated with outstanding 19C ceramic tiles.

•➡ *First R c del Bon Succés leads to* **pl del Bon Succés**.

**No 3**, since 1952 the administrative office of the Ciutat Vella district, was formerly the Bon Succés convent. Completed in 1635, its façade is built of Montjuïc stone.

A Gothic roof gallery is retained.

The Majorcan **Miquel Perello** added the Baroque doorway. His name, in Latin, is inscribed above this, and its completion date, 1690, appears below the balconied window.

•➡ *Continue westward to c d'Elisabets.*

| Location 3 | **CARRER D'ELISABETS** |
| --- | --- |

The convent of Santa Elisabets, which occupied much of the area, 1554–1880, has given the street its name.

**No 6** bears a ceramic plaque, L of the door, 'Iglesia de Nostra Senyora de Miserí', recording that it was formerly a church dedicated to Our Lady of Mercy. Constructed in 1693, the building has been converted to a warehouse.

Above the doorway's lintel, two angels support the arms of the city.

•➡ *Continue westward passing four great palm trees that stand in line. Proceed to the patio adjacent to No 12 and follow the passage R to the gateway ahead.*

**Nos 8** and **10** are entered from this gateway, which bears the arms of Barcelona. A stone plaque inset R, dated 1733, records that No 10 was formerly a charity hospital for the poor, dedicated to Nostra Senyora de Miserí.

•➡ *Return to the street R.*

**No 12** was built as the College of Sant Guillem d'Aquitania, an Augustinian monastery founded in 1587.

The portal, with Baroque carving above, survives from the former church, which lies immediately behind, now adapted as a library.

**No 19**, a herbalist's, displays ancient pharmacy bottles in its window. Within, the small interior is beamed.

•➡ *Continue ahead to pl dels Àngels.*

Remains of the **Convent dels Àngels** occupy the west side of the street. In 1990, this former monastery was restored and adapted to house a library for the city's art museums.

Fronting the former chapel, the Classical portal was built in 1680 but remodelled in 1785.

*◆● Follow c dels Àngels that runs southward from the square.*

Passed R is the long wall of the monastery.

An inset plaque depicts angels supporting a coat of arms.

Below are restored figure corbels.

*◆● Return northward to c d'Elisabets, first R, and continue to La Rambla, fifth R.*

| Location 4 | **RAMBLA DELS ESTUDIS** |
|---|---|

In the 14C, the northern section of La Rambla was divided from the remainder by the westward extension of the wall, which crossed the thoroughfare at this point to link with the Santa Anna gate on the east side. The section of wall straddling the road was replaced by the Estudis General (University) in the mid 16C. Later converted to a barracks by Philip V, the obstruction was finally demolished in 1843 but its name is commemorated by this stretch of La Rambla. A caged-bird market has given the Rambla Estudis the alternative name of Ocells (birds).

*◆● Proceed southward.*

| Location 5 | **ROYAL ACADEMY OF THE SCIENCES AND ARTS** (REIAL ACADÈMIA DE CIÈNCIAS I ARTS) *Domènech i Estapà 1883* |
|---|---|
| 115 La Rambla | The architect was twenty-six when he designed this theatre. His early works were basically functional but with idiosyncratic touches and he later embraced the Colossal style. Added in 1888, the clock was the first public timepiece in Barcelona and, beneath it, the words *Hora Official* (Official Time) denote its authoritative status. |

*◆● Enter the building.*

Columns support the vestibule's star-shaped coffered ceiling.

Incorporated in the same building, immediately north of the vestibule, **Viena**, a fast food outlet, displays painted panels and a decorative ceiling evoking the Belle Epoque.

*◆● Exit and continue southward.*

| Location 6 | **MARE DE DÉU DE BETLEM** *Josep Juli 1680–1729* |
|---|---|
| 2 Carrer del Carme | Only the exterior of this church, dedicated to the Mother of God of Bethlehem, is of interest, its once sumptuous Baroque interior having been totally destroyed by arsonists in 1936. |

A Jesuit convent stretched northward from Carrer del Carme to Carrer del Bon Succés and its church was built, facing La Rambla, in 1533. The church burnt down in 1671 and was rebuilt in Baroque style by **Josep Juli**. In 1767, the Jesuits were expelled from Spain and Mare de Déu de Betlem, generally known simply as Betlem, became a parish church.

**Exterior** The outstanding feature of the building is its external ashlar stonework, which is interspersed with diamond-shaped strips, providing a sense of great solidity and strength.

Both doorways facing La Rambla are the Baroque work of **Franciso Santacruz**. Virtually identical in design, they are only distinguishable because the cherubic figures face opposite directions: the north doorway represents the youthful John the Baptist and the south doorway, Christ.

•● *First R c del Carme.*

The Carrer del Carme façade was completed by 1690.

Flanking the main entrance, between twisted columns, are the figures of St Ignatius of Loyola and St Francis of Borja.

Above them, a relief depicts the Nativity.

At the Carrer d'Enxucla corner (first R), a figure of St Francis Xavier occupies a niche.

•● *Enter the church.*

It is difficult to appreciate that the present unexceptional interior was, before the 1936 fire, the most sumptuous Baroque example in Barcelona. A visit to La Verge de la Mercè (page 102) will give some indication of what has been lost.

•● *Exit L c del Carme. Return to La Rambla and cross to the east side.*

| Location 7 | **MOJA PALACE** *1790* |
| --- | --- |

| 118 La Rambla<br><br>*Grand salon open for exhibitions only.* | A severely Classical building, the palace possesses one of the finest Baroque salons in Barcelona, decorated by **'El Vigatà'**. |

**History** An earlier palace on the site was erected in 1702 for Pere de Cartella. This was one of the first structures permitted to be built against the 13C wall, its owner even being allowed to insert windows in the north tower of the ancient Portaferrissa gateway and incorporate it in the palace. Cartella's niece inherited the building, deciding, on her marriage to the Marquis of Moja, that it should be rebuilt. Advantage was then taken of the permission to demolish the 13C wall that had been given in 1704.

Juan Carlos, the present King of Spain, spent his first night in Barcelona in the Blue Room of the palace.

**Exterior** Immediately to the north of the building, a warehouse was constructed over the garden in 1934. However, the 18C two-storey loggia at the end of the garden, built by **Antoni Rovira**, survives and may be glimpsed from La Rambla.

The La Rambla and garden façades of the palace were built by 1778, but it was another twelve years before the remainder was completed. Early in the 19C, **Josep Flaugier** enlivened the street façades with brightly coloured murals, but nothing survives on La Rambla.

Shops were fitted at ground-floor level in 1934.

•● *First L c Portaferrissa*

Outlines of **Flaugier**'s murals survive on this façade.

•● *Enter the building (if an exhibition is in progress).*

•● *Alternatively, proceed to location 8.*

Unfortunately, the **Grand Salon**, which occupies the

first and second floors, may be viewed only when an exhibition is held and then, of course, much of its beauty is concealed. Regarded as one of Barcelona's finest Classical interiors, it is the late-18C work of **Francesc Pla**, known as 'El Vigatà' due to his birth at Vic.

The upper level is galleried.

Other rooms, some containing 18C work by **Pau Montanya**, are rarely open to the public.

➤ *Exit R and cross to the west end of c Portaferrissa.*

A fountain marks the position of the Portaferrissa gate in the 13C wall. This was demolished in 1774, although one of its flanking towers survived until 1818.

Above, a ceramic plaque designed by **Joan Guivernou** in 1959 illustrates the gateway.

➤ *Exit R. First R La Rambla.*

| Location 8 | **RAMBLA DE SANT JOSEP** |
| --- | --- |

The name of this stretch commemorates the monastery of Sant Josep that originally occupied its west side.

However, the flower kiosks that predominate have given it an alternative nickname, Rambla de las Flors (flowers). In the 19C, this was the only place in Barcelona where flowers could be purchased. The kiosks were then of cast iron but from the middle of the present century they have been constructed primarily of glass. Completely new designs were proposed in 1990. One of the flower-sellers became the favourite model, and later the wife, of Ramon Casas, the painter who introduced Impressionism to Catalonia.

Newspaper kiosks, an important feature of La Rambla, also appear side by side with the flower sellers.

**No 105**, on the Carrer del Carme corner, displays Ionic pilasters surmounted by stone putti on plinths, with pottery medallions above: work from the 'Romantic' period.

**No 116** retains 18C sgraffiti.

**No 114** Inset in the façade, at second-floor level, is a Baroque Virgin and Child.

| Location 9 | **VICEREINE'S PALACE**<br>(PALAU DE LA VIRREINA) *1777* |
| --- | --- |

| 99 La Rambla | **History** Manuel d'Amat i Junyent, Spain's Viceroy in Peru, commissioned this building for his retirement in Barcelona but died before its completion. However, his wife, the Vicereine, did occupy the building and its name still commemorates her residency. |
| --- | --- |
| *Open for temporary exhibitions Tuesday–Sunday 10.00–14.00 and 16.30–21.00. Admission charge.* | |

**Exterior** It is believed that architectural drawings, known to be ready by 1770, were sent to Peru for approval by the viceroy before his death. Their designer is unknown but **Josep Ribes** has been suggested. Construction began in 1772, under the general direction of **Pedro Cermeno**. **Carles Grau** was responsible for the street façade and decor.

The style of the La Rambla façade, completed in 1775, is reminiscent of the work of Louis XIV's great architect, Charles le Brun, although more exuberantly decorated with sculptures – urns, trophies, etc. – to accord with the contemporary taste in the city.

Towers were built for viewing purposes, as was fashionable in Barcelona at the time. These can be seen from the east side of La Rambla, rising above the balustrade.

•● *Enter the vaulted vestibule and proceed to the patio.*

With its Corinthian pilasters and carved trophies, the patio, like the façade, follows the Louis XIV style.

•● *Return to the vestibule and ascend the stairs R.*

A Rococo dining-room, much of it the work of **Francesc Serra**, is the most imposing interior in the palace; it is generally open during temporary exhibitions.

•● *Exit R. The central entrance of the adjacent building, No 95, marks the commencement of the market.*

| Location 10 | **SANT JOSEP MARKET 'LA BOQUERIA'** |
| --- | --- |

La Rambla

*Open Monday–Saturday 08.00–13.00 and 17.00–20.00.*

Barcelona's famous food market is, for many visitors, the most convenient venue in which to purchase items such as charcuterie, cheese and fruit. The choice is vast, the setting attractive and the prices competitive.

Between 1836 and 1840, **Francesc Daniel Molina** laid out a square, Plaça Sant Josep, where the St Josep Convent had stood from 1593 until it was demolished in 1835. Colonnaded façades, identical in design, appear to have been inspired by the Regency terraces of **John Nash** in London.

Gradually, market buildings, of slatted-iron construction, were erected in the centre of the square by various architects, and its elegance was lost. In London's Covent Garden a similar process took place, but the area was much larger and the market buildings remained a separate entity.

Officially, the market is named Sant Josep but it is always referred to as 'La Boqueria' due to its proximity to Pla de la Boqueria.

•● *Follow La Rambla southward.*

**Casa Cuinart Mantequeria, No 91**, offers one of the widest ranges of hams and cheeses in the market.

•● *Proceed to the market's main entrance.*

This entrance displays the arms of Barcelona in stained glass, suspended from the apex.

•● *Enter the market.*

Most visitors will wish to make a general tour of the 'Boqueria'. Charcuterie and dairy produce tend to be at the La Rambla end, followed by fresh fruit and vegetables; behind come nuts, dried fruit and meat; odoriferous fish is restricted to the far end.

•● *Exit from the west end of the market. R c de*

*Jerusalem. Third L c del Carme. Continue ahead to the former Hospital de la Santa Creu.*

| | |
|---|---|
| Location 11 | **FORMER HOSPITAL DE LA SANTA CREU** |

47 Carrer del Carme

*Libraries and cloisters open Monday–Friday 09.00–20.00, Saturday 09.00–14.00.*

*Academy of Medicine open Monday–Friday 09.00–13.00 and 16.00–18.00.*

*Admission to everything is free.*

Dating from the early 15C, this group of buildings and cloisters is one of the oldest hospital complexes in the world to survive. Most of the former wards now accommodate public libraries. The exquisite mid-18C dissecting room of the Royal Academy of Medicine may be visited when convenient.

**History** Guitardus founded this hospital near Barcelona cathedral in the 10C and, owing to the sponsorship of the cathedral chapter, it was similarly dedicated dually to the Santa Creu (Holy Cross) and Santa Eulalia. By the 11C, shelter was provided for pilgrims to the Holy Land and the King, Ramon Berenguer I, gave the hospital his support. A move was made to the present site in 1219, when an existing building was converted for its use. In 1401, three other hospitals were combined with Santa Creu and a great rebuilding scheme begun to provide four wings round a cloister. In the late 15C, all Barcelona hospitals were amalgamated here and the cloister was extended southward to accommodate them, almost doubling the size of the complex.

Sensitive restoration and conversion of the buildings to cultural use began in 1929; they have been little altered.

Two blocks, linked by the hospital's gateway, face Carrer del Carme. To the east lies the ashlar façade of the **Royal Academy of Medicine and Surgery**, whose nameplate, in Spanish not Catalan, Real Academia de Medicina y Cirugía, is fixed beside the doorway.

This austere mid-18C building replaced the Anatomy Hall built in 1403 for the College of Surgeons, founded by Martí I two years earlier.

The gateway to the complex bears the arms of the hospital and the date 1680 in Latin.

West of the gateway stretches the rough-stone façade of the early-17C **Convalescence House**, now shared by the Institute of Catalan Studies and the Library of Catalonia. Their brass nameplates, in Catalan, 'Institut d'Estudis Catalans' and 'Biblioteca de Catalunya' are fixed to the wall.

•➡ *Enter the gateway.*

**Royal Academy of Medicine and Surgery** Immediately L, the ashlar stonework of the Royal Academy's main façade is in Classical style, built under the direction of a Madrid architect, **Ventura Rodriguez**, in 1764. Most of the building accommodates the former dissecting room, which is lit primarily from its cupola to minimize shadows. Only one window, therefore, has been inserted in this façade; the others are false.

A large stone plaque, surmounted by the royal arms, stands in the second bay south of the doorway. This commemorates the presentation of the building to the College of Surgeons by Carlos III.

•➡ *Ring the white bell beside the door to view the* **Dissecting Room** *(with guide).*

Within the entrance hall stands a copy of a statue of

Asclepius, Homer's 'peerless physician' of the *Iliad*.

Although small, the circular dissecting room possesses one of the most attractive interiors in Barcelona. Its object was the instruction of students, not the performance of operations, but now the room is used primarily for the ceremony of interviewing prospective new members of the Academy.

The original marble dissecting table stands in the centre.

Rococo armchairs form the two front tiers.

Above them, stone benches, originally students' seating, are now occupied by members of the public during the interviewing ceremony.

The gallery is protected by a gilded, wrought-iron balustrade.

Windows in the cupola and its lantern provide top illumination to the room.

Alfonso XIII presented the Venetian crystal chandelier in 1929, following the restoration of the building.

Above the entrance is a bust of Alfonso XIII.

Above the opposite door is a bust of Carlos III.

Other busts are: L of the entrance, Pere Virgils, 1697–1767, the surgeon for whom the Academy was built, and R of the entrance, Doctor Gimbernut, 1734–1811.

•● *Exit from the building immediately ahead to the former Convalescence House.*

**Convalescence House** Various legacies provided funds for the construction of this late-Gothic/ Renaissance masterpiece, built 1629–80.

It was to one of its beds that Gaudí was rushed on 4 June 1926, after being struck by a tram. Hospital staff did not realize who he was until the following morning, and no treatment was given to him during the night. The great architect died three days later.

A simple façade to the building is enlivened by a marble doorway with Ionic pilasters and the mutilated arms of the hospital above.

•● *Enter the* **vestibule**.

The boss of the groin vault bears the much-restored arms of the building's founder, **Pau Ferrer**.

Ten ceramic panels, illustrating the life of St Paul, are the work of **Llorens Passolles**, 1681.

•● *Proceed ahead to the* **Convalescence House Cloister**.

Basically Renaissance in style, the only Gothic feature of the cloister, built 1655–78, is provided by the gargoyles.

Square Tuscan columns of the arcade support the gallery, which has double the former's number of arches.

The balustrade of the gallery introduces a Baroque note.

Ceramic work around the passages is again by **Passolles**.

In the centre of the cloister, the well, built of Montjuïc stone in 1677, incorporates a large figure of St Paul.

All the sculptures of the well, by **Lluís Bonifàs**, were originally coloured.

Two stairways lead to the gallery; that in the north-west corner is generally closed.

*Proceed to the stairway in the south-east corner, L of the entrance.*

Although the ground-floor ceramics are by **Passolles**, the work illustrating fruit and flowers around a balustrade, that surrounds the staircase, is by **Bernat Roig**.

*Ascend to the gallery level and follow the west passage.*

This passage leads to a roof garden.

*Return to the gallery R and proceed to the reception room in the corner.*

Request permission here to view the Chapel of the Convalescence House (La Capella de la Casa de Convalesencia). Permission depends on convenience at the time and the availability of a guide.

*Alternatively, proceed from the reception room to the Biblioteca de Catalunya.*

**Convalescence House Chapel** Ceramics in the chapel are the earliest work of **Passolles** in the hospital, but the altar frontal, depicting St Paul, is by **Ramon Porcioles**.

The gilded reredos is an 18C Baroque piece.

**Viladomat** is believed to have painted the *Coronation of the Virgin* scene on the vault.

*Return to the reception room and proceed to the library. Visitors may enter but not tour the area.*

**Catalonia Library (Biblioteca de Catalunya)** The library has been installed in the wards that originally occupied the entire first floor of the hospital, begun in 1406. Three of its four wings survive.

Simple, pointed arches of stone support the timber roof.

Traces of Gothic decoration survive, e.g. above the entrance, and it appears that originally each bay and arch was brightly painted. The dazzling scene must have been quite a shock to patients recovering from a medieval operation.

*Return to the cloister and exit R.*

The buttressed 15C wall of the hospital stands immediately ahead.

*Proceed through the arch and enter the **Biblioteca de Sant Pere** (St Peter's Library), immediately R.*

Lying below the 15C wards, this is typical of the hospital's ground floor.

Bosses punctuate the low rib vault.

*Exit directly ahead to the **Biblioteca Infantil** (Children's Library).*

The area is practically identical to that occupied by St Peter's Library.

•● *Exit L and proceed to the main cloister of the hospital.*

**Cloister  Guillem Abiell** completed the cloister in 1417, incorporating stone that had been cut for a new royal palace at the south end of La Rambla; Martí I had decided not to proceed with the project and presented the stone to the hospital.

Originally, the cloister was much smaller and closed by an earlier south wing, since demolished.

Immediately L of the entrance, a Latin plaque commemorates the rebuilding.

Rib vaults and their bosses in the passages have been completely restored.

Romanesque-style capitals in the Gothic arcade are entirely modern work.

•● *Proceed to the cross in the centre of the garden.*

Simple buttresses between the arches support the arcade.

The 17C Baroque cross on its twisted marble column marks the point where the cloister's south wing stood. The cloister's extension southward began in 1509, but little Gothic work is now visible because of subsequent rebuilding.

External stairways to the first floor were built in 1585, entailing the complete remodelling of the last two bays of both side wings.

The newel-post to the west stairway R is carved with an allegorical figure of Charity.

Immediately R is the protective grille of the former **Pharmacy**.

The newel-post of the opposite stairway L is carved with the figure of St Roc, patron saint of the hospital.

Immediately to the south, two bays of a Gothic arcade are a survival from the 15C **archives building**.

A modern structure of brick surmounts this block, incorporating the belfry.

To the rear, three bays of a colonnade are decorated with antique ceramic tiles.

The remaining **east block**, built in front of, and therefore obscuring, the hospital's chapel, was built in 1830: the date is inscribed above the second door L.

Traces of sgraffiti remain.

The **south range** was also built in 1830. It stands against a 16C structure.

Accommodating, on its upper floor, the **Massana School**, the west range appears to be 17C work.

The name of the school, which is described as 'a municipal conservatory of the opulent arts', is inscribed in ceramics above the door.

Above this, a Baroque Virgin and Child occupy a niche.

Standing in front of this building is the structure of a Gothic well, dated 1537, but not in its original position.

At the south end, the range incorporates a 15C balcony with Flamboyant apertures, which is supported by three arches.

A Gothic doorway to the balcony of the **south wall** is now blocked.

●● *Proceed through the* **archway** *in the south range.*

The first section passed was added in 1830; the second, 16C work, retains two small windows with original corbels.

●● *Cross to the south side of c de Hospital.*

Most of the **south façade** was built in the 16C.

Its doorway is characteristic Catalan Renaissance work, with Grotesque Italianate pilasters and a tympanum in the form of the shell of St James, which incorporates the arms of the hospital.

West of the doorway, gargoyles and a window survive from the 14C **Hospital del Colom**, which was incorporated in the complex at an early stage.

●● *Proceed eastward to the Plaça del Canonge Colom corner (first L).*

| | |
|---|---|
| Location 12 | **FORMER CHAPEL OF THE HOSPITAL DE LA SANTA CREU** |

| | |
|---|---|
| 56 Carrer de Hospital | Now an art gallery, where temporary exhibitions are held, only three bays within retain Gothic detailing. |
| *Open Monday–Friday 10.00–15.00 and 17.00–21.00. Saturday 10.00–15.00. Admission free.* | The chapel, built 1406–44 as a free-standing building, was almost completely remodelled in the 18C. Restoration took place in 1951, when it was adapted to serve as an exhibition gallery. |

Above the chapel rises a galleried tower.

The arms of the hospital are carved above the 16C doorway.

Above this stands an 18C allegorical figure of *Charity*, by **Pere Costa**.

●● *Enter the chapel.*

Two skylights and a lantern provide the only natural light to the building, the north window now being blocked.

The barrel vault was rebuilt in the 18C.

A wooden balustrade protects the south gallery.

Gothic vaults and bosses survive in the fourth and fifth bays.

Rich Flamboyant work decorates the eighth bay.

●● *Exit L c Hospital.*

| | |
|---|---|
| Location 13 | **CARRER HOSPITAL** |

Carrer Hospital passes the south end of the former Hospital de la Santa Creu, which gave the street its name. Buildings, particularly the shops, are in far better condition here than in the streets to the south and this part of the El Rayal quarter has definitely gone up-market. On 11 May, the area celebrates the

Feast Day of Saint Ponç, its patron, and stalls, from where honey, preserved fruits and herbs may be purchased, are set up in the specially decorated street; Sant Ponç, it must be emphasized, is not the patron saint of the district's prostitutes.

•● *First L pl del Canonge Colom leads to c de les Floristes de la Rambla, which skirts the east side of the hospital.*

The creeper-covered east wall of the hospital's chapel is passed; its 18C lantern, with red and green tiles, rises above.

•● First L **Jardins del Doctor Fleming**.

Alexander Fleming, the Scottish discoverer of penicillin, is commemorated by the name of these gardens, which are appropriately situated adjacent to the ancient hospital. The doctor's bronze bust, against the wall of the last block L, was presented by the city. Above it are inscribed the words *Barcelona a Sir Alexander Fleming.*

The commemorative plaque L was given by Barcelona firemen.

A similar plaque R was donated by the Montepio Union de Empleados del Matadero de Barcelona (Organization for the Welfare of Abattoir Workers). Presumably, their members were particularly prone to bacterial infection.

•● *R c del Carme.*

| Location 14 | **CARRER DEL CARME** |

An attractive shopping street, Carrer del Carme has none of the sleaziness that prevails further south in El Rayal's 'Chinese' quarter. Its name commemorates the Carmelite monastery that formerly occupied the site of the 'Boqueria' market.

**No 31**, an 18C mansion, was pierced by a shopping arcade in 1800. Its sgraffiti, depicting mythological themes, have almost disappeared.

**El Indio, No 24**, a linen retailer, has emphasized its name by displaying two identical cast-iron busts of a Red Indian chieftain in the centre of the 1922 shop front.

**Vda De M Garrigo** (Vda is an abbreviation meaning widow), **No 3**, purveyors of coffee, tea and confectionery, retains its delicate, wooden shop front and internal stained glass, all unaltered since the business was founded in 1850.

•● *First R La Rambla. Continue southward, passing the market entrances, to the junction with c de la Petxina (first R).*

**Antigua Casa Figueras, No 83**, bakers and confectioners, on the corner with Carrer de la Petxina, was founded in 1820. Its ground-floor marble façade, by **Antoni Ros i Güell**, 1902, was restored in 1986.

**Promoció de Ciutat Vella, No 77**, originally a pharmacy, preserves its Gothic Revival mosaic façade by **Sagnier**, 1911.

**Casa Bruno Quadras, No 82**, occupies the Carrer

Cardenal Casanyas corner. Built as an apartment block in 1896, the architect, **Josep Vilaseca i Casanoves**, who was a follower of **Domènech i Montaner**, extended his mentor's eclecticism further and in this building incorporates Colossal features inspired by ancient Egyptian architecture.

The cast-iron dragon is an expression of the fashion for chinoiserie created by Barcelona's international exhibition in 1888. Originally, an umbrella shop occupied the ground floor, and the dragon still holds an umbrella.

●● *Cross to the west side of La Rambla and follow c de Hospital directly ahead.*

**No 10** Terracotta reliefs gradually replaced sgraffiti as decoration to Barcelona façades in the 19C, and there are several examples in Carrer de Hospital. Winged ballerinas are featured on this house.

●● *Continue westward. First L pl Sant Agustí.*

| Location 15 | **SANT AGUSTÍ** *Pere Bertran 1728–50* |
| --- | --- |
| 2 Plaça Sant Agustí | Dedicated to Saint Augustine, this unusually large parish church is of interest chiefly due to the contrast between the unfinished exterior, which gives an immediate impression of a ruinous building, and the completely finished interior. |

**History** Construction began in 1728 and the building was consecrated within twenty-two years, great speed for such a large church. **Bertran** originally intended that the nave would stretch further into the square but, in 1748, a reduction of its length was ordered on grounds of economy. A Baroque exterior of stone was designed by **Pere Costa**, but with only the lower section of the west front and the crossing tower completed money ran out and the building has remained in its unfinished state ever since.

**Exterior** The railings of the portico were designed by **Rogent**.

Above the central gate are the arms of Barcelona.

●● *Enter the church.*

**Interior** An exercise in academic Classicism, most of the detailing is restoration work, following fires in 1835 and 1936. Corinthian pilasters decorate the walls of the nave.

Balustrades add a Baroque note to the north wall of the nave and the galleries.

The extensive crossing is surmounted by a cupola.

Transepts are unusually large for a Barcelona church.

A gilded Baroque reredos stands in the west transept R.

Matching doorways to both transepts are Renaissance in style.

Above the doorway L is an early-19C Nativity painting by **Claudio Lorenzale**.

Two more works by this artist enliven the sanctuary.

●● *Exit R. First R c de l'Arc de Sant Agustí.*

Passed R is the unfinished east wall of the church.

*•* *Continue to c de Sant Pau and cross immediately to its south side.*

---

| Location 16 | **HOTEL ESPAÑA** |

9–11 Carrer de Sant Pau

Of little interest externally this hotel, which specializes in economically priced package tours, retains its outstanding ground-floor décor, the work of **Domènech i Montaner**. Visitors are welcome.

In 1902, **Domènech** was commissioned to renew the interiors of the public rooms of what was then called the Fonda Espanya, an existing hotel. The sculptor **Eusebi Arnau** and the painter **Ramon Casas** were responsible for much of the detailing.

Immediately left of the vestibule is the bar, inappropriately 'embellished' with large photographic murals of Paris!

The **public dining room** (not the one reserved for hotel guests) possesses the finest décor. Its marine sgraffiti were executed by **Casas**.

*•* *Exit R and continue ahead to La Rambla. Immediately L is pla de la Boqueria.*

---

| Location 17 | **PLA DE LA BOQUERIA** |

This small square was formed in 1824 on the site of the Boqueria gate in the 13C wall, which had been demolished in 1760. Outside the gate, in the Boqueria plain (pla), meat-sellers (bocateria) set up their stalls early in the 13C, giving their name to the area. By the 14C, the flat land had been paved with stone and a gallows set up. During the 15C, the plain became notorious for its gambling tables. The development of the east side of La Rambla began around this point in 1704 and street lighting was installed between here and the theatre to the south in the late 18C.

The Classical fountain was set in the south wall when the square was established in 1824.

*•* *Return to the central promenade of La Rambla.*

A mosaic designed by **Joan Miró** forms the pavement.

*•* *Proceed to the south end of pla de la Boqueria.*

---

| Location 18 | **RAMBLA DELS CAPUTXINS** |

Between the Boqueria and Ollers Gates (entrance to Carrer dels Escudellers) stood a Capuchin monastery that gave its name to this stretch of La Rambla.

**Hotel International, No 80**, is dated 1894 on its roof cresting. Uniquely in La Rambla, the hotel possesses an upper terrace from which clients may gaze down on the lively scene. Officially the terrace is reserved for hotel guests, but non-residents appear to have little difficulty in obtaining service.

**Cafeteria de la Opera, No 74**, is the most fashionable café on La Rambla. Its panelled interior is full to bursting point at night. Thick, hot chocolate is the speciality. The café's terrace, like most in La Rambla, is situated on the promenade.

*•* *Cross to the Liceu Theatre directly opposite.*

| Location 19 | **LICEU THEATRE** |

63 La Rambla

*Tours Monday–Friday 11.30–12.15. Box office open for* **advance** *bookings in Carrer Sant Pau; for the* **day's performance** *in La Rambla, Monday–Friday 08.00–15.00, Saturday 09.00–13.00.*

The Liceu is one of the world's leading venues for opera and ballet, but a relatively insignificant exterior fails to hint that its auditorium is the largest in Europe.

**History** Inspired by French opera houses, **Miquel Garriga i Roca** designed the Liceu as part of the celebration of the Catalan Renaissance. Formerly, its site had been occupied by the College of Barefoot Trinitarians. Work began in 1845 and was completed by **Josep Oriol Mestres** in 1847. Fourteen years later the building was gutted by fire, the roof falling in. Some areas survived, however, and the Liceu reopened 20 April 1862 having been rebuilt by **Mestres**. In 1893 a fanatical anarchist, Santiago Salvador, threw two bombs on the stalls, killing twenty.

The simple façade, a faithful copy of the original, fronts a theatre that is only exceeded in size in Europe by La Scala, Milan.

*•➡ Enter the building.*

The foyer, staircase and first-floor lounge survived the fire and are little altered.

The **lounge** (Saló de Descanso) is also known as the Hall of Mirrors (Saló dels Miralls). Its Neo-Pompeiian style emulates the French taste during the Second Empire.

Rooms that lead off this lounge belong to a private, very fashionable club, founded in 1847, the Cercle del Liceu; these rooms, exquisitely redecorated in Modernist style early in the present century, also escaped the fire.

Comprising stalls with five tiers above, the Classical **amphitheatre** has an audience capacity of 2,700, even greater than La Scala's.

Structural columns have been set back so that no spectator's view is obscured.

The lamps are original but have been adapted from gas to electricity.

A school of music, the Liceu Conservatory, is also accommodated in the building.

*•➡ Exit R, proceed to the central promenade and continue southward passing c de La Unió (first R).*

More seats for hire are provided in this sector.

**Hotel Oriente**, Nos 45–47, is built around the Franciscan monastic college of Sant Bonaventura, founded in 1652.

*•➡ Enter the vestibule and proceed through the central doorway ahead to the lounge.*

The **lounge** has been created in the centre of the former cloister, built by **Pere Serra i Bachs** in 1670. Originally, of course, the cloister was open to the sky.

*•➡ Exit R. First R c Nou de la Rambla. Proceed to No 6, Fernanda Costura.*

From outside this shop can best be seen the chimneys of the Güell Palace, on the opposite side of the road.

In their surfaces, for the first time, **Gaudí** embedded pieces of broken ceramics to form abstract patterns.

*•• Proceed to the palace.*

| | |
|---|---|
| Location 20 | **GÜELL PALACE** (PALAU GÜELL) *Gaudí, 1890* |

3–5 Carrer Nou de la Rambla

*Open Monday–Saturday 11.00–14.00 and 17.00–20.00. Admission charge.*

The only **Gaudí** building in the old city, the palace is also the only example of the architect's domestic interiors that may be visited.

**History** **Gaudí**'s friend and patron, Count Eusebi Güell, commissioned the palace as a private residence. When built, it adjoined the family's existing town house. Güell, educated in England, was a successful industrialist and a civic leader who felt it his duty to sponsor the innovative arts. It is said that the palace was built partly to commemorate his Italian-born mother, and there are internal elements that appear to have been inspired by Italian Gothic work.

Construction began in 1885, but the extravagant interior was not completed until five years later. The Güell family occupied the unfinished house for only two years, as they decided to move away from the city centre in 1886. In 1945, the descendants of the Count presented the building to the city. It was adapted to form part of the Theatre Museum in 1975 but its future use is uncertain.

**Exterior** **Gaudí** inaugurated his mature period with this building, although his delicate use of colour and complete freedom of line were reserved for later work.

Gothic and Mudéjar elements are incorporated in the design. The decorative chimneys, already described, the imaginative ironwork and the parabolic vaults of the entrance proclaim the architect's originality.

*•• Enter the building.*

**Interior** None of the original furnishings survive. Columns and the arch R show Art-Nouveau influence.

From the rear of the **vestibule**, a ramp descends to the former stables in the brick-built basement.

The monumental **staircase** is of polished marble from nearby Garraf.

*•• Ascend the stairs.*

A **reception hall** occupies the mezzanine level.

*•• Continue to the first floor.*

Three **living rooms** face the street. Their columns and sinuous arches, set back from the windows, are typical of **Gaudí**'s late style.

*•• Proceed behind them to the chapel.*

Three storeys high, the **chapel** with its parabolic vault occupies the entire atrium of the building, a feature much favoured by **Gaudí**. Ironwork provides the main decorative feature.

*•• Proceed to the rear of the chapel.*

Woodwork in the **dining-room** is inspired by the Mediterranean Gothic style.

*•• Return to the chapel and ascend the side stairs.*

Areas above first-floor level were reserved for
**bedrooms**. In some of them, the ironwork around the
columns is partly gilded.

 ●● *Exit R and return to the La Rambla promenade R.*

**Hotel de las Cuatro Naciones, No 40**, was built early in
the 19C. It was later remodelled to become
Barcelona's leading hotel; a position that it held for
over a century.

**No 33** combines ceramic tiles and terracotta
medallions in its 19C façade.

 ●● *From the east side of La Rambla follow c dels
Escudellers eastward.*

| Location 21 | **CARRER DELS ESCUDELLERS** |
|---|---|

In the Middle Ages, potters operating in the area
were known as Escudellers, because of the type of
popular cooking vessel that they made. During the
18C, the street became famous for its small hotels.
This and the surrounding streets are now the haunt of
prostitutes, mostly well past their prime. If
approached by a mature, smiling lady, remember
that she is almost certainly not begging, but offering
to sell you her charms. Most of the bars are clip-joints
with the 'girls' much in evidence. However, the street
is certainly animated night and day and there are
some good restaurants to suit all pockets.

**Grill Room, No 8**, has a splendid Modernist façade,
designed in Gothic Revival style which continues
internally.

 ●● *Continue eastward.*

| Location 22 | **LOS CARACOLES RESTAURANT** |
|---|---|

14 Carrer dels
Escudellers

*Open daily.*

Probably Barcelona's most famous restaurant, Los
Caracoles, as its name suggests, always has snails on
the menu, but its real speciality is the succulent spit-
roasted chicken 'pollo al ast', cooked on the street in
full view of the passers-by, both to lure them in and
to dispose of a great deal of heat (see page 213).

 ●● *Exit L and return to La Rambla L. Continue
directly ahead to pl del Teatre.*

| Location 23 | **PLAÇA DEL TEATRE** |
|---|---|

The square occupies the site of the potters'
workshops, which stood just outside the Portal dels
Ollers that formerly closed Carrer dels Escudellers.
From this point, the entire stretch of the 13C wall to
the sea was demolished in 1774.

The **monument to Frederic Soler**, playwright and
founder of the modern Catalan theatre, was made by
**Falqués** in 1900; its figure is by **Querol**. Formerly, a
huge fountain known as the 'Font del Vell' stood in
its place, portraying Hercules, the mythical founder
of Barcelona: this was demolished in the late 19C.

| Location 24 | **TEATRE PRINCIPAL** |
|---|---|

27 La Rambla

Teatre Principal is no longer the city's principal
theatre and is currently rented by the Liceu for
rehearsals.

The Hospital de la Santa Creu was granted

permission to build a theatre by Philip II in 1568, taxes on the admission charges supporting the foundation. Completed in 1603, on the site of the present building, the theatre was built of wood. It was rebuilt in 1778 but burnt down nine years later. In 1790 its Baroque replacement, known as the Casas de la Comedias, staged Italian opera for the first time in Spain. Restoration in 1840 destroyed most of the Baroque decoration and the present, rather severe, Classical building emerged. A fire in 1924 gutted the interior.

•● *Continue southward.*

| Location 25 | **RAMBLA DE SANTA MÒNICA** |

Stretching from Plaça del Teatre to the sea, this is the most southerly section of La Rambla. Its name commemorates the convent of Santa Mònica that stood on the west side.

•● *Continue southward.*

**Centre d'Art Santa Mònica, No 7** Formerly, this building was occupied by the Augustinian Descalzos (discalced or barefoot), which had been founded as a dependency of the Santa Mònica convent in 1636. Adapted to an art gallery for temporary exhibitions in 1988, the original church tower and cloister survive.

•● *Ascend the ramp and enter the building.*

The main exhibition area (usually an entry charge) is formed by the rather severe **cloister**, now covered.

•● *Exit from the building R and cross to the east side of La Rambla.*

From the 15C to the 17C the east side of Rambla Santa Mònica was almost entirely occupied by the Fundació de Canons, where bronze cannon were manufactured for the militia.

**Palau March, No 8** Now the Cultural Department of the Generalitat, this austere Classical building was commissioned in 1776 by Francesc March, a wealthy merchant from Reus, and probably designed by **Soler i Farreca**. In the early 19C Napoléon's military representative, General Dehesme, made this his residence, transferring from the Fiveller Palace.

•● *Continue southward. First L ptge de la Banca (between Nos 4–6).*

| Location 26 | **WAXWORK MUSEUM** (MUSEU DE CERA) |

Passatge de la Banca

*Open,* **winter** *Monday–Friday 10.00–13.30 and 16.00–19.30, Saturday, Sunday and holidays 10.00–20.00;* **summer** *daily 10.00–20.00. Admission charge.*

As far as most foreign visitors are concerned, this will be of interest only to those who are charged with amusing a child on a wet day. The exhibition features both Spanish and internationally known subjects. Understandably, Madame Tussaud's in London and Musée Grevin in Paris are more impressive.

•● *Return to La Rambla. Cross directly to the west side and M Drassanes. Take line 3 in the direction of Zona Universitària and travel one stop to Paral-lel. Exit to the east side of av del Paral-lel (even numbers) and proceed southward to the c Nou de la Rambla junction (third L).*

NB the highlight of this part of the route is the

Romanesque church of Sant Pau del Camp. Its interior may be viewed only at 19.30 unless an appointment has been made.

| Location 27 | **CHINESE QUARTER** (BARRI XINÈS) |

Europe's most famous (and feared) red-light district is not for the timid. Carrer Nou de la Rambla and Carrer de Sant Pau, which runs parallel with it to the north, are the twin 'high streets' of the quarter.

The name, adopted around 1900, is unofficial and its limits debatable, but the zone roughly forms the southern sector of the El Raval quarter, between Carrer de Hospital and the sea: some even insist it spreads east of La Rambla. No Chinatown ever existed here, but its proximity to the port ensured that Chinese sailors, who seem to have dominated the merchant seamen's profession in the late 19C, were frequent visitors to the bars and brothels.

Much larger, much naughtier and much more dangerous than any other comparable area in a European city, the Barri Xinès, at least its side streets, must be treated with extreme caution by anyone who looks as though he or she might rank above pauper level. At nightfall, no cameras, handbags or jewellery should be carried. Having said that, the area is fully policed and no danger should be experienced in the main streets from the knife-wielding junkies who are the prime offenders.

The main attraction of this red-light district is, of course, cheap sex, but remarks already made regarding the whores that frequent the old city still apply.

**Bagdad, No 103** Carrer Nou de la Rambla, offers the most outrageous live-sex porno show in Europe. There are two performances each night (23.00 and 01.30) and the spectacle is lavish for this type of entertainment. Obviously, only the broadest minded visitor, or those carrying out research (like the author), will be attracted. Audience participation is not discouraged!

•● *Return to av del Paral-lel R and proceed northward.*

| Location 28 | **AVINGUDA DEL PARAL-LEL** |

Originally, the street was called Avinguda de Francesc Layret, but on discovering that by chance it ran exactly parallel with latitude north 40°44′, the street was given its present name.

It was around Paral-lel in the mid 19C that the industrialization of Barcelona began. Early in the present century, the area around the junction with Carrer Nou de la Rambla became the 'Place Pigalle' of Barcelona, with its revue theatres and cabarets.

**El Molino, No 99** This cabaret theatre began life as the Moulin Rouge during the late 19C. Closed throughout the Civil War, it reopened in 1939 under the present name, El Molino (The Windmill). Its decor is in the French Belle Epoque style. A knowledge of Spanish helps.

•● *Return to av del Paral-lel. Directly ahead (running eastward from rda de Sant Pau) follow c de Sant Pau.*

| Location 29 | SANT PAU DEL CAMP |
|---|---|

Carrer de Sant Pau

*Open Monday–Saturday 19.30 (prior to vespers at 20.00), Sunday 18.30 (prior to Mass at 19.00). Other times by arrangement (telephone 241 00 01).*

Although a few Romanesque details survive within other buildings in the city, Sant Pau del Camp retains the only virtually complete interior in this style. Its exquisite 12C cloister is one of Barcelona's greatest treasures.

**History** Parts of the fabric of the church pre-date the 7C and it is quite possible that Sant Pau del Camp was founded in the Roman period. Moorish raiders led by Al-Mansur almost certainly destroyed an existing monastic church on the site in 985 and twenty years later it is known that the Almoravides set fire to its replacement. The monastery of Sant Pau del Camp (St Paul in the Field) was refounded in 1117 and the present building dates from this time. Until the 14C the monastery stood outside the city wall, its rural situation being reflected in the name. Abandoned in the 19C, the building served as an army barracks in 1904, but was eventually restored by the municipal authorities.

**Exterior** Although small, the west front possesses a great deal of original sculpture. Supporting the doorway's side lintels are marble capitals from the Visigothic period, carved between the 7C and 8C and reused from an earlier building.

All the lintels are carved with symbolic circles.

Directly above the door, a Latin inscription on the lintel refers to saints Paulus and Petrus (Paul and Peter). On the same lintel, the Latin names Renardus and Raimunda have been deciphered; it is not known who they were.

Flanking the tympanum, corbels depict, in a crude style, the winged-lion emblem of St Mark and the winged-bull emblem of St Luke.

Set on either side of the doorway's arch are the winged-man emblem of St Matthew and the eagle emblem of St John the Evangelist.

Between them is the stylized hand of God, with the usual pointing fingers.

Both Lombard friezes are decorated with corbels of varying designs.

Remains of castellation survive on the apex of the gable, a reminder that medieval churches were commonly fortified.

**•➡** *Proceed clockwise round the exterior.*

The door of the north transept is a Gothic addition.

At the east end of the church, apses form the chancel and flanking chapels of both transepts.

Lombard friezes decorate all three apses, but most of their corbels have been lost.

The southern extension is modern work: behind this lies the chapter house and cloister.

**•➡** *Return to the west front and enter the church.*

**Interior** The building is not very different internally from those Norman churches in England that escaped Gothic remodelling. Most of the short **nave** has been refaced, because of the damage caused by arson during the 'Tragic Week' of 1909, when protesters against conscription in the war with Morocco rioted.

The shallow apse, lit by three small windows, serves as the sanctuary.

Each **transept** has an east apsidal chapel lit by one small window.

The original barrel-vaulted roof of the church survives, but the early–13C exterior to the **south transept** R is rib-vaulted.

●● *Proceed through the south chapel to the former chapter house.*

Now a chapel, the Gothic **chapter house** was built c.1300. The original rib-vault and its boss survive.

Against the east wall L stands the gravestone of Guifre Borrell, d.911, an early member of the dynasty that ruled Barcelona for five hundred years. Discovered in the church in 1596, the stone's Latin inscription on the reverse side indicates that it originally commemorated a Roman.

Two-light Flamboyant windows flank the doorway to the cloister.

●● *Proceed to the* **cloister**.

On the cloister side, the round-headed doorway is Transitional in style, with beasts decorating its capitals.

Although the Gothic cloister of Barcelona Cathedral also has Moorish-style arches to its arcades, those of Sant Pau are a unique Romanesque example.

Capitals are decorated with men, beasts and plants.

Medieval gravestones and tomb chests line the cloister's passages, set in Gothic niches or supported by brackets.

●● *Exit from the church.*

A modern building links the church with the former **Abbot's House**, now the rectory, built in 14C style. This was much remodelled in the 18C and its windows renewed.

●● *Exit to c de Sant Pau R.*

**No 114**, facing the Abbot's House, is the only building in the long street to be decorated with sgraffiti; it is a late example of this work.

Passed R, immediately east of the church, is the garden that was laid out in 1989 above an underground car park. The intention was to regain for Sant Pau a semblance of its original 'in the field' position, but the obtrusive dividing wall has been greatly criticized.

●● *Continue ahead to c d'Espalter (fourth L).*

**Farmàcia Masana, No 67**, on the corner, is yet another chemist's shop that retains its original 19C decor.

●● *First L c Robador. Third L c de Hospital. First R c dels Egipciaques.*

Immediately R, a figure of St Paul occupies a niche on the corner with c del Carme.

A large building, the **Col·legi Públic Milà i Fontanals**, occupies the north side of c del Carme, continuing northward along c dels Àngels. Designed by the Modernist **Goday**, *c*.1900, it is decorated with terracotta reliefs.

•• *Follow c del Carme westward.*

**No 59** is decorated with terracotta and fussy iron balconies.

**Farmàcia del Carme, No 84 bis**, retains its Art-Nouveau shop front with mosaic panels. Its interior, however, is modern.

**Ca l'Erasme, No 106**, a Classical 18C building in Louis XVI style, was commissioned by Erasme de Gonima. Its patio, usually shut, is a good example of Catalan Baroque. The first-floor salon (not open) is attributed to **Flaugier**.

•• *Continue ahead. First L pl del Pedró.*

| | |
|---|---|
| Location 30 | **FORMER CHAPEL OF SANT LLATZER** |
| 2 bis Plaça del Pedró | Although so little of this former chapel survives, it is mid-12C work and, therefore, of historic importance. |

Two-thirds of the building's Romanesque west façade remains on the east side of the square. The chapel was originally surrounded by fields and served a monastic leprosy hospital, Hospital de Malalts Mesells, founded by Bishop Guillem de Torroja in the mid 12C. St Lazarus was adopted as the hospital's patron saint in the 14C and its name changed. What remains served as a chapel until 1913.

A small section of the doorway, a Baroque niche and the bell-tower are preserved on the west façade.

The east apse of the church, with some decorative features, now forms part of the private patio to No 109 Carrer del Carme and can rarely be seen.

•• *Follow c de Sant Antoni Abad westward from pl del Pedró.*

The **Carme church** R is a large brick building, designed by **Josep Maria Pericas** in 1913. It replaced a 15C convent church demolished four years earlier.

**No 54**, a 16C house, retains its portal and one window that are original. Above them are the arms of St George, contemporary with the building.

**No 61**, opposite, now a shop, incorporates part of the 15C façade and vestibule of the former church of **Sant Antoni Abad**, built as the chapel of a congregation of canons, founded here in 1430 to seek a cure for leprosy.

The spandrels of the three arches bear the arms of St Anthony, the city of Barcelona and Alfonso the Magnificent and his consort, María of Castile.

Only the upper window L is original. Three corbels survive at ground-floor level.

•• *Proceed through the doorway.*

Carved bosses decorate the rib vault of the vestibule.

Part of the tympanum of the nave's entrance remains.

Foliated capitals and two angel corbels also survive.

Arsonists completely destroyed the interior of the church in 1909 and it was not rebuilt. The famous 15C reredos to the high altar, by **Jaume Huguet**, was lost during the fire.

●● *Exit L and continue ahead to rda Sant Pau. Cross the road.*

**Saint Anthony's Market** (Mercat de Sant Antoni), built by **Rovira i Trias** in 1859, is regarded as an outstanding example of Catalan ironwork. It was probably inspired by London's Crystal Palace, completed eight years earlier. Various produce is sold, the emphasis within being on provisions. Sunday morning is particularly lively.

●● *Follow c de Manso, that runs westward from the south side of the market, to av del Paral-lel and M Poble Sec.*

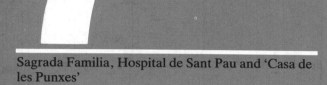

## Sagrada Familia, Hospital de Sant Pau and 'Casa de les Punxes'

Gaudí's great unfinished church, the Sagrada Familia, unofficial symbol of Barcelona, is the highlight of this route which, apart from the rebuilt medieval church, La Concepció, is devoted to important Modernist works. These include major projects by the two best-known Modernists after Gaudí, Domènech i Montaner and Puig i Cadafalch. The entire route lies within the Eixample, Barcelona's extension, begun in the 19C.

*Timing:* Both the Sagrada Familia and the Hospital de Sant Pau remain open throughout the day, every day, a welcome rarity in the city.

The Montaner Palace is open Saturday 09.00–13.00.

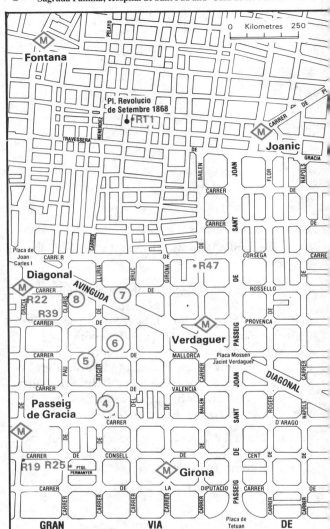

Locations
1 Hospital de la Santa Creu i de Sant Pau
2 Avinguda de Gaudí
3 Sagrada Familia
4 La Concepció
5 Montaner Palace
6 Casa Thomas
7 Casa Terrades 'de les Punxes'
8 Music Museum

**Start** *M Hospital de Sant Pau, line 5. Leave by the Cartagena exit L and follow c de Cartagena northward to its junction with c de Sant Antoni Maria Claret (first R).*

| Location 1 | **HOSPITAL DE LA SANTA CREU I DE SANT PAU** *Domènech i Montaner 1902–10* |
|---|---|

167 Carrer de Sant Antoni Maria Claret

*Grounds open dawn to dusk.*

This is by far the largest project undertaken by **Domènech**, and nowhere else can so many outstanding Modernist buildings be seen in such close proximity.

**History** A bequest led to the development of this great complex of hospital buildings, laid out on a site of 100,000 square metres. Officially, it is called the Hospital de la Santa Creu i de Sant Pau (Holy Cross and St Paul) but is generally referred to simply as Sant Pau. Domènech began its design in 1902, influenced by the vogue for garden cities and the sanitary advantages of physically separating the hospital's functions. A series of pavilions was built, some of them linked by subterranean passages, and the grounds were landscaped. Between 1912 and 1930, the architect's son, **Pere Domènech i Roura**, continued his father's work, closely following the original style, but with budget limitations restricting the decorative element.

**Exterior** The brick-built entrance pavilion is surmounted by a needle spire rising above its clock tower.

Angled side wings flank the structure.

*•• Ascend the steps.*

A monument commemorates Pere Gil, founder of the hospital.

Sculptures within the vestibule are early examples of the work of **Pau Gargallo**. Themes include flower capitals and angels.

*•• Proceed through the entrance to the grounds ahead.*

Four pavilions are symmetrically placed on either side of the central tree-lined area; all are the work of **Domènech i Montaner** and terminate in a circular tower, roofed by a cupola.

*•• Proceed northward, following the west group of pavilions L.*

Colourful ceramic tiles and mosaics impart a Byzantine appearance.

*•• After the fourth pavilion has been passed, turn R and proceed to the east façade of the Cafeteria L.*

The Baroque façade, dated 1733, the work of **Carles Grau i Bover**, came from the chapel of the Hospital de los Peregrinos de Santa Marta, the remainder of which was demolished in 1909.

Other buildings to the north are the work of Domènech i Montaner's son.

*•• Return westward and follow, first L, the east range of pavilions southward. Exit from the hospital complex. Continue directly ahead and follow the central promenade of av de Gaudí southward.*

| Location 2 | **AVINGUDA DE GAUDÍ** |

This is by far the best approach to the Sagrada Familia, and one of the most moving experiences that Barcelona has to offer. It has transpired that the two leading Modernist architects, **Gaudí** and **Domènech i Montaner**, pay homage to each other in the Avinguda de Gaudí, with their most ambitious works closing the vistas at both ends. Few of Barcelona's major thoroughfares end in great vistas, and it seems almost an indecent luxury that this avenue should possess two.

From the Hospital de Sant Pau, the route tracks downhill, with the towers of the Sagrada Familia gradually dominating the view as they are approached.

**☛** *Continue to the c de la Indústria junction (first L).*

At this point, the first of six identical **street lamps**, designed by **Pere Falqués** c.1900, is reached. Each lamp, of maroon-painted iron and fixed to an obelisk-shaped stone base, has recently been restored to its original appearance.

**☛** *Continue ahead to the Sagrada Familia.*

| Location 3 | **SAGRADA FAMILIA** *Gaudí 1884* |

115 Plaça de la Sagrada Familia

*Open January– March 09.00–19.00; April–June 09.00– 20.00; July and August 09.00– 21.00; September– December 09.00– 20.00. Admission charge.*

*Lift to the top of the east façade's tower operates daily 10.00–13.45 and 15.00–18.45. Nominal charge.*

The unfinished Sagrada Familia church, on which **Gaudí** worked for more than half his life, has become the symbol both of Barcelona and of Modernism. Only the apse, crypt, east façade and one tower had been completed at the time of **Gaudí**'s death in 1926. Work is continuing, based on the architect's models and sketches and it is possible that the building will be completed, basically as envisaged by **Gaudí**, during the first quarter of the twenty-first century. Apart from the crypt, the interior of the church is as yet little more than a building site.

**History** Due to its architectural importance, many wrongly believe that this great church, called by its full title, the Templo Expiatorio de la Sagrada Familia (Expiatory Temple of the Holy Family), is a cathedral. Barcelona's cathedral has been established probably since the Roman period and it was never intended that the Sagrada Familia should usurp its function. In 1869, Josep Bocabella founded an association dedicated to Saint Joseph. A major aim was to bridge the widening gulf developing between workers and employers, inspired by the example of Jesus who worked as a carpenter for Joseph, his father. In 1882, Bocabella commissioned **Francesc de Paula Villar i Lozano** to design a church for the association, and work was begun in the Gothic-Revival style.

In the following year, irreconcilable disputes between the architect and his client led to the appointment of the twenty-nine-year-old **Gaudí** as a replacement.

**Gaudí** made changes to the crypt, the only feature that had been built, and constructed the apse in Gothic-Revival style. It was not until the east façade was begun in 1891 that the 'Gaudí' style of the building, with its Art-Nouveau characteristics, was firmly established. In 1910, age fifty-eight, **Gaudí** completed the Casa Milà and decided to accept no further commissions, so that he could concentrate on the Sagrada Familia. His assistants included **Joan Rubió i Bellver, Francesc Berenguer i Mestres, Domingo Sugranyes** and **Francesc Quintana**, all craftsmen and all very poorly paid, averaging 1.5 pesetas per day, seven days a week. **Gaudí** himself received only 200 pesetas per month, but eventually refused any payment at all, his other projects having earned him sufficient to live on. For the last eight months of his life, **Gaudí** resided on the site in one of the builder's huts.

The east façade of the church, together with its south tower, was completed before **Gaudí**'s death in 1926. Ten years later, when work came to a halt, the remaining three towers of this façade had been built. Construction resumed in 1952: the west façade is now finished and the south façade well under way. **Jordi Bonet** became responsible for the project in 1984 and it is estimated that with modern production methods and materials it should be possible to complete the Sagrada Familia by 2020.

Since resumption began in 1952, the project has been controversial. There are those who believe that construction should continue, at present the official policy; those who would prefer work to stop when the three façades with their towers have been completed; and the most drastic group, those who would like all post-Gaudí work to be demolished. The 'stop work before completion' factions argue that **Gaudí**'s models and drawing are flimsy evidence for what the architect intended, and that in any case he was an intuitive designer, who would have made changes as work progressed. They also believe that there is no need for a new church of such large dimensions in a less religious age and that the money would be better spent on more useful projects. In addition, they postulate that the switch from stone to concrete would have been frowned on by **Gaudí**, as the texture and colour of the man-made material is very different. At present, however, money is pouring in from many sources and there seems no doubt that if the project is continued as planned there will be no lack of finance. Supporters of completion explain that **Gaudí** never expected to finish more than a section of the church in his lifetime, estimating that if stone were used throughout, approximately two hundred years would be needed. They point out that **Gaudí** completed one tower and one façade as a guide to future architects, intending that they should follow his overall plan but not insisting on **Gaudí** pastiche. But perhaps, when all is said and done, it is the pride of the Barcelonans that will ensure its continuation. 'Would Parisians have accepted the Eiffel Tower without its upper stages?' a supporter has asked.

**Exterior** An additional advantage in approaching the church from the north is that the work completed in Gaudí's lifetime is seen first.

Immediately ahead, the east, **Nativity façade**, 1891–1900, is one of the three projected by **Gaudí** but the only one that he finished.

Each of the façades is to be surmounted by four towers, representing the twelve apostles, part of the medieval-style symbolism applied throughout the building. **Gaudí** established the shape of the famous towers in 1902, but a recent visitor from the NASA space research station remarked on the similarity in shape between them and the Saturn rocket, a demonstration, perhaps, of the timeless aspect of **Gaudí**'s late work.

Towers of four different heights are planned, those of the façades, although each over 100m high, being the shortest.

In order of height the others, on which work has not yet started, are: four surrounding the crossing, representing the Evangelists; one rising from the apse, representing the Virgin; and a central tower, representing Christ, that will rise from the crossing to 170m, almost half as high again as the existing towers.

**Gaudí** completed the most southerly tower L in 1921, the only one to be finished before his death in 1926. However, work had begun on the remaining three that surmount the east façade and these were built by 1936, when work was halted because of the Civil War.

Polychrome mosaics decorate the upper section of the towers.

Detailing of the east façade is described on the next page, when the building has been entered and it can be approached more closely.

●● *Proceed anticlockwise to the north apse.*

Surprisingly banal Gothic-Revival work, northern Gothic at that, leads many to believe that this apse was initiated by **Villar**, the original architect, but it is, in fact, early work by **Gaudí**, 1884–93.

●● *Continue ahead to the west façade.*

Work began on this façade in 1952 and was completed in 1990.

Carving by the internationally renowned Catalan sculptor, **Josep Maria Subirachs**, depicts the Passion and Death of Christ, the theme chosen by **Gaudí**.

●● *Continue southward. First L c de Mallorca. Enter the small car park immediately L.*

A cottage-like building, with green paintwork R, is the **Parish School** built by **Gaudí** in 1909. Its address is 401 Carrer de Mallorca, but a wall conceals the street façade. The building is not open to the public.

The major façade of the church will be on this, the south side: although under construction, work is hidden from view at the time of writing. Its theme of Christ in Glory is being carved by **Subirachs**.

●● *Return to the west façade and enter the church.*

Plans of the Sagrada Familia and a model, not by **Gaudí**, of the west façade are displayed at the entrance.

●● *Proceed to the centre of the church.*

Visitors remark on the limited number of workmen to be seen. This has always been the case, **Gaudí** preferring a small team of craftsmen. 'My client (God) is in no hurry' he is reported as saying.

Immediately L is the high altar.

●● *Continue to the apse.*

Stairs within the **apse** descend to the crypt which, at the time of writing, is only open for services.

**Gaudí** added windows and a rib vault to the **crypt**, which was partly finished when he took over the project. The great architect lies here. His tomb was forced open during the anti-clerical vandalism of 1936, when the crypt was burnt.

●● *Continue eastward to the most northerly tower of the east façade. Ascend by lift.*

Views are gained of internal construction work, if in progress, but of greater interest is the opportunity to inspect closely the structure of the stone-built towers.

●● *Descend and proceed eastward outside the building to view the only façade completed by Gaudí.*

This depicts the **Nativity** and was built 1891–1900.

Three doorways, apparently surmounted by stalactites, represent, from L to R, *Hope*, *Charity* and *Faith*.

**Hope doorway** Biblical scenes depict the daily life of the Holy Family.

**Charity doorway** The family tree of the House of Jesse is carved on the great lintel above the door.

At the top of the window is an Annunciation scene.

Below, on the central entrance, large figures represent those attending the Nativity.

On the first apex is a Coronation of the Virgin scene.

Carved at upper level is the Chi Ro emblem of Jesus.

**Faith doorway** Sculptures above depict the Nativity and, below, scenes from the childhood of Jesus.

Grapes and cereals are carved on the pinnacle.

●● *Return towards the entrance and follow the signs to the museum (Museu del Temple Expiatori) situated in the south-east corner of the church. Entry is free.*

Progress of the work, beginning with the north apse, is illustrated. **Gaudí** produced models of the interior and the exterior of the Sagrada Familia; in 1936, they were smashed by iconoclasts but subsequently pieced together as accurately as possible and are exhibited here. Some drawings, however, were lost completely.

●● *Exit from the church L c de Sardenya.*

Immediately R are the gardens of the Plaça de la Sagrada Familia.

●● *First R c de Mallorca. First L c de Sicilia. Third R av de Diagonal.*

On the corner, at **No 332 Diagonal**, stands the **Casa Planells**, by **Josep Jujol**, 1924. Jujol, basically a painter, was responsible for the design of much of the decorative mosaic and ceramic work of **Gaudí**'s later buildings, Güell Park being the most famous example. This apartment block is a rare example of his architecture. The curved façade suggests inspiration from **Gaudí**'s *La Pedrera*, completed in 1910.

*●● Continue westward. Third R pas de Sant Joan.*

**Casa Macaya, No 108** Built by **Puig i Cadafalch** in 1901 as a large residence, but now the headquarters of Centre Cultural de la Caixa de Pensions, this building, in Flamboyant Gothic Revival style, has been given a Catalan tower and roof gallery (filled).

Sgraffiti decorate the first and second floors of the façade.

Particularly charming is the oriel window R, clad with ceramics.

The courtyard (note the unusual staircase) leads to an exhibition room.

*●● Return southward to the Diagonal junction which forms Plaça Mossèn Jacinct Verdaguer.*

The central **column** commemorates the Catalan poet, Verdaguer, 1845–1902. It was designed by **Josep Pericas** and built 1913–24, with sculptures by the **Oslé** brothers.

An outstanding Grecian-inspired frieze is incorporated.

*●● Follow pas de St Joan southward to the junction (first R) with c de València.*

Ahead, on the east side of the street at **No 92**, is the **Saleses Church**, by **Joan Martorell i Montelles**, 1885. Influenced by the German Gothic style, its zigzag patterned roof is reminiscent of Stefansdom in Vienna. **Gaudí** admired **Martorell**'s early architectural use of colour.

*●● First R c de València. Proceed to the junction (first R) with c de Bailen.*

Occupying the west corner block is **Casa Llopis i Bofill**, an apartment building by **Antoni Gallissà i Soque**, 1903. Protruding bays are an early example of Rationalism.

Subdued sgraffiti decorate the walls, and the roof gallery, of Mudéjar-style brickwork, is blocked with ceramics.

*●● Continue westward. First R c de Girona.*

**Casa Lamadrid, No 113**, is an unusually restrained work by **Domènech i Montaner**, 1902, bearing few decorative features. Floral capitals to the ground-floor columns and ceramics to the first floor balconies are the most noteworthy features.

Small rosettes carved above the windows are reminiscent of **Domènech**'s Casa Thomas (Location 6).

The roof-level crest bears the completion date, 1902, in Roman numerals. It is flanked by a floral balustrade.

*●● Cross to the east side of c de Girona and proceed northward.*

**No 122**, an apartment block by **Jeroni Granell i Manresa**, 1903, is noteworthy for its delicate green and violet sgraffiti. There are Art-Nouveau features, particularly at ground-floor level and within the pretty hall, which may generally be entered.

*●* *Return southward. First R c de València.*

Immediately L, the north entrance to **Mercat Concepció**, a food market, is flanked by colourful florists' kiosks.

*●* *Continue westward. First L c del Bruc.*

**Escola Municipal de Música**, on the corner, at **No 110**, was built by **Antoni de Falguera** in 1910. Much influenced by Puig i Cadafalch, the staircase and 'La Peixera' room with its stained-glass skylight are of interest.

*●* *Exit L and proceed southward. First R c d'Aragó.*

| Location 4 | **LA CONCEPCIÓ** |
|---|---|
| 299 Carrer d'Aragó | |

When Via Laietana was laid out through the old city in the 19C, one of the most important losses was the Santa Maria de Jonqueres monastery, which stood, until 1868, where the road is now joined by Carrer Jonqueres. However, its church, 1293–1448, together with the cloister, was rebuilt here as the church of La Concepció (the Conception), under the guidance of **Jeroni Granell**, 1871–88. The campanile was added, employing stones from that of the church of Sant Miquel, also demolished in the 19C for road improvements. Meant to be a facsimile of Sant Miquel's, the campanile of La Concepció is more fancifully decorated.

*●* *Enter the church.*

The aisleless nave has six side chapels, each with a 19C Gothic-Revival reredos.

Walls are decorated with the arms of the kings of Aragon and other protectors of the convent.

*●* *Proceed to the cloister, which adjoins the west side of the church.*

Due to lack of space, the rebuilt cloister had to be reduced in size; it is, therefore, rectangular rather than square and there are fewer bays. The lower storey was built in 1450 and the upper storey, now glazed, in the second half of the 15C.

*●* *Exit from the west side of the cloister R c de Roger de Llúria.*

**Nos 72–74**, an apartment block, is Modernist work.

**Casa Vilanova**, **Nos 76–80**, occupies the south-east corner with Carrer de Valencia. Designed as apartments by **Juli Fossas i Martinez** in 1907, the building incorporates Art-Nouveau features, particularly the central range of loggias, which is surmounted by a cupola with a short spire. Gaudí's contemporary work appears to have influenced the architect.

*●* *Continue northward.*

**No 82**, on the north-east corner with Carrer de València, displays great stained-glass bays.

**No 84** is decorated with geometrical sgraffiti.

First and second floors retain their stained-glass bays, but the glass of the third floor has been lost. Balustrades to the balconies and the ground-floor stonework are Art-Nouveau work.

*•● Continue ahead to the south-west corner with c de Mallorca (first left).*

| | |
|---|---|
| **Location 5** | **MONTANER PALACE** (PALAU MONTANER) |

99–101 Carrer de
Roger de Llúria

*Open Saturday
09.00–13.00.
Admission free.*

This elegant mansion was designed as a family residence for a partner in the publishing company of Montaner i Simon. **Domènech i Estapà** began the work in 1885 but, possibly due to a dispute, or to fraternal pressure, **Domènech i Montaner**, the client's elder brother, completed the project in 1893. The building remained in the possession of the Montaner family until the end of the Civil War, when it was adapted to government offices; the Delegación General del Gobierno now occupies the premises.

Three great timber eaves project at roof level.

Beneath them, polychrome ceramic figures were added by **Domènech i Montaner**.

Lower floors are the work of **Domènech i Estapa**.

*•● Enter the building.*

A great staircase rises two storeys from the vestibule. It is the most important feature of the building and entirely the work of **Domènech i Montaner**. Balustrades are carved with typical examples of the designer's floral themes.

A stained-glass window, reminiscent of the same architect's Palau de la Música Catalana, lights the staircase.

*•● Exit L and cross to the north-west corner with c de Mallorca opposite.*

**Col·legi Oficial d'Advocats, No 283**, is a rare example in Barcelona of an Italian style building.

*•● Follow c de Mallorca eastward.*

| | |
|---|---|
| **Location 6** | **CASA THOMAS** |

291–293 Carrer de
Mallorca

**Domènech i Montaner** built Casa Thomas in 1898 as a two-storey structure. Fourteen years later it was heightened by his son-in-law, **Francesc Guardia i Vial**, who kept to the spirit of the original work, retaining the ground floor and virtually reproducing the original second storey with its twin turrets, but at fourth-storey level. If, therefore, one can 'demolish' in the mind's eye the three central storeys, **Domènech**'s original building may be pictured. Casa Thomas marked an important development in the architect's work as, for the first time, two of his 'trademarks', ceramics with button-like reliefs and floral balustrades, made an appearance.

A glass screen now protects the ground floor's ironwork and stained glass.

*•● Continue eastward. First L c del Bruc. Second L av Diagonal.*

| | |
|---|---|
| **Location 7** | **CASA TERRADES 'DE LES PUNXES'** *Puig i Cadafalch 1905* |

416–420 Avinguda
Diagonal

**Puig** was given an irregular island site for this huge apartment block, the largest of the famous architect's projects. In spite of this, apart from the high south-west corner tower, he managed to design a series of symmetrical façades, united by steeply pitched gables

and pointed conical roofs to the towers.

Slender finials, surmounting the towers and gables, add to the spiky effect and have gained for the building the nickname 'Casa de les Punxes' (House of Spires).

**Puig** had studied Nordic Gothic architecture and its influence on Casa Terrades is apparent. Large areas of brickwork give a monumental effect, but the series of four-storey bays that punctuate the façades and the entire ground floor are of stone.

•● *Follow av Diagonal westward and cross to the south side.*

| Location 8 | **MUSIC MUSEUM** (MUSEU DE LA MÚSICA)<br>*Puig i Cadafalch 1904* |
|---|---|

Palau Quadras
373 Avinguda
Diagonal

*Open daily 09.00–14.00. Admission charge except Sunday and public holidays.*

A strange but delightful building, commissioned by the Baron of Quadras as his private residence. Here, **Puig** most successfully combines varying styles.

Rustic eaves and dormer windows of timber surmount the structure.

Above the first-floor window a stone screen, intricately carved with medieval themes, dominates the façade.

A gallery runs at upper level.

Within the building is displayed a collection of ancient musical instruments. Of particular interest are the guitars.

•● *Exit L and cross to the north side of av Diagonal.*

**Casa Comalat, No 442**, was built by **Salvador Valeri i Pupurull** in 1911.

The cupola's decoration is Rococo, whilst the remainder of the façade is basically Baroque.

•● *Enter the hallway.*

Ochre and violet predominate, highlighted by mosaics and stained glass.

•● *Exit and continue westward. First R c de Còrsega.*

**No 316**, surprisingly, is the rear of Casa Comalat and, equally surprisingly, the work of the same architect – no sign of Baroque or Rococo here, **Valeri** apparently being influenced, on this façade, by **Gaudí**'s Casa Batlló. Angled windows are shuttered, giving the impression of a giant accordion.

•● *Return westward. First L av Diagonal and M Diagonal.*

8

## Domestic Modernism and Shopping Streets

The finest domestic buildings of Gaudí, Domènech i Montaner and Puig i Cadafalch are seen, many of them situated in Passeig de Gràcia, Barcelona's foremost shopping street.

*Timing:* Most of the fashionable stores remain open throughout the afternoon but, of course, shut Sunday, when the shopping streets are rather lifeless.

Gaudí's Casa Milà may be visited Monday–Friday on the hour from 10.00 to 13.00 and 16.00–18.00; also Saturday and Sunday (from 11.00), but not after 13.00.

Domènech's Casa Lleó Morera, now partly occupied by the Tourist Office, is open to visitors Monday–Thursday, 16.30–17.30, by prior arrangement.

Puig's Casa Ametller is open Monday–Friday, 10.00–14.00 and 16.00–20.00.

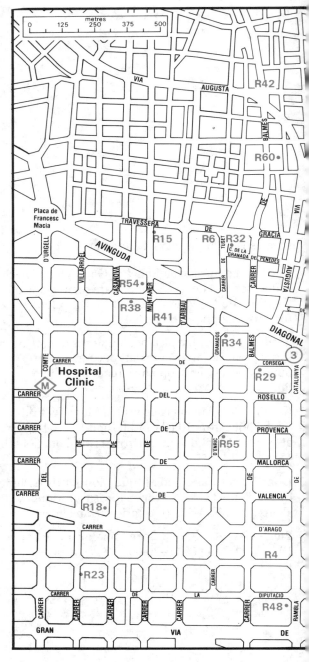

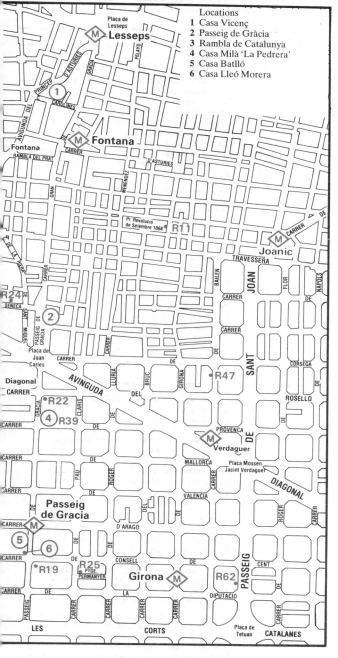

Locations
1 Casa Vicenç
2 Passeig de Gràcia
3 Rambla de Catalunya
4 Casa Milà 'La Pedrera'
5 Casa Batlló
6 Casa Lleó Morera

**Start** *M Lesseps, line 3. Exit from the station R av Princep Asturies. First L c Carolines.*

| Location 1 | **CASA VICENÇ** *Gaudí 1883–88* |
|---|---|
| 22 Carrer Carolines | Regarded as a formative Modernist work, Casa Vicenç was **Gaudí**'s first important project. |

A wealthy builders' merchant commissioned the villa for his summer-house, to be constructed on the hillside slopes to the north of the city. It was possibly his client's commercial interest in building materials that permitted **Gaudí** to blend bricks, ceramics and stonework in such a polychromatic way. Certainly, nothing like it had been seen before. An Islamic influence is apparent in the Mudéjar-style detailing, albeit applied in an idiosyncratic way.

Subterranean floors are rarely found in the city, but the architect appreciated their relative coolness in the hot Barcelona summer and often incorporated a basement. Other examples are at Güell Palace, Casa Milà and Casa Batlló.

Ironwork, designed to represent small fan palms, possesses the usual spikiness that **Gaudí** favoured.

In 1926, the house was extended westward at the rear for its conversion to flats, and most of the splendid garden was lost. **De Serra Martinez** was responsible for the work, sensitively continuing **Gaudí**'s style.

*Continue eastward. First R c Gran de Gràcia. Proceed to M Fontana and train southward to M Diagonal (one stop). Exit and follow pas de Gràcia northward.*

*Alternatively, follow c Gran de Gràcia southward to its junction with pas de Gràcia. Turn L and proceed to No 132, Casa Fuster.*

| Location 2 | **PASSEIG DE GRÀCIA** |
|---|---|

Although bargains are rarely to be found, Passeig de Gràcia boasts some of the most luxurious shops in the city, many international fashion houses being represented. Due to its width and the limited extent of its central promenade, repeated crossing from side to side is not practicable. Moreover, it is recommended that the thoroughfare should be explored by individual sectors; to walk up one side and then down the other is a very tiring and, in part, monotonous experience.

Passeig de Gràcia follows the dead-straight route, between fields and orchards, of the old road that led from Barcelona to the village of Gràcia. Lacking any buildings until 1824, Passeig de Gràcia had become a five-track thoroughfare three years later, with the central track, unlike today, entirely reserved for pedestrians. In 1852, gas lighting was installed, and the street was destined to become the most important north/south artery of the Eixample.

Residences, mainly for the upper middle class but also for a limited number of aristocrats, were built from *c.*1880; few incorporated shops. By 1925, however, many ground floors were being leased to retailers and the development of Passeig de Gràcia as a commercial street was under way.

●● *Continue northward.*

This, the most northerly stretch of Passeig de Gràcia, is the only one to retain a central promenade. An underground car park has been constructed beneath it.

Projecting on the east side is **Casa Fuster, No 132**, with its main façade looking south. This was almost the last domestic building in the city to be designed by **Domènech i Montaner**, who completed it in 1910.

A Nordic roof line crowns the building.

Below, Catalan Gothic windows are the main decorative feature.

At first-floor level, the loggia is Classically inspired.

Pink and white marble, it has been observed, gives the apartment block a Venetian feel.

●● *Return southward. First R av de Diagonal.*

The **Pompeia Church** and convent, **No 450**, were built by **Sagnier**, 1907–15. Of brick and stone, influenced by Catalan Gothic work, the uninspired building is rarely open.

●● *Cross to the south side of av de Diagonal and continue westward.*

**Fargas, No 391**, confectioners and bakers, serve luxurious refreshments at their snack bar.

●● *Exit L.*

Immediately west of Fargas, a sign in Catalan, frequently seen in Barcelona, proclaims *US EXCLUSIU BOMBERS*. Don't be alarmed. No American president in a fit of madness has suddenly declared war on Spain. It simply indicates the existence of a water supply, reserved for the exclusive use of firemen (*bombers*).

●● *Continue westward. First L Rambla de Catalunya.*

| Location 3 | **RAMBLA DE CATALUNYA** |
|---|---|

This charming tree-lined street, with a central promenade, is reminiscent of La Rambla but very much smarter, if a little less lively.

A metal structure supports an awning, providing shade for those taking refreshments on the café's terraces. Unlike La Rambla, free public seating is provided. At Christmas time, a poultry market is held in the street.

There is a wider range of shops here than in Passeig de Gràcia even though fashion boutiques still predominate.

**Casa Serra, No 126**, occupies the north-east corner with Avinguda Diagonal. Built by **Puig i Cadafalch** in 1903 as the Serra family's residence, it was never completed for them, and from 1908–69 accommodated the Congregation of Santa Teresa de Jesús. Now the headquarters of the Diputació that administers the Barcelona provinces, it is linked with their dominating modern office block at the rear.

A 'medieval' tower and roof gallery are typical **Puig** themes, but the first floor windows are Renaissance, an unusual style for this architect to adopt.

On the central promenade, at the Avinguda Diagonal junction, is *Reclining Giraffe*, a tongue-in-cheek modern sculpture by **Josep Granyer** that gently satirizes the reclining-nude theme favoured by many artists.

●● *Proceed southward. First L c de Còrsega. First R pas de Gràcia.*

**Palau Robert, No 107**, is a beautifully proportioned Neo-Baroque building, occupying the south-west corner with Avinguda Diagonal. It was designed by **Henry Grandpierre** in 1903. The Presidencia's Department of the Generalitat occupies the premises, and temporary exhibitions, free of charge, permit visitors to view the interior of the ground floor.

To the rear is one of the largest private gardens in central Barcelona.

●● *Exit from the palace.*

The junction of Avinguda Diagonal, Passeig de Gràcia and Carrer de Còrsega forms Plaça de Joan Carles (the Catalan name of King Juan Carlos). In its centre, the obelisk designed by **Viladomat** was originally crowned with an allegorical statue *The Republic* but this was removed following the Civil War.

**Marés** added *Victory* to the base.

●● *Follow pas de Gràcia southward.*

The street lamp/bench, on the west side of the street, is one of a famous set designed in Art-Nouveau style by **Pere Falqués**, the municipal architect, *c.*1900. Incorporated in the design are the arms of the city. Aided by the patronage of large companies, these are being restored.

●● *Continue southward to the north-east corner with c de Provença.*

| | |
|---|---|
| Location 4 | **CASA MILÀ 'LA PEDRERA'** *Gaudí 1906–10* |

92 Passeig de Gràcia

*Guided tours in English Monday–Friday 10.00, 11.00, 12.00, 13.00, 16.00, 17.00 and 18.00; also Saturday, but not after 13.00, Sunday 11.00, 12.00 and 13.00 only. Admission free.*

Regarded by many as **Gaudí**'s masterpiece, this apartment block of white stone is renowned for its overall sculptured appearance and the originality of its chimneys.

**History** With this building, **Gaudí** broke away completely from the Catalan architectural heritage that had inspired the Modernists. The treatment of the design as a sculpture in stone (hence its nickname 'La Pedrera' – the stone quarry) is uniquely Gaudíesque. Casa Milà was the precursor of Expressionist architecture and a progenitor of abstract sculpture.

On its completion, **Gaudí** accepted no more commissions, devoting the remainder of his life to the Sagrada Familia church.

**Exterior** Restored externally in 1989, Casa Milà's formerly grimy stonework is once more gleaming white.

Cerdá's grid system for the Eixample specified that every corner building should be chamfered. **Gaudí** had to follow this rule but overcame its rigidity by designing an undulating façade.

Originally, the project was even more ambitious, **Gaudí** planning to surmount the roof with a large *Virgin of Grace*, carved in the same stone as the façade, and thereby giving the building the appearance of a homogeneous sculpture. Eventually, however, lack of finance precluded this.

Columns and window apertures bear an Art-Nouveau influence.

The ironwork to the balconies owes much of its detailing to **Jujol**.

*Enter the building and await the guide.*

**Interior** **Gaudí** wanted the patios to be as extensive as possible, and the building has no common stairway; all apartments must be reached by lift or, in an emergency, the service stairs.

Traces of colourful decoration within the atrium survive, particularly where it has been protected by the balconies, and restoration is planned based on existing photographs; however, none of the original work had been commissioned by **Gaudí**.

As at Güell Palace, a ramp descends to the former stables in the basement.

*Ascend the service stairs, with guide, to the top floor (the small lift is restricted to use by the elderly or infirm).*

Upper-floor flats were added to the block during the 1950s.

Some ceilings by **Gaudí** survive in the original apartments, but little else. Pere Milà i Camps, who commissioned the development, lived in a first-floor apartment, with décor by **Gaudí**. However, his wife Roser, who detested the architect's work, ripped this out following her husband's death.

*Ascend more steps to roof level.*

**Gaudí**'s famous chimneys provide a sculpture gallery of *espantabruixas* (witch scarers). Similarities with antique military helmets have been suggested, but there is no record of the source of **Gaudí**'s inspiration. It was originally intended that the chimneys should be clad with polychromatic ceramics, as at Casa Batlló, but there was insufficient money.

*Descend and exit from the building. Follow pas de Gràcia southward.*

**Comtes de Barcelona Hotel, No 75**, was built as Casa Enric Batlló, an apartment building, by **Josep Vilaseca** in 1896. Ceramics and ironwork are outstanding.

The vestibule, which may be entered, leads to a central atrium.

*Exit R. Second R c de València.*

**Farmàcia J de Bolos, No 256**, is yet another fine example of a Modernist pharmacy. Stained glass is outstanding.

*Return eastward. First R rbla de Catalunya.*

**Artespana, No 75**, are renowned stockists of contemporary Spanish furniture.

●● *Continue southward.*

**Colmado Quillez, No 63**, stock a good selection of groceries and Catalan wines, including cavas.

**Casa del Dr Fargus, No 47**, by **Sagnier**, 1904, a remarkable sober work by this eclectic designer, shows Gaudí's influence in its Baroque, curved lines.

The hall displays Art-Nouveau woodwork.

**Forn de Sant Jaume, No 50**, is one of the most popular confectionery and pastry shops in Barcelona. There is an internal café in addition to the terrace.

**Joan Prats Gallery, No 54**, specializes in modern works of art: all are for sale.

●● *Return northward. First R c d'Aragó.*

**Fundació Tàpies, No 255**, an early work of **Domènech i Montaner**, was designed in 1880 as commercial premises for his brother, a partner in the publishing company, Montaner i Simon. For the first time in Barcelona, an iron structural frame was used for a building that was neither a market nor a railway station. Clad with brick, and terracotta reliefs, a strong Mudéjar influence will be noted.

Restored in 1990, the building has been crowned with a giant sculpture in aluminium and metal fabric, *Cloud and Chair*, by Tàpies, founder of the art study centre.

Open Tuesday–Sunday, 11.00–20.00. Admission charge, temporary and permanent works are exhibited.

●● *Continue eastward. First R pas de Gràcia.*

Opposite, on the west side of Passeig de Gràcia, the block between Carrer d'Aragó and Carrer del Consell de Cent comprises the most famous group of Modernist buildings in Barcelona – virtually a museum of Modernism. The six adjacent façades consist of work by **Gaudí**, **Sagnier**, **Puig i Cadafalch** and **Domènech i Montaner**. Due to the disparity of styles employed, the block is known as 'The Apple of Discord' (block of houses and apple in Spanish being the same word – *Manzana*). The buildings are best viewed initially as a group from this side of the road: they are floodlit at night and a return visit is recommended then, particularly to see Casa Batlló, which appears even more enchanting when illuminated.

| | |
|---|---|
| Location 5 | **CASA BATLLÓ** *Gaudí 1907* |
| 43 Passeig de Gràcia | This is the best-known component of the 'Apple of Discord'. Its sinuous form, delicate colouring, romantic turret and cottage-style roof give Casa Batlló more the appearance of a fairy-tale mansion than the apartment block that it now is. |

**Gaudí** was commissioned to redesign the stairway, first floor and façade of an existing building as the town residence of the Batlló family, work which took two years.

The undulating façade was a foretaste of 'La Pedrera', which **Gaudí** worked on at the same time but finished three years later.

As a famous example of architectural 'good manners' **Gaudí** lowered the roof line so that **Puig**'s adjoining gables could be seen to better effect.

As was usual at this period, **Jujol** was responsible for the polychromatic decoration of the façade, restored in 1988.

An effect of wet sand dripping from a sand-castle, observed in the stonework, was soon to be repeated even more dramatically by **Gaudí** in the east façade of the Sagrada Familia.

It has been suggested, perhaps rather fancifully, that the legend of Catalonia's patron, St George, inspired the design of the building. The roof, with its scale-like tiles, depicts the dragon's back and the cross that pierces the turret the lance of St George. Balustrades of the balconies are said to represent the bones of the dragon's victims.

*●● Enter the building through its south archway.*

The atrium, a favourite device of **Gaudí**'s, has been designed to create an impression of height: the walls taper, windows are gradually reduced in size and the tone of the blue ceramics decreases in intensity towards the light.

*●● Exit R.*

**Casa Ametller**, which adjoins Casa Batlló, at **No 41**, was completed in 1900, the first building in the block to appear as it does today. Its architect, **Puig i Cadafalch**, introduced a Flemish gable to combine with his more usual Catalan Gothic details. Puig, an historian and archaeologist before later becoming a politician was, in some ways, the best qualified of all the Modernists when it came to following medieval styles.

Visitors may view the original Gothic-Revival interior of the first-floor premises of Institut Ametller d'Art Hispanic. Open Monday–Friday 10.00–14.00 and 16.00–20.00. Admission free.

The next two buildings, originally influenced by the Louis XVI style, were later modernized and adapted by **Sagnier**.

*●● Continue southward to the c del Consell de Cent corner (first R).*

| Location 6 | **CASA LLEÓ MORERA** *Domènech i Montaner 1905* |
|---|---|

35 Passeig de Gràcia

*Open Monday– Thursday by prior arrangement. Admission free. Offices closed at 15.00 in summer.*

The first floor of this, the most southerly building in the 'Apple of Discord', now accommodates the Patronat de Turisme de Barcelona.
Without doubt, the building is best viewed externally from the opposite side of Passeig de Gràcia, as its ground floor has been completely altered by the insertion of shop windows. Nevertheless, the romantic adoption of Gothic fenestration and tracery and a delicate corner turret make this one of the most appealing of **Domènech**'s buildings.

On the second floor, stone carvings depict late-19C inventions, such as the gramophone and telephone.

*●● Enter the main doorway, on the corner, and ascend the stairs to the first floor (the concierge does not approve of the lift being commandeered for such a*

*short expedition). Ring the entry bell.*

Miraculously, the internal fixtures of this, the most splendid floor in the building, have been little altered. Stained glass, carved woodwork, ceramic tiles and parquet flooring survive, all very much in **Domènech**'s unique style. Visitors will be shown the vestibule and the former living-room, overlooking Passeig de Gràcia; other areas depend on convenience at the time.

← *Exit from the building L and follow pas de Gràcia northward to M Passeig de Gràcia.*

# 9

## University and the Bullring

A west to east route follows the central section of Gran Via, Barcelona's longest thoroughfare. The original university, Plaça de Catalunya, which is the largest square in the city, and the bullring are seen, together with a variety of Modernist buildings.

*Timing:* The Geological Laboratory and Museum of the Seminary is open Monday–Friday.

The Bullfighting Museum may not be visited during a *corrida* (bullfight) and can only be visited as a member of a group during the winter months.

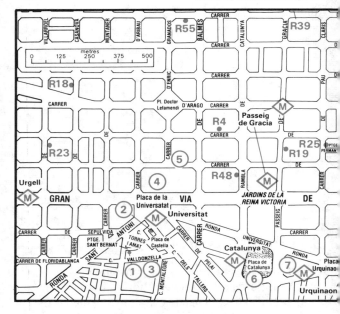

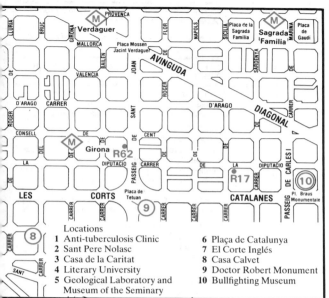

Locations

1 Anti-tuberculosis Clinic
2 Sant Pere Nolasc
3 Casa de la Caritat
4 Literary University
5 Geological Laboratory and
  Museum of the Seminary

6 Plaça de Catalunya
7 El Corte Inglés
8 Casa Calvet
9 Doctor Robert Monument
10 Bullfighting Museum

**Start** *M Universitat, line 1. Leave by the rda Sant Antoni exit and proceed ahead. First L c Torres i Amat. First R ptge Sant Bernat.*

*Alternatively, to shorten the route, leave by the Gran Via exit and proceed immediately to location 4.*

| | |
|---|---|
| Location 1 | **ANTI-TUBERCULOSIS CLINIC** (DISPENSARIO ANTITUBERCULOSO) *GATPAC 1938* |

| | |
|---|---|
| 10 Pasatge Sant Bernat | Although lacking overwhelming interest for the average visitor, this tubercular clinic is regarded as one of the most important Rationalist examples of architecture in Europe. |

Followers of Le Corbusier had introduced Rationalism to the city in 1928, but this was the first public building to adopt the style. It was commissioned by the Generalitat in 1934 but, due to the Civil War, not completed until four years later. The designers of the complex belonged to a practice called GATPAC, comprising **Josep Lluís Sert, Josep Torres Clavé** and **Joan Baptista Subirana**.

Four-storey blocks have been grouped around a courtyard, in a traditional manner for hospitals, but modern building materials were employed and the plan of each block was dictated precisely by its function.

•● *Return to c Torres i Amat R. Second R pl de Cartellà.*

| | |
|---|---|
| Location 2 | **SANT PERE NOLASC** 1710–16 |

| | |
|---|---|
| Plaça de Cartellà

*Open 18.30 (prior to Vespers at 19.00)* | When built, as the church of the convent of the fathers of Paules de la Mision, Sant Pere was dedicated to Sant Sever and Sant Carles Borromeu. Following the monastic closures in the 19C, the convent became a tobacco factory and later a military hospital, with the church serving as its chapel. |

In 1939, the domestic buildings of the convent were demolished and replaced by the present square: Sant Pere became the parish church.

A fragment of the Tuscan monastic cloister survives on the square's façade.

This is the only Baroque church in Barcelona designed with twin towers.

Behind them rises the cupola, clad with mosaics, like that of the Ciutadella's church.

The high altar's reredos is an 18C Baroque example.

Behind this, the wall is painted with grisaille work.

A *Coronation of the Virgin* scene by **Joseph Flaugier**, a French artist born near Marseilles and a contemporary of David, decorates the cupola.

•● *Exit from the church directly ahead to the north side of the square. R c dels Tallers. First R c Valldonzella. First l c Montalegre.*

| | |
|---|---|
| Location 3 | **CASA DE LA CARITAT** |

| | |
|---|---|
| 5 Carrer Montalegre | A long, salmon-pink façade – partly 18C, partly modern – marks the site of the mid-13C monastic house of Augustinian Canonesses, dedicated to Nuestra Senyora de Montalegre. In 1598 the complex was occupied by a seminary, but this was transferred |

to La Rambla in 1803 and replaced by a hospital, Casa de la Caritat (House of Charity). Abandoned in 1957, remodelling of the buildings began in 1986 to provide offices for the Cultural Department of the Diputació. A Museum of Contemporary Art is to be incorporated.

•● *Enter the first doorway R.*

Information regarding the province of Barcelona is provided within the vestibule.

Immediately behind lies the Pati Manning, a two-storey cloister completed in 1743 and the oldest section of the seminary to survive.

Ceramics line the base of the walls, which are decorated above with restored sgraffiti.

Tuscan columns support both levels.

•● *Exit L. R c Valldonzella. L c dels Tallers. Continue ahead to pl Universitat and cross to the long university building on the north side.*

---

| Location 4 | **LITERARY UNIVERSITY** (UNIVERSITAT LITERARIA) *Rogent 1863–72* |
|---|---|
| Plaça Universitat | Until the move to Avinguda Diagonal in 1958, all the departments of Barcelona's University, except Medicine, were accommodated here. Now the building houses the great library and the faculties of Geology and Philology. |

**Rogent** was inspired by Catalan Romanesque architecture, the façade and main vestibule echoing Poblet monastery.

At both corners, towers are built in the form of campaniles.

•● *Enter the first doorway and ascend to the first-floor library, at the west end of the building.*

The **library** contains more than 250,000 documents, many of them dating from the Medieval and Renaissance periods, which were taken by the state from the monasteries following their abolition in 1835.

•● *Proceed eastward to the centrally sited auditorium.*

A huge Romanesque-style doorway provides the entrance to the **auditorium.**

Paintings illustrate historic events.

Decoration is Mudéjar inspired.

•● *Descend to the ground floor.*

Buildings are grouped around linked patios.

The monumental central vestibule once more repeats themes from Poblet monastery.

•● *Exit from the building L. First L c de Balmes, First L c de la Diputació. Immediately R is the Geological Museum.*

# 9

| | |
|---|---|
| Location 5 | **GEOLOGICAL LABORATORY AND MUSEUM OF THE SEMINARY** (MUSEU GEOLOGIC DEL SEMINARI) *Rogent 1878–88* |

231 Carrer de la Diputació

*Open Monday–Friday 11.00–13.00 and 17.00–19.00. Closed in August. Admission free.*

This building, the last work of **Rogent**, was built as a seminary and still accommodates the Institute of Catholic Social Studies.

Geological exhibits include precious and semi-precious stones.

*•● Exit L. First R c de Balmes. First L Gran Via.*

**Gran Via de les Cortes Catalanes** 'Gran Via', the longest thoroughfare in Barcelona, commences just outside the airport and runs in a north-easterly direction. More than six miles of its route is built-up, but commercial blocks dominate and the visitor will find only short stretches of interest, e.g. here in the city centre, and at Pedralbes.

**Cine Coliseum, No 595**, was built by **Nebot i Torrens** in 1923, but follows the Neo-Baroque, turn-of-the-century style inspired by L'Opéra in Paris, with its dome, statues and columns. Dictator Primo de Rivera was responsible for encouraging this academic revival.

*•● First L rbla de Catalunya.*

**Casa Pia Batlló, No 17**, occupies the south-west corner. This apartment block is the Modernist work of **Josep Vilaseca**, 1891–1906.

Small lanterns decorate the upper level.

Exposed iron girders are given a decorative application.

*•● Proceed to the extreme south end of the central Promenade.*

*Pensive Bull*, a statue by **Josep Granyer**, matches his *Reclining Giraffe* at the north end of the thoroughfare (see page 152). This satirizes serious art in a similar way, referring to Rodin's *The Thinker*. Both statues were presented by the Association of the Friends of Rambla de Catalunya in 1972.

*•● Continue northward.*

**Casa Heribert Pons, Nos 19–21**, built as an apartment block by **Alexandre Soler i March**, 1909, is decorated with an allegorical relief paying homage to the arts. It now accommodates offices of the Generalitat.

*•● Return southward., First L Gran Via.*

In the pedestrianized centre of the street are the **Jardins de la Reina Victoria**, incorporating monuments to Eusebi Güell, sponsor of **Gaudí**, by **Marés**, and on the south side, to designer Francesc Soler i Rovirosa.

*•● Follow rbla de Catalunya southward to pl de Catalunya.*

| | |
|---|---|
| Location 6 | **PLAÇA DE CATALUNYA** |

Although a Barcelona landmark, this extensive square, linking the old city and the Eixample, is undoubtedly an architectural let-down. Uninspired commercial buildings enclose it, the only exception to mediocrity being the Modernist office buildings on the east side of Passeig de Gràcia. How unfortunate that the late Don Ramón Areces, the multibillionaire owner of the El Corte Inglés stores, seems to have cared not a jot about the disfiguring effect of his windowless edifice that glowers over the square from the east side. The central gardens serve as a focal point for major celebrations, such as the national day of Catalonia, 11 September; St John's Day, 24 June, and the feast day of the Virgin of Mercy, patron saint of the city, 27 September.

When the medieval wall of Barcelona was demolished in 1859 and the development of the Eixample begun, the site of Plaça de Catalunya was a large field outside the city, between the ancient Portal de l'Àngel gate and the recently opened Portal d'Isabel II gate, at the north end of La Rambla. **Cerdá** planned to extend La Rambla through it and create a huge square further north, between Gran Via and Carrer del Consell de Cent, but the municipality opposed this, preferring a square that would link the old city directly with the new. Incessant disputes between the municipality, the state and private landowners were settled by an intermediary Fabra i Ledesma, who decided on the present scheme and ordered that all structures then existing on the site should be demolished.

Most present buildings date from the comprehensive redevelopment of **Francesc Nebot** in 1927.

*➥ Proceed anticlockwise around the square.*

On the south-west corner, facing La Rambla, is the **Zurich Café**, with its fashionable terrace.

*➥ Cross to the central garden.*

The **garden** is laid out with evergreen oak trees and brightly coloured paths. Sculptures include *Deessa*, by **Josep Clara**, in the south-west corner, and *Shepherd with a Flute*, by **Pau Gargallo**, to the north. There is an abundance of free public seating.

*➥ Cross to the east side of the square.*

| Location 7 | **EL CORTE INGLÉS** |
|---|---|
| 14 Plaça de Catalunya | The El Corte Inglés chain of department stores, now represented in most large Spanish cities, has gained an international reputation. Barcelona possesses two branches, the newest and largest being in Diagonal (see page 173). |

The quality of goods sold is not dissimilar to London's Selfridges, but in no way do the stores aspire to be a 'Spanish Harrods'. Surprisingly, the food halls in this branch are on the sixth rather than the more usual ground floor.

A top-floor cafeteria and open terrace provide spectacular views.

The name, El Corte Inglés (The English Cut), puzzles British tourists. It is inherited from the original small tailor's shop in Madrid that gave birth to the chain and was so named because it purchased cloth from England. Don Ramón Areces borrowed £800 to buy the shop in 1934 and developed it so successfully that his empire now comprises more than twenty branches, with a 1989 turnover of £2 billion.

Areces died in July 1989, the richest man in Europe.

*●● Exit R and follow pas de Gràcia northward.*

On the east side of the stretch between Plaça de Catalunya and Gran Via are groups of Modernist office buildings. Particularly outstanding is the group north of Carrer de Casp, designed by **Mestres, Bassegoda** and **Bonaventura** in the late 19C.

*●● Continue ahead crossing to the north side of Gran Via.*

**Cine Comedia, No 13**, on the south-west Passeig de Gràcia corner, was built as the Mariet Palace.

*●● Follow Gran Via eastward and cross to the south side.*

**Farmàcia Vilardell, No 650**, occupies the south-east corner with Carrer de Pau Claris. Built in Medievalist style in the late 19C, original woodwork, well restored, survives.

**Casa Mulleras, No 654**, is a rare example of **Sagnier** under the influence of Domènech i Montaner. Completed in 1904, the façade bears attractive sgraffiti depicting dancing ladies.

The gallery is of an unusual design.

*●● Return westward. First R c de Pau Claris, Second R ptge de Permanyer.*

**Passatge de Permanyer** is a delightful terrace of single-storey houses. Londoners might well think they have magically stumbled on a Chelsea mews, with cherry trees replaced by palms.

*●● First R c de Roger de Llúria. Second L Gran Via.*

**Ritz Hotel, No 668**, founded by César Ritz in 1911, remains the finest 'old-style' hotel in Barcelona. Naturally, five-star rated, there are 314 rooms.

Facing the Ritz, in the middle of Gran Via, stands the **Diana Fountain**.

**No 670**, adjoining the Ritz, is a severely Classical building, constructed as the Boada Palace, by **Rogent**, in the late 19C.

*●● Return westward. First L c de Roger de Lluria.*

**Casa Cabot, Nos 8–14**, was designed by **Vilaseca i Casanoves** in 1905. Fanciful floral decoration and an exuberant roof cornice decorate these apartment buildings, now in dire need of cleaning.

The rose-coloured sgraffiti façade of **Nos 12–14** has been repainted.

**Nos 8–10** have an outstanding decorative doorway.

*●● Return northward. First R c de Casp.*

| Location 8 | **CASA CALVET** *Gaudí 1899* |
| --- | --- |
| 48 Carrer de Casp | Designed just prior to Gaudí's formulation of his idiosyncratic style, Casa Calvet is a relatively restrained example of Baroque Modernism. |
| | Above the doorway extends a rather jolly central bay. |
| | Perhaps the most Gaudíesque element is the spiky iron sculpture protruding from the apertures in the 'Dutch' gables. |

●● *Enter the vestibule.*

A protective concierge may well emphasize the privacy of this apartment block. Better to indicate absolute noncomprehension, while quickly observing the tiny atrium, ceramic tiles and lift, designed by Gaudí, which is flanked by twisted columns.

●● *Exit R and follow c de Casp eastward. Second R c de Girona. First R c d'Ausiàs Marc.*

**Casa Roger Vidal**, Nos 33–35, occupying the north-west corner, is an architectural nightmare, the unmistakable eclecticism of **Enric Sagnier**, built in 1890. In descending order are observed: a Gothic rosette above an Ionic pilaster above bisected Romanesque windows!

An enormous Greek key frieze decorates the roof line at the sides.

●● *Follow c d'Ausiàs Marc eastward.*

**Nos 37, 41** and **46** (note the tree trunk columns) are interesting examples of Modernism.

●● *Second L pas de Sant Joan. Proceed northward to pl Tetuan and cross to the central monument.*

| | |
|---|---|
| Location 9 | **DOCTOR ROBERT MONUMENT** <br> *Josep Llimona 1904–10* |
| Plaça Tetuan | An outstanding example of Modernist sculpture, this large monument commemorates Dr Bartomeu Robert, 1842–1902, a popular mayor of the city. Originally, the memorial stood in Plaça de la Universitat but was dismantled by order of Franco as he feared that it might serve as a rallying point for nationalistic Catalan rebels: the monument was re-erected here in 1979. The style and quality of the stone base have led many to believe Gaudí was involved in its design – he was not. |

Whereas Doctor Robert is merely represented by a stone bust, splendid allegorical figures have been cast full length in bronze. One of these, an elegant lady, appears to be whispering her commiserations in the doctor's ear.

●● *From the south-east corner of pl Tetuan take bus 6, 7, 18, 35 or 62 eastward to pas de Carles I (two stops) and proceed to the bullring on the north-east corner with Gran Via.*

●● *Alternatively, to terminate the route, follow pas de Sant Joan northward. Second L c del Consell de Cent and M Girona.*

| | |
|---|---|
| Location 10 | **BULLFIGHTING MUSEUM** (Museu Tauri) |
| Plaça de Braus Monumentala <br><br> 749 Gran Via de les Corts Catalanes | Those wishing to visit a bullring and see the bulls and horses, without suffering the bloody trauma of a bullfight, are catered for in this museum, which is situated within the complex. |
| *Open daily April– September 10.00– 14.00 and 16.00– 19.00 (not if a bullfight day). Other periods, groups only and by* | Inspired by Islamic architecture, **Ignasi Mas** and **Joaquim Raspall** designed the façade of this, now Barcelona's only bullring, in brick and ceramics. <br><br> Completed in 1915, the first corrida took place in February the following year. |

●● *Enter the building and turn L to the ticket office.*

*arrangement.
admission charge.*

Before entering the museum block, visitors are permitted to view the bullring. Its gravel ground is reminiscent of a beach at one of the nearby Costa Brava resorts.

•→ *Continue clockwise to the museum.*

Exhibits include photographs, posters and costumes.

The career of Spain's legendary bullfighter, Manolete, is traced and the poster advertising his last fight at Lérida displayed: Manolete was fatally wounded in that city's ring, aged 30, in 1947.

From the terrace, visitors can view the bulls in the bullyard and the horses in their stables.

•→ *Exit from the bullring R and cross pas de Carles I. From the north side of Gran Via take bus 7 westward to rbla de Catalunya (three stops). From the bus stop return eastward to M Passeig de Gràcia.*

# 10

## Pedralbes Monastery and Montjuïc

Barcelona's most complete medieval monastery is visited, followed by a Gaudí gateway, Pedralbes Palace and the stadium of Barcelona Football Club. A journey by Metro is then made to the foot of Montjuïc. Although most locations of interest on Montjuïc are described, it is impossible to appreciate them all during one visit. Many will prefer to visit the museums on the north slope on one day, and the summit, with its parkland, viewpoints and Olympic Games complex, on another.

*Timing:* Pedralbes Monastery is closed Monday.

Barcelona Football Club's museum is closed Sunday in summer, Monday in winter and on match days.

The Magic Fountain is illuminated on Thursday, Saturday and Sunday and on public holidays from 21.00; in winter, weekends only from 20.00.

The Museum of Catalan Art is closed for restoration until 1992.

The Ethnological Museum is closed Sunday afternoon.

The Archeological Museum is closed Monday.

The Joan Miró Foundation Museum is closed Monday, and Sunday at 14.30.

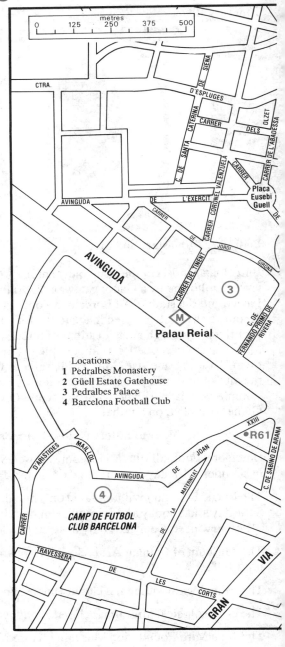

Locations
1 Pedralbes Monastery
2 Güell Estate Gatehouse
3 Pedralbes Palace
4 Barcelona Football Club

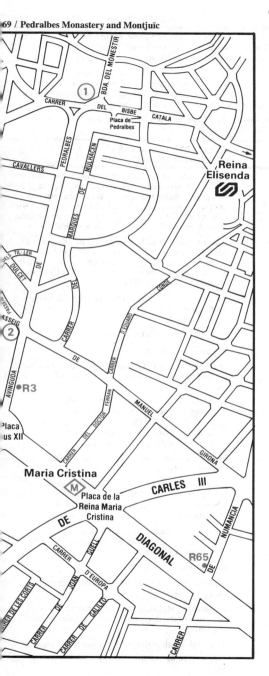

**Start** *M Reina Elisenda FF.CC. Generalitat line. From the station ascend the steps, exit L and take bus 22, 64 or 75 westbound, two stops, to pl de Pedralbes. From the bus stop proceed westward, following c del Bisbe Català. First R bda del Monestir.*

*Alternatively, if outside the rush hour, take bus 22 from the south end of pas de Gràcia travelling northward, or bus 64 from the La Rambla end of pas de Colom travelling westward to pl de Pedralbes, then proceed as above.*

*Alternatively, alight at Pedralbes from bus 100 operated by the Barcelona Patronat de Turisme (see page xvi).*

| Location 1 | **PEDRALBES MONASTERY**<br>(MONESTIR DE PEDRALBES) |
|---|---|

Baixada de Monestir

*Open Tuesday–Sunday 09.30–14.00 and 17.00–19.00. Church open 10.00–13.00 (Sunday Mass at 12.00). Admission charge, but free to minors and Spaniards.*

Pedralbes Monastery, constructed in the 14C and 15C, is not only the best-preserved example of a monastic complex to survive in Barcelona, but was built with such speed that the buildings possess a rare unity of style. Pedralbes is regarded as an outstanding example of Catalan Gothic's mature period.

**History** Elisenda de Montcada, the fourth and last wife of Jaume I, founded the monastery in 1326. **Ferrer Peiró** and **Domènec Granyer** were responsible for the work and, due to support from the King, the church was consecrated in 1327.

Fronted by the Gardens of Queen Elisenda L is the south section of the wall that originally enclosed the entire complex.

The south gateway's tower was built in the 15C.

●● *Enter the gateway.*

Immediately R is El Conventet (small convent), built for the Franciscans, who were appointed to serve the nuns.

Romanesque features from the demolished 11C monastery of Santa Maria del Besalu have been added to the façade. These include: the gallery, round-headed windows, the doorway with its tympanum and the gateway to the garden.

●● *Pass the entrance to the cloister L and follow the east façade of the church.*

Consecrated in 1327, the church, with its octagonal bell tower, is designed with a Gothic simplicity much admired by Le Corbusier, the 20C father of Rationalism.

The doorway's lintel is carved with the shield of Elisenda, the arms of the Montcada family and the royal arms of Barcelona.

●● *Enter the church.*

The church is north/south orientated, with the high altar at the south end.

Immediately R, behind the grille, the nuns' nave is restricted to the thirty nuns that still reside in the convent.

The nave, south of the grille, is open to the public.

A central choir was created for the Franciscans in the 15C.

At the south end of the church, tombs are inserted in the wall so that they may be venerated both from within the church and from the cloister.

Fitted in the most southerly west chapel, just before the sanctuary, are the tombs of two queens, Constança de Cardom and Elionor de Pinos.

Queen Elisenda, founder of the monastery, lies in the sarcophagus borne by three lions, which is inserted in a vaulted niche immediately R of the high altar.

The Queen's reclining figure, guarded by censing angels, is depicted wearing royal dress. The tomb was made before Elisenda's death in 1361.

From the sanctuary may best be viewed the nuns' gallery, which lies behind the organ at the north end of the church.

Within the apse hangs a mid-14C Calvary painting.

Two paintings depict Saint Francis of Assisi and Saint Lluís de Tolosa.

•● *Exit from the church L.*

Steps lead to the 15C crenellated tower of the north gateway, once the monastic penitentiary.

The north wall continues on either side of the gateway.

•● *Return southward.*

Baixada del Monestir now divides the former monastic grounds. Originally, to the north and east of the square, stood domestic accommodation for the secular clergy.

•● *Continue ahead past the apse of the church and enter the cloister R. Proceed anticlockwise following the east passage, which abuts the church.*

The cloister, linking the nuns' domestic accommodation, was built in the 14C. Originally two storeys high, its third storey was added in the 15C.

The royal and the Montcada family arms are carved in the passageways.

Immediately R is the Sant Miquel Chapel, originally the cell of Abbess Francisca Sa-Portella. Its walls are completely covered with murals depicting scenes from the *Passion*, by **Ferrer Bassa**, 1343. **Bassa**, who studied art in Italy, was greatly impressed by contemporary Tuscan schools and this is an early example of Renaissance influenced work in Catalonia.

•● *Exit R.*

Immediately R is the reverse side of the tomb of Queen Elisenda, her reclining figure dressed in nun's habit.

Flamboyant Gothic niches in the wall R accommodate the reverse sides of the tombs of Queen Constança and Elionor.

The north passage fronts the former monastic dormitory.

•● *Follow the west passage and enter the doorway R.*

**Martorell** renovated the **refectory**, which lies behind the cloister's west passage, in 1894. It was last used for dining purposes in 1983.

To the rear lie the original **kitchens**.

In the south-west corner of the cloister stands a Plateresque cistern, made in 1584 but remodelled in the 18C.

•● *Follow the south passage and enter the doorway R.*

Most of this range served as the infirmary.

•● *Continue to the south-east corner and enter the former chapter house.*

The square, vaulted chapter house was built in 1316.

Its stained glass, including the rose windows, was made in 1419 but has been much restored.

Exhibited are models of the monastery and the chapter house.

•● *Exit from the monastery R bda del Monestir. First R c del Bisbe Català. Continue ahead, passing both spurs L of av de Pedralbes and cross to the bus stop on the south side, just before the intersection, first L, with c d'Esplugues. Take bus BC, B1 or SJ in an eastward direction, two stops, to ptge Manuel Girona. From the bus stop proceed southward passing, first L, ptge Manuel Girona. Cross to the west side of av de Pedralbes, where it forms a chamfered junction with pas dels Til·lers.*

| Location 2 | **GÜELL ESTATE GATE** (FINCA GÜELL) <br> *Gaudí 1887* |
|---|---|
| 7 Avinguda de Pedralbes | Eusebi Güell commissioned **Gaudí** to design this gatehouse to his estate, whilst working for him on the Güell Palace, just off La Rambla. <br><br> At the time, the architect was still influenced by Islamic architecture, and ceramics alternate with Mudéjar-style brickwork. <br><br> The iron gate is known as 'the Dragon of Pedralbes'. <br><br> •● *Follow ptge Manuel Girona, which continues westward from the gatehouse. First L c Fernando Primo de Rivera. First R av Diagonal. First R enter the Parc de Pedralbes and proceed ahead to the palace at the north end.* |

| Location 3 | **PEDRALBES PALACE** <br> (PALAU DE PEDRALBES) |
|---|---|
| Pedralbes Park <br> 686 Avinguda Diagonal <br> (Tel. 204.63.19) <br><br> *Museums planned: Decorative Arts, Postal Museum– Cambó Collection (after restoration); Ceramic Museum open Tuesday– Sunday, 09.00– 14.00. Admission charge.* | A pavilion belonging to the counts of Güell was purchased by the municipality and expanded to provide a suitable palace for Alfonso XIII during his visits to Barcelona. The palace was completed and its grounds laid out in 1925. However, Alfonso, who had affectionately referred to the unpopular dictator, Primo de Rivera, as 'my Mussolini', was forced to abdicate in 1931 and the building was adapted to accommodate the Museum of Fine Arts. Following the Civil War, Franco acquired the palace as his Barcelona residence. <br><br> The building is being adapted to house museums and its gardens are now a public park. <br><br> •● *Exit from the grounds L, cross to the south side of av Diagonal and proceed eastward.* <br><br> Flanking Pedralbes Park and lining the southern side of Avinguda Diagonal are most of the buildings of |

the faculties that comprise **Barcelona Universitat**. All were built in the present century, breaking away from the Universitat Central in Plaça de la Universitat.

*•➡ First R av de Joan XXIII.*

The south-east corner is occupied by the **Hotel Princesa**, five-star rated and one of the most luxurious modern hotels in Barcelona.

*•➡ Cross to the west side of the road.*

Forming the entrance to the Facultat de Farmacia is a brick gateway, designed in Mudéjar style by **Gaudí**. It was transferred here from the Güell estate.

*•➡ Continue southward to the football stadium, which is entered from the west side. Follow the signs to the museum (museu).*

---

| Location 4 | **BARCELONA FOOTBALL CLUB** |
|---|---|

Camp de Futbol Club Barcelona Avinguda de Joan XXIII (for the museum and matches) Travessera de les Corts (for tickets) Museum open April–September, Monday–Saturday 10.00–13.00 and 15.00–18.00, holidays 10.00–13.00; October–March, Tuesday–Friday, 10.00–13.00 and 16.00–18.00. Saturday, Sunday and holidays 10.00–13.00. Admission charge.

Barcelona F.C. (Barça), the world's wealthiest football club, play few matches in July and August, the peak tourist season, but their stadium may be viewed, and the club's museum remains open.

Built in 1957, with a capacity of 90,000, the stadium was extended for the World Cup and, later, the 1992 Olympic Games: 133,000 spectators can now be accommodated, all seated, but not all under cover.

The museum was opened in 1984; first seen is the royal box, built of marble, from which the entire stadium may be viewed.

An Aladdin's cave of trophies won by the club is displayed in the room above.

*•➡ Ascend the stairs to the museum R.*

Exhibits include programmes, photographs and an audio-visual presentation (in Spanish only). Schoolboy-size versions of the club's kit may be purchased.

Spanish championship matches end in June, but from the third week in August a tournament between four international club teams is held in the stadium.

Tickets for all matches are sold to non-members Wednesday–Sunday 10.00–13.00 and 16.00–20.00, during the week prior to each fixture. The ticket office, situated on the south-west corner of the complex, facing Travessera de les Corts, is most easily approached from M Collblanc.

*•➡ Exit from the stadium R, av de Joan XIII, and return to av Diagonal R.*

**Caixa de Pensions**, 621–29 Avinguda Diagonal, occupy twin, linked blocks, clad with black glass. They were built as the company's head office, 1978–83, by **Coderch de Sentmemat**, and accommodate 1,000 staff.

*•➡ Continue eastward, passing pl de la Reina Maria Cristina.*

Immediately R is Barcelona's second **El Corte Inglés** store, the larger of the two branches in the city.

*•➡ Return westward to M Maria Cristina, line 3, and train five stops to M Espanya. Exit and proceed to the north side of pl d'Espanya.*

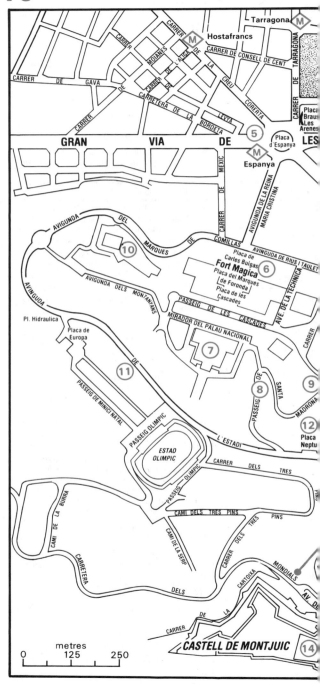

Hostafrancs

CARRER DE CONSELL DE CENT

CARRER · DE · GAVA

CARRETERA DE LA BORDETA

GRAN VIA DE

LES

Placa
d'Espanya

Espanya

AVINGUDA DEL MARQUES DE COMILLAS

AVINGUDA DE RIUS I TAULET

Placa de
Carles Buigas

Fort Magica

Placa del Marques
de Foronda

Placa de les
Cascades

AVINGUDA DELS MONTANYANS

Pl. Hidraulica

Placa de
Europa

PASSEIG DE LES CASCADES

MIRADOR DEL PALAU NACIONAL

PASSEIG DE MINICI NATAL

ESTAD
OLIMPIC

PASSEIG OLIMPIC

L'ESTADI

CARRER DELS TRES

CAMI DELS TRES PINS

CAMI DE LA BURRA

CAMI DE LA SERP

CARRETERA DELS

CARTOIXA

CARRER DE LA

CASTELL DE MONTJUIC

metres
0    125    250

Locations

5 Plaça d'Espanya
6 Magic Fountain
7 Museum of Catalan Art
8 Ethnological Museum
9 Archeological Museum

10 Spanish Village
11 Olympic Games Complex
12 Joan Miró Foundation/Museum
13 Montjuïc Park
14 Army Museum

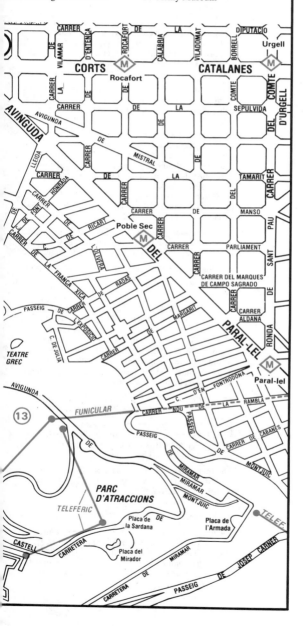

| Location 5 | PLAÇA D'ESPANYA |
|---|---|

It is from this square that visitors usually approach the 'magic' fountain and the exhibitions and museums that occupy much of the north slope of Montjuïc hill. Apart from the late-19C former bullring to the north, the square owes most of its present appearance to buildings constructed for the International Exhibition of 1929.

In the late Middle Ages a cross, known as the Creu Coberta (covered cross), gave its name to the locality, and windmills stood on the higher ground. This was also the site of the gallows until it was transferred to Ciutadella in 1715.

Brick buildings on the north side were constructed by **Rubio i Tuduri** as hotels for visitors to the 1929 exhibition, but have been adapted for other purposes.

Although no longer used as such Barcelona's oldest bullring, **Plaça de les Arenes**, stands at the junction of c de Tarragona and Gran Via. Built in 1899 by **Font i Carreras**, its design, utilizing brickwork, did much to determine the present appearance of the Plaça d'Espanya. Adaptation to incorporate a pavilion for the Barcelona Trade Fair, but maintaining the façade, is planned. All bullfights are now held at the Plaça Braus Monumentale (see page 165).

In the centre of the square, the **fountain** was designed by **Gaudí**'s follower, **Josep Jujol**, apparently influenced by the Baroque fountains of Bernini.

Its allegorical sculptures are the work of **Miquel Blay.**

●● *Follow c de Tarragona northward, passing the bullring.*

**Parc de Joan Miró**, on the east side, is laid out with palm trees and gravel paths, where the locals play the French game, *petanque*, at weekends. Rising from a rectangular pond is an enormous polychromatic sculpture by **Joan Miró**, 1893–1983, whom the park commemorates. Apparently, from a distance, made of papier-mâché, closer inspection reveals that the sculpture is, in fact, clad with ceramics.

●● *Return to pl d'Espanya and proceed to av de la Reina Maria Cristina, which leads from its south side.*

Flanking the avenue, the two brick towers that signalled the entrance to the International Exhibition were designed by **Ramon Raventos**, influenced by the campanile of St Mark's, Venice.

The **Iberia terminal** on the east side L, originally an exhibition structure, was built in Nou Centism style by **Jujol** and **Andreu Colzada.**

A similar building to the west was the work of **Adolf Forensa** and **Felix de Azua.**

●● *Follow av de la Reina Maria Cristina southward if open. Exasperatingly, the municipality authorizes the closure of this road to the public if a major exhibition, such as the Auto Fair, wishes to spread across it, thus making pedestrian access to the Montjuïc museums less convenient.*

•● *If the avenue is closed, follow Gran Via westward. First L c de Mèxic and the Cuartel de Policia Nacional (page 179).*

| Location 6 | **MAGIC FOUNTAIN** (FONT MÀGICA)<br>*Buïgas 1929* |
|---|---|
| Plaça de Font Màgica)<br><br>*Fountain illuminated, to musical accompaniment, Thursday, Saturday, Sunday and public holidays from 21.00; in winter, weekends only from 20.00. Admission free.* | This is one of the most memorable free shows in Europe and a great favourite with day trippers from the nearby coastal resorts. The central jet shoots 165 feet into the air, water flowing at 624 gallons per second. Music, mostly Baroque, accompanies the spectacle.<br><br>Until replaced by dictator Primo de Rivera in 1928, **Puig i Cadafalch** was responsible for planning the International Exhibition. Both palaces on the south side of Plaça de Carles Buïgas were built to his designs, their towers being copies of buildings in Valencia and Caldes de Montbui.<br><br>•● *If the Museum of Catalan Art is open ascend the steps to the Palau Nacional.*<br><br>•● *Alternatively, return to the north side of Plaça de Carles Buïgas and turn L. First R c de Mèxic and the Cuartel de Policia Nacional (page 179).* |

| Location 7 | **MUSEUM OF CATALAN ART**<br>(MUSEU D'ART DE CATALUNYA) |
|---|---|
| Palau Nacional<br>Parc de Montjuïc<br><br>*The museum is closed for restoration until 1992.* | Catalan art from many periods is represented in the museum, but its chief glory is the unrivalled collection of Romanesque murals brought from ancient churches in the province.<br><br>This museum, founded by the municipality in 1891, initially occupied the former Arsenal on the Ciutadella, but transferred to the Palau Nacional in 1934. The two-storey palace had been built by **Pedro Cendoya Oscoz** and **Enric Cata** for the 1929 exhibition, and was adapted to house the museum when it ended.<br><br>Originally it was intended to exhibit copies of the Romanesque murals, leaving the originals *in situ*, but as so many were in danger of deterioration or removal to other countries, they were stripped from the walls of the churches and brought to Barcelona in 1919, under the direction of an Italian, Franco Staffanoni: replicas were made for the churches.<br><br>Private collections supplemented the exhibits in 1932 and 1952 and it is expected that eventually the museum will be extended further, by incorporating modern works by Catalan artists currently exhibited in the Museum of Modern Art at the Ciutadella.<br><br>A comprehensive remodelling of the museum was planned in 1989, which will incorporate air-conditioning, essential for the preservation of many of the exhibits. It has been mooted that longer opening hours will be operated and an adjacent Metro station built.<br><br>As many exhibits are to be relocated it is not possible to give more than a general indication of their whereabouts. However, it is expected that the |

Romanesque, Gothic and Renaissance/Classical exhibits will remain as individual sections, probably occupying their present areas.

*•▶ Enter the Romanesque section R of the main entrance.*

Due to its dry, unpolluted air, the Pyrenees mountain range provides ideal conditions for the preservation of works of art, and most examples displayed here come from village churches that have stood in their valleys from the 10C. The largest murals were painted on the shallow curved apses, which enclose the sanctuaries. Byzantine iconography was generally adopted with, from top to bottom: God surrounded by the four Evangelists, or the emblems representing them; the disciples and the Virgin; mythical beasts. From the 13C, it was common to replace the figure of God with the Virgin and Child.

Other exhibits include paintings, altar frontals, sculptures and furnishings.

Particularly outstanding are the murals from Sant Quirze de Pedret, Sant Climent de Taüll and Santa Maria de Taüll.

*•▶ Continue to the rooms east of the main entrance.*

Catalan Gothic art is represented in its three stages of French, Italian and Flemish/French influence.

In the Gothic period, great carved reredoses painted with religious themes, replaced the apsidal murals behind the high altars. Particularly outstanding are the 15C examples by **Jaume Huguet.**

The Renaissance and Classicism coincided with the transfer of trading importance from Barcelona to Seville and this was mirrored by the decline in Catalan art. **Antoni Viladomat** is regarded as the leading Catalan painter in the Classical style and his scenes from the life of St Francis, painted in the 18C for the Sant Francesc convent in Barcelona, are exhibited.

Entered from Room 20, on the upper floor, is the **Ceramics Museum** (Museu de Cèramica), where examples from the 12C to the 20C are displayed.

*•▶ Exit from the museum R and follow Mirador del Palau Nacional eastward. Continue uphill and bear R at the pas de Santa Madrona junction.*

*•▶ Alternatively, to shorten the route, exit ahead from the museum and descend to pl de Carles Buïgas. First L av del Marquès de Comillas. First R c de Mèxic. Immediately L is the brick-built Cuartel de la Policia Nacional (page 179).*

| Location 8 | **ETHNOLOGICAL MUSEUM** (MUSEU ETNELOGIC) |
|---|---|
| Passeig de Santa Madrona | Early man-made artefacts, obtained mainly from expeditions sponsored by the museum, are exhibited. |
| *Open daily 09.00– 20.30 but closed Sunday at 14.00. Admission charge but free to minors and Spaniards.* | Created in 1940, the museum's present building was completed in 1973. |
| | Outstanding objects from Japan and Guatemala are exhibited on the first floor, from New Guinea and the Philippines on the second floor. |

*•● Exit R and follow pas de Santa Madrona
eastward. At the junction (L) do not return to the
Palau Nacional but continue ahead.*

| | |
|---|---|
| Location 9 | **ARCHEOLOGICAL MUSEUM**<br>(MUSEU ARQUEOLÒGIC) |

Passeig de Santa
Madrona

*Open Tuesday–
Saturday 09.30–
13.00 and 16.00–
19.00. Sunday and
holidays 09.30–
14.00. Admission
charge except
Sunday.*

Created in 1935, the museum is housed in the
Florentine-style pavilion built as the Palace of
Graphic Arts for the 1929 exhibition.

Items from pre-history and the Greco-Roman
periods are displayed.

A model of the Empuriés excavation on the Costa
Brava is exhibited, together with many of the
important finds from this city. These include the
Venus of Empuriés and a torso of Aphrodite.

*•● Exit R.*

The **Greek Theatre** (Teatre Grec) lies immediately L.

Modelled on Epidaurus, this open-air theatre was
designed by **Ramon Raventos** in 1929. Performances,
in the summer months, include ancient Greek plays.

*•● Pass on the north side of the Archeological
Museum. Second R av de la Tècnica. First L av de
Rius i Taulet. Second R c de Mèxic.*

*•● Alternatively, to shorten the route, follow pas de
Santa Madrona westward and then, first L, continue
southward to pl Neptú and the Joan Miró
Foundation's Museum (location 12).*

The brick-built **Cuartel de la Policia Nacional**, at Nos
36–44 c de Mèxic, was originally built as Fàbrica
Casarramona, a spinning mill, by **Puig i Cadafalch**, in
1911. Here, **Puig** abandons his usual Moorish-
influenced style. A greater continuity of appearance
is thereby achieved.

*•● Return to av del Marquès del Comillas R and cross
to the south side. Follow the path L immediately
before the avenue curves L.*

The German Pavilion for the 1929 exhibition,
designed by **Ludwig Mies van der Rohe**, was
dismantled following its termination. However, such
is the current fame of this architect that it was
decided to re-erect the building as a permanent
fixture, the **Mies van der Rohe Pavilion**, work being
completed in 1986 (open daily, free of charge, 10.00–
19.30 in summer, 10.00–18.00 winter).

A combination of marble panels, tinted glass,
textured stone and shallow pools creates an air of
cool tranquillity, particularly appreciated by visitors
who are about to ascend Montjuïc on a hot summer's
day. **Mies** originally borrowed the marble from his
father's quarry, and the present marble comes from
the same source.

*•● Exit and return to av del Marquès de Comillas L.*

Location 10 | **SPANISH VILLAGE** (POBLE ESPANYOL)

Avinguda del Marquès de Comillas

*Open Sunday, Monday and holidays 09.00–02.00; Tuesday and Wednesday 09.00–04.00; Thursday and Saturday 09.00–06.00. Admission charge but free to minors and Spaniards.*

*A double-decker London bus operates a free service between the Village and the pl d'Espanya end of av de la Reina María Cristina.*

Time has imparted a patina to this sixty-year-old 'village' and a 'Disneyland' effect, on the whole, is avoided. Youngsters, in particular, enjoy the toy-town atmosphere.

Created in conjunction with the International Exhibition, the Spanish Village was completed in 1928 under the direction of a group that included Miguel Utrillo, the art critic, who gave his name to the fatherless Maurice Utrillo, famed for his 'white' paintings of Montmartre early in the present century.

The architects were **Francesc Folguera** and **Ramon Raventos.**

Buildings from all parts of Spain are reproduced, to provide a 'museum' of Spanish architecture. None, however, are original. Initially, crafts were demonstrated in many of the buildings, but this aspect has lapsed in recent years.

The entrance is a replica of the San Vincente gateway in Ávila.

Immediately L, a free plan of the village is provided by the Tourist Office. From the Castilian precinct, the traditional Spanish main square (Plaza Mayor) is entered. No one style is followed here, each province contributing its own features.

The town hall, which dominates the square, was inspired by the example in Valderrobes.

•● *R of the town hall follow c del Alcalde de Zalamea.*

The street leads to the area based on buildings in the pilgrimage city of Santiago de Compostela.

•● *Ascend the stairs to the church.*

Designed in Mudéjar style, the building reproduces a church at Alcaniz. Stretching eastward are replicas of buildings from Aragon, Andalucia, Majorca and Catalonia, ending with the façade of a Romanesque palace from Tárrega and the fortified Montblanc gateway.

•● *Return westward following c del Principe de Viana.*

Picturesque galleried houses from the Basque and Navarre regions are reproduced.

Stone houses from Extremadura line c de la Caballeros.

•● *Exit from the Spanish Village L and cross to the north side of av del Marquès de Comillas. Take bus 61 or 201 two stops to the Olympic Games complex at L'Anella Olímpica.*

•● *Alternatively, continue in the same buses to the Joan Miró Foundation (four stops) or the cable-car station at Viver Tres Pins (five stops).*

Location 11 | **OLYMPIC GAMES COMPLEX**

L'Anella Olímpica | The Olympic Ring (L'Anella Olímpica) was created on the Montjuïc plain to accommodate many of the major events of the 1992 Olympic Games. Three separate venues have been designed to house athletics, indoor events and swimming; there is, in addition, a University of Sport.

First seen from the west is the new INEF **University of Sport**, designed by **Ricardo Bofill**. It is a Post-Modernist structure, inspired by Palladian work. Approximately 1,000 students can be accommodated, facilities including a lecture hall, classrooms, offices and a library. Changing rooms lead directly to the external sports grounds.

**Plaça de Europa**, immediately to the east, is an arcaded circus, reconstructed above a new reservoir which supplies 50,000 Barcelona residents with drinking water.

The **Olympic Pool** lies to the north-east of the circus. Terraces on two levels connect the pool with the **Palau d'Esports Sant Jordi**, a covered stadium which seats 17,000. Its Japanese architect, **Arata Isozaki**, designed the building so that the roof could be assembled at ground level before being raised by hydraulic jacks. Measuring 160m by 110m, it is the largest roof ever to have been erected in this way.

*Guided tours in English at 13.00, 15.00, 17.00, Monday to Friday, if no sporting or concert event is taking place. (Tel. 4240508)*

The 70,000 capacity **Olympic Stadium** (Estadi Olimpic) at the south-east extremity of the complex and built on the highest point of Montjuïc, is an adaptation of the stadium that was created in 1936 from the chief venue of the 1929 International Exhibition.

Whilst maintaining the original façade of the structure, its interior was completely rebuilt, and 15,000 additional seats created by lowering the arena's ground level and reducing its area. The stadium has been designed primarily to accommodate the athletic events, and the opening and closing ceremonies of the 1992 Olympic Games.

●● *Exit from the complex R and follow av de l'Estadi eastward to pl Neptú.*

---

Location 12

**JOAN MIRÓ FOUNDATION/MUSEUM** (FUNDACIÓ JOAN MIRÓ) *Josep Lluis Sert 1975*

---

Plaça Neptú

*Open Tuesday-Saturday 11.00–19.00 (closed Thursday at 21.30). Sunday and holidays 10.30–14.30. Admission charge.*

The Foundation displays works by the Barcelona artist, Joan Miró, most of which were presented by him, together with temporary exhibitions. It also houses the Centre for Studies and Experimentation in the Plastic Arts.

Miró and Salvador Dalí are undoubtedly the best-known modern artists from Catalonia, but whereas Dalí sympathized with the Franco regime, Miró dissented and was virtually exiled to Majorca, dying there, aged 90, on Christmas Day 1983. His body was returned to Barcelona, where he was born in 1893, and interred on the slopes of Montjuïc.

Paintings date from 1914 to 1979, mostly exhibiting the thick black outlines and bright primary colours favoured by the artists.

An enormous tapestry, Tapiz de la Fundació, appears to be inspired by the figure of a cat.

Some of Miró's contemporaries, including **Matisse**, **Léger** and **Sam Francis**, are also represented.

●● *Exit from the Foundation to pl Neptú L. Follow av de Miramar eastward to the cable-car station. Ascend by cable car (two stages) to Montjuïc Castle.*

*•● Alternatively (for those uneasy in cable cars), from the same station take the funicular railway, which entails a short walk up from its terminal to the castle.*

---

| Location 13 | **MONTJUÏC PARK** |

Montjuïc hill's position, rising steeply from the Mediterranean, dominates the Barcelona skyline to the south. Its name is believed to commemorate an ancient Jewish cemetery, but could be a corruption of Mont Jovis (Jupiter), referring to a Roman temple on the hill's summit. A settlement that existed on Montjuïc, even before the Roman occupation, was linked by a road to the walled city on Mons Taber in the 3C. For centuries, a watch-tower on the summit provided navigational assistance to shipping until, in 1640, it was replaced by the first castle. In the same year, the Catalans defeated the army of Philip IV at the foot of the hill.

*•● Proceed to the castle.*

---

| Location 14 | **ARMY MUSEUM** (MUSEU MILITAR) |

Castell de Montjuïc

*Open Monday–Saturday 09.30–13.30 and 16.00–1900; Sunday and holidays 10.00–14.00. Admission charge.*

First built in 1640, construction taking just thirty days, Montjuïc Castle has been extended and remodelled several times. Lord Peterborough captured it in 1705, during the War of Succession, and the castle was blown up the following year by the troops of Philip IV. **Vauban** rebuilt and enlarged the fortress for the Bourbons and it is basically this 18C structure that survives.

In 1808, General Dufresnes evicted the Spanish troops from Montjuïc and captured Barcelona for Napoléon. During the Civil War the castle became a prison, and it was here that the leader of the Catalan government in exile, Lluís Companys, was shot after his forcible return from Vichy France in 1940. Montjuïc castle was given to the municipality in 1960 and converted to accommodate the Army Museum.

*•● Enter the museum.*

Of greatest interest to many will be the models of Catalan castles. The arms collection of Frederic Marés forms an important part of the collection.

*•● Exit and return by foot or cable car to the next cable-car stage downhill. Continue eastward to pl de la Sardana.*

A sculpture celebrates the *Sardana*, Catalonia's national dance.

From **Plaça del Mirador**, immediately R, may be gained the most spectacular views across the harbour.

Facing the Mirador is the entrance to the **Amusement Park** (Parc d'Atraccions). The park, similar to that on Tibidabo, is dominated by a big wheel.

*•● Descend by cable car and funicular to M Paral·lel.*

*•● Alternatively, follow ctra de Montjuïc eastward until it joins av de Miramar, then proceed westward to pl de Dante and take bus 61 or 201 to pl d'Espanya and M Espanya.*

**11**

Ciutadella Park and Barceloneta

Very much an open-air route, combining the only park in the city centre with Barcelona's beach area: a fine day is essential. Situated within Ciutadella Park are the Museum of Modern Art, the Parliament of Catalónia and an attractive zoo.

Apart from its beach, much of which is being improved, Barceloneta is popular due to its many lively fish restaurants, most of which overlook the sea.

*Timing:* The Zoological Museum is closed Monday. Most fish restaurants in Barceloneta are closed Sunday evening.

**Arc de Triomf**

CARRER

DE

TRAFALGAR

ARC D
TRIOM

Locations
1  Arc del Triomf
2  Palace of Justice
3  Zoological Museum
4  Ciutadella Park
5  Ciutadella Chapel
6  Former Governor's Palace
7  Museum of Modern Art
8  Parliament of Catalonia
9  Zoo
10 Barceloneta Beach and
   Olympic Village
11 Barceloneta Quarter
12 Sant Miquel del Port

PASSEIG DE

PICASSO

CARRER PORTAL NO

COMERC

Plta.
Comerc

PASSE

PASSE

PRINCESA

CARRER    DE    LA

Jaume I

CARRER MONCADA

DEL

CARRER FUSINIA

CARRER

COMERCIAL

PTGE
MERCANTIL

PASSEIG DE

R45

R50

R43

CARRER    DE    LA    RIBERA

CARRER

L'ARGENTERA

DE

AVINGUDA    MARQUES

DE

PASSEIG

ESTACIO
RODALIA

Barceloneta

AVINGUDA

MOLL DE LA BARCELONETA

NACIONAL

CARRER    MAR

CARRER

MIQUEL

CARRER

BALBOA

DE    L'ATLANTIDA    DE

GINEBRA

Placa
de la
Font

DE—MAQUINISTA

Pl.
Barceloneta

12

CARRER—D'ANDREA—DORIA

CARRER    DE

SANT

BALUARD

SANT

11

CARLES

PASSEIG

PASSEIG

CARRER    ALMIRAL

L CARRER

CERVERA

CARRER

CARRER    ALMIRAL

ALXADA

CARRER

CARRER
JUDICI

R10

PLATJA DE SANT MIQUEL

TORRE
SANT SEBASTIA

Locations

| | |
|---|---|
| **1** Arc del Triomf | **7** Museum of Modern Art |
| **2** Palace of Justice | **8** Parliament of Catalonia |
| **3** Zoological Museum | **9** Zoo |
| **4** Ciutadella Park | **10** Barceloneta Beach and |
| **5** Ciutadella Chapel | Olympic Village |
| **6** Former Governor's Palace | **11** Barceloneta Quarter |
| | **12** Sant Miquel del Port |

**Start** *M Arc de Triomf, line 1. Leave by the c Trafalgar exit and proceed southward.*

| | |
|---|---|
| Location 1 | **ARC DEL TRIOMF** *Vilaseca 1888* |

Passeig de Sant
Joan

This brick archway, which provided the entrance to the Universal Exhibition of 1888, remains a Barcelona landmark. It was contemporary with Gaudí's Casa Vicenç and, like that building, adopts Mudéjar-style features.

The arch is decorated with statues and iron urns that punctuate its balustrade.

Running southward from the archway, the gardens now commemorate Lluís Companys, the Catalan president at the outbreak of the Civil War. Originally, they were paved with mosaics designed by Falqués, but these were lost when the underground car park was excavated.

**••** *Proceed to the east side of pas de Lluís Companys.*

| | |
|---|---|
| Location 2 | **PALACE OF JUSTICE** (PALAU DE JUSTICIA) *Sagnier and Domènech i Estapà 1887–1908* |

14 Passeig de Lluís
Companys

A very long façade of Montjuïc stone, punctuated by towers with cupolas, proclaims Barcelona's law courts. A youthful work of the two architects, who were both twenty-nine when designing the building, this was one of the earliest examples of Modernism. **Sagnier**'s eclectic taste is already apparent, Parisian touches being combined with an English style that had recently distinguished London's museums at Kensington.

**••** *Enter the building.*

A broad staircase, lit by a stained glass ceiling, leads to the first floor and the **Saló Pasos Perdidos** (Hall of the Lost Steps), named to commemorate the hall above the Conciergerie in Paris, where prisoners, sentenced by the Revolutionary Tribunal, passed through on their way to the tumbrils.

The high vault is an iron structure; side windows are of stained glass.

Murals were painted by **Josep Maria Sert**.

**••** *Exit from the building L. First R pas de Pujades. First L pas de Picasso.*

| | |
|---|---|
| Location 3 | **ZOOLOGICAL MUSEUM** (MUSEU DE ZOOLÓGIA) *Domènech i Montaner 1888* |

Passeig de Picasso

*Open Tuesday–
Sunday 09.00–
14.00. Admission
charge.*

Originally, the museum was built as a café/restaurant for the Universal Exhibition. After it ended Domènech, together with Antoni Maria Gallissà and others, operated an Arts and Crafts workshop in the building, which was then called the Castell dels Tres Dragons (Castle of the Three Dragons), an allusion to a contemporary play. Parliament assembled here in 1917.

Brick cladding, in Mudéjar style, disguises an iron frame, with much of the decoration, including ceramic plaques at upper level, the work of **Antoni Gallissà**.

The stained glass has been lost.

Fossils and stuffed animals are exhibited within.

**••** *Proceed through the building to the park.*

# 11

Location 4      **CIUTADELLA PARK**
(PARC DE LA CIUTADELLA)

*Open daily 08.00–*
*21.00. Admission*
*free.*

Missed by many visitors due to its peripheral
location, this is the only park in Barcelona that can
easily be reached from the city centre. Two
museums, the Parliament House and Barcelona Zoo
lie within the park, which covers almost three times
the area of the walled Roman city.

Streets were laid out in this part of Barcelona in the
13C and the quarter was first known as Vilanova
(new town). Later, it spread to the sea and the name
was changed to Ribera (shore). The area remained
outside the city wall until 1438, and in 1513 a bulwark
was constructed to protect it from seaward attacks.

The Catalans, supported by the English and the
Genoese, opposed the claim of the Bourbon, Philip
V, to the Spanish throne during the War of
Succession, and he besieged the city for thirteen
months until it surrendered in 1714. As punishment,
and to ensure that any future revolts could be
quelled, Philip ordered that a great citadel
(Ciutadella) should be built in the Ribera district;
**Prospéro Verboom** began its construction in 1715.

More than 1,200 houses were demolished to provide
the site, no compensation was paid to the owners and
it was not until Barceloneta was laid out after 1750
that they were adequately rehoused. Also lost was
the great Santa Clara Convent, the site of which was
originally expected to be sufficient to accommodate
the citadel. However, the nuns were given the
ancient Tinell Hall of the royal palace in exchange.
When completed in 1727, the star-shaped citadel,
which could accommodate 8,000 troops, is believed
to have been the largest in Europe, but it never
housed a garrison; instead, the complex became a
civil prison.

In 1808, Napoléon's troops captured the fortress. It
was demolished in 1841 but rebuilt two years later.
General Prim, in 1869, declared that the Citadel
should belong to the city. **Josep Fontseré** won the
international competition to create a park on the site
and much of his layout remains, including tree-lined
walks in the English style. Buildings retained from
the citadel and still surviving are: the governor's
palace, the chapel and the arsenal.

In 1888, the Universal Exhibition was held in the
park and some of its structures have proved to be
permanent, significantly altering Fontseré's plan.
More recently, the creation of the Zoo at the south
end has led to further changes.

•● *Follow any of the paths that lead to the north-east*
*corner of the park.*

The **Cascade** (La Cascada) was built 1871–81 in the
form of a white marble triumphal arch, with water
descending from a projecting structure. It was
designed by **Fontseré** assisted by the youthful **Gaudí**,
who had yet to gain his architectural diploma. **Gaudí**
worked on some of the reliefs and the fountain's
system.

An iron quadriga surmounts the arch.

No water has flowed for some time, but the fountain

is expected to be restored to working order.

*•• Proceed southward to the small lake and turn R. Continue to pas de Picasso on the west side of the Palm House.*

Immediately L is the **Geological Museum** (Museu de Geologica) open Tuesday–Sunday.

Continue southward to the Palm House, opposite ptge Mercantil. The **glass cube** outside the Palm House L, enclosing old chairs and a sofa, together with steel joists draped with cloth, pays homage to the Cubist works of Pablo Picasso and was composed by the Catalan sculptor **Antoni Tàpies**. It was discovered that the cube had to be cooled by running water in order to combat the build-up of solar heat within; air-conditioning has since been installed to prevent the glass cracking.

*•• Follow pas de Picasso southward and re-enter the park L at the junction with av Marquès de l'Argentera (second R).*

Immediately ahead is the equestrian monument to General Prim, by **Puigjaner**. This commemorates the man responsible for presenting the site of the citadel to the municipality. The monument was damaged during the Civil War but has been restored.

*•• Follow the second path L to the chapel.*

*•• Alternatively, take bus OF ZOO, east of the monument, direct to the Zoo (Location 9).*

| Location 5 | **CIUTADELLA CHAPEL** (CAPELLA DE LA CIUTADELLA) *Alejandro de Rez 1716–27* |
|---|---|
| Plaça d'Armes Parc de la Ciutadella | First seen R is the cylindrical **campanile** at the rear of the apse. |

The chapel was built in Classical style for worship by members of the garrison, but never used as such. By 1928, the building had fallen into disrepair and restoration was put in hand.

The **cupola** is clad with polychrome ceramics.

With its simple but harmonious façade, this chapel had a great influence on the design of many 18C religious buildings in Barcelona.

*•• Continue northward to the adjoining building.*

| Location 6 | **FORMER GOVERNOR'S PALACE** *Verboom 1748* |
|---|---|
| Plaça d'Armes Parc de la Ciutadella | An early Classical work in Barcelona, the austere design of the palace was influenced by contemporary French architecture. It is now a school, Institut de Batxillerat Verdaguer. |

The Bourbon coat of arms surmounts the building.

Projecting from the sides are the earliest dormer windows to be built in Barcelona.

*•• Proceed clockwise around the small pond to the large block opposite.*

| Location 7 | **MUSEUM OF MODERN ART**<br>(MUSEU D'ART MODERN) |
|---|---|

Plaça d'Armes
Parc de la
Ciutadella

*Open Sunday
10.00–15.00,
Monday 15.00–
19.30. Tuesday–
Saturday 09.00–
19.30. Admission
charge but free to
minors and
Spaniards.*

Occupying part of the former arsenal, the museum is scheduled to transfer eventually to the Museum of Catalan Art on Montjuïc. Those expecting to find dazzling examples of work by Miró, Dalí and Clavé will be sadly disappointed; few works by internationally known artists are exhibited. In general, modern Catalan paintings, which never reached the heights of Catalan architecture, must be judged parochial.

**History** When completed *c.*1843 the building, which was intended to house the arsenal, overlooked the parade ground, now laid out as a garden. In the late 19C, it was refurbished by **Falqués** and **Gallissà** as a royal palace. Adaptations were made in 1902 to accommodate the Barcelona Museum of Fine Arts, and this, together with the Archeological Museum, remained here from 1907 to 1932, when both were transferred to Montjuïc.

The entire building was then adapted by **Santiago Marco** to house the Catalan Parliament, which sat here from 1932 to 1939; it then became a barracks. In 1945, the Museum of Modern Art was created in the north wing. For a brief period works by Picasso were included, but in 1968 these were transferred to the new Picasso Museum in Carrer Montcada.

The bulk of the building was converted once more, this time to house the Catalan Parliament following the return of democracy to Spain; the first Home Rule Parliament since the Civil War was convened in 1980.

●● *Enter the museum by the first doorway L. Turn L and proceed clockwise.*

Exhibited are works, mainly by Catalan artists, created in the late 19C and early 20C. As has previously been said, few examples by artists of international renown are on view and the museum is chiefly, therefore, of specialist interest.

However, **Santiago Russinyol** and **Ramon Casas**, both born in the 1860s, have their admirers, the latter being regarded as Catalonia's first Impressionist.

**Room 9** displays Art-Nouveau furniture.

In the central courtyard, unusual wood sculptures and mobiles, reminiscent of totem poles, are the work of **Josep Guinovart i Bertras**, 1976–9.

The perceptive may locate one work each by **Sisley** and **Bonnard**.

●● *Exit from the museum L.*

| Location 8 | **PARLIAMENT OF CATALONIA** (PARLAMENT DE CATALUNYA) *Plaça d'Armes* |
|---|---|

Parc de la
Ciutadella.
(Tel. 300.62.63.)

*Open by
appointment, two
days in advance,
Monday–Friday*

The sgraffiti, the upper section of the pavilion and the magnificent doorway to the main entrance are the late-19C work of **Falqués** and **Gallissà**.

Administrative power in Barcelona is divided in a complicated way with, since 1979, separate bodies representing the city of Barcelona (Ajuntament), province of Barcelona (Diputació), region of

*10.00–14.00 and
16.00–19.00,
Thursday 10.00–
14.00. Admission
free.*

Catalonia (Generalitat) and the semi-autonomous
nation of Catalonia (Parliament). In Parliament, the
president and counsellors of the Generalitat attend
sessions, together with the president and members of
the government. All proceedings, naturally, are in
Catalan. More space for members is now required
and this will be provided by the eventual transfer of
the Modern Art Museum to the Palau Nacional on
Montjuïc. The entire complex will then become
Parliament House.

*•● Exit L and follow the signs to the Zoo (Parc
Zoológic).*

| Location 9 | **ZOO** (PARC ZOOLÒGIC) |

Parc de la
Ciutadella

*Open daily January
and February
10.00–17.00, March
10.00–18.00, April
10.00–19.00, May
to August 0930–
19.00, September
10.00–18.00,
October to
December 10.00–
17.00.*

*A mini-train tours
the zoo area
(additional charge)*

This zoo, the most important in Catalonia, is a post-
Civil War addition to the park's entertainments. It is
well laid out and the animals are separated from
spectators in the modern manner by moats rather
than iron bars. Particularly strong in primates, the
zoo's biggest attraction is Snowflake, the only known
albino gorilla.

A recent addition to the complex is the aquarium,
which includes a whale and dolphin show at intervals.
The great mammals can at other times be viewed
swimming under water, through glass panels in the
sides of their pool.

A fountain near the entrance to the zoo is crowned by
the figure, *Lady with Umbrella*, by **Roig i Soler**, a
work that is regarded with great affection by all
Barcelonans.

*•● Exit from the zoo R and return towards the
Parliament of Catalonia. Leave the park from the exit
behind the building. R c de Wellington. At the end of
the street follow the signs to M Ciutadella R. Continue
ahead to pas Marítim and Barceloneta beach.*

*•● Alternatively, if not wishing to visit the beach,
from M Ciutadella train one stop in the Roquetas
direction to M Barceloneta. Exit L and follow pas
Nacional southward (Location 11).*

| Location 10 | **BARCELONETA BEACH AND OLYMPIC VILLAGE** |

It surprises many to discover that a beach can be
reached so easily from the centre of Barcelona, as it is
not visible from the harbour and there is little publicity
for its existence. Always crowded on summer weekends,
the rather sleazy ambience is not so different from
Brighton's, on the south coast of England, although
there is coarse sand rather than pebbles and, at the
south end, fish restaurants extend on to it.

*•● Turn L and follow pas Marítim northward to its
termination.*

A formerly bleak area of railway lines, gasometers
and light industrial buildings has been cleared to
provide the site for gardens and the Olympic Village
(Vila Olímpica), built to accommodate the
competitors in the Summer Olympic Games of 1992.
The beach that skirts the zone is being greatly
improved, and a brand new yacht marina and
conference centre incorporated. Two skyscrapers, at

136m the tallest buildings in Barcelona, will dominate the area. Eventually, the 'Village' buildings will be sold to private purchasers and the area opened to the public. Barcelona will then possess a beach of high quality on its doorstep, a rare facility for a major European city.

●● *Return southward following pas Marítim.*

The established beach of Barceloneta includes a few private areas, most of which are open, on payment, to visitors. However, apart from increased security and the privacy afforded by changing cubicles, their advantages are limited. High chicken-wire fences keep out those who have not paid, and create a concentration camp effect that does little to enhance the appearance of the beach. If utilizing them, men must take note of the rather sexist 'women only' sections, denoted by 'Reservado Señoras' signs. There are no 'men only' equivalents for misogynists.

●● *Continue to the south end of pas Marítim. Descend the steps to the beach and continue ahead.*

From this point the famous beachside restaurants of Barceloneta begin to appear, their vivacity making this the most appealing part of the beach. In summer, tables and chairs will spread from their terraces on to the sand itself. The fish appears to be of a uniformly high standard, with paella and zarzuela popular favourites. Dress is most informal and no one minds if diners wish to remain in their bikinis. Sunday lunch on Barceloneta beach on a hot summer's day should not be missed: none of the coastal resorts nearby offer an equivalent gastronomic experience.

Although the sand is coarse in parts, the beach itself is surprisingly clean, considering its proximity to the port. Non-swimmers and those with young children should bear in mind, however, that the sand drops at a steep incline immediately the water is reached.

●● *Leave the beach and proceed southward towards the cable car tower ahead.*

This tower, **Torre de Sant Sebastia**, was built in 1930 to provide access to the cable-car service across the harbour to the lower slopes of Montjuïc. There is a half-way stage at a similar tower.

●● *If not taking the cable car, proceed to the roundabout at the south end of Passeig Nacional, from where buses leave for various parts of the city e.g. OF 17 to pl de Catalunya, OF 39 to pl Urquinaona, OF 57 and 64 to Drassanes at the south end of La Rambla. All pass M Barceloneta.*

●● *Alternatively, to view more of Barceloneta, follow any of the streets that run parallel with pas Nacional northward. Fourth L c Sant Carles. Continue to its end. R pas Nacional.*

| Location 11 | **BARCELONETA QUARTER** |

Barceloneta is famed for its fish restaurants, which abound throughout the quarter, not only on the sea front. The beach gives it a seaside atmosphere lacking in other waterfront areas of the city, which are separated from the open sea by a series of moles.

Most of the triangular spur of land on which

Barceloneta stands has been reclaimed from the sea, a prime reason for its construction being the rehousing of those who lost had their properties when the Citadel was built. Planned by **Prospéro Verboom**, work did not begin until 1753, but in thirty months eight streets had been completed. A simple grid plan was followed, with long, very narrow blocks permitting each room to face the street. To increase further the natural light to each property, building heights were limited to two storeys and transgressors were made to demolish their extensions in 1861. However, by 1871 four floors were permitted, and it is now rare to find an original two-storey house in Barceloneta.

When completed, 1,300 residents were accommodated, a few more than had lost their houses for the Citadel development.

Passeig Nacional, the main thoroughfare, is lined on its landward side with restaurants, but uninteresting harbour buildings on the opposite side block views of the water, rather spoiling the ambience.

*First R pl Barceloneta.*

| | |
|---|---|
| Location 12 | **SANT MIQUEL DEL PORT** *Francesc Paredes* and *Damià Ribas 1755* |
| Plaça de la Barceloneta | The city's oldest Baroque church, Sant Miquel is the only building of architectural importance in Barceloneta. |

It was built under the direction of the military engineer, **Pedro Cermeño,** and completed in two years.

The sculptural ornamentation of the façade is the work of **Pere Costa**.

*Enter the church.*

Originally, the plan of the building was exactly square, with one central cupola supported by four pillars, but in 1863 **Elies Rogent** extended the building eastward, greatly increasing its capacity, although following the existing style.

A further cupola was added.

Restoration took place in 1912.

*Exit L.*

**No 41**, **Carrer Sant Miquel** was the residence of Ferdinand de Lesseps, entrepreneur of the Suez and Panama canals, when he served as France's Consul-General in Barcelona during the 1840s. A terracotta wall-plaque with floral decoration records his occupancy.

*Return to pas Nacional R.*

This, the northern section of Passeig Nacional, is its liveliest. On the feast day of Saint Michael, 29 September, the thoroughfare is closed and a festival takes place.

*Continue northward to M Barceloneta.*

# 12

## Güell Park and Tibidabo

The work of Gaudí and Jujol at Güell Park achieved a fairy-tale quality that would be unmatched until Disneyland was created, on another continent, more than half a century later.

Mount Tibidabo is visited primarily for its views, the most extensive in Barcelona, and for its relative coolness in the hot summer months.

*Timing:* Fine weather is essential and there is little point in visiting Tibidabo unless the air is clear. Best visibility is generally in the early evening and in summer it is then that the Amusement Park opens. Both Güell Park and Tibidabo Park are on the Tourist Bus Route 100, the ticket for which includes the not inconsiderable cost of the bus and funicular to the summit of the latter. In addition, the entry price to the Amusement Park at Tibidabo is reduced.

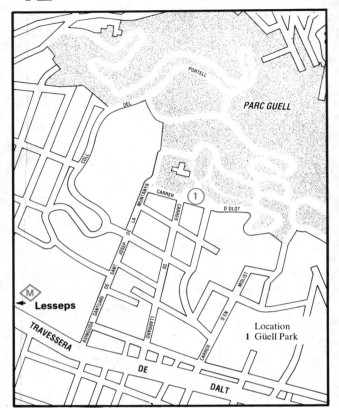

PORTELL

PARC GUELL

DEL

COLL

MUNTANYA

CARRER

CARRER

D'OLOT

DE LA

SANT JOSEP

30

MOLIST

D'EN

SANTUARI

LLOBBANT]

CARRER

AVINGUDA

DE

M Lesseps

Location
1 Güell Park

TRAVESSERA

DE

DALT

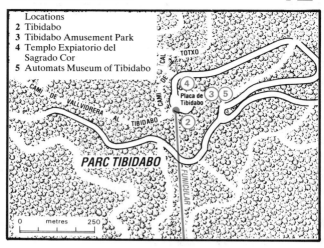

Locations
2 Tibidabo
3 Tibidabo Amusement Park
4 Templo Expiatorio del
  Sagrado Cor
5 Automats Museum of Tibidabo

**Start**  *Take bus 24 from pl de Catalunya (outside El Corte Inglés) to Parc Güell.*

*Alternatively, M Lesseps, line 3. Exit and proceed to the east side of pl Lesseps. Follow trav de Dalt eastward. Take bus 24 in an eastward direction to Parc Güell.*

*Alternatively, alight at the stop from bus 100, run for the Barcelona Patronat de Turisme. (See page xvi).*

| Location 1 | **GÜELL PARK** (PARC GÜELL) *Gaudí 1890–1914* |
| --- | --- |

*Open daily: summer 09.00–21.00; spring 09.00–19.00; autumn and winter 09.00–17.00. Admission free.*

Structures in this hillside park, the most colourful of **Gaudí**'s output, owe much to the ceramics of one of the architect's assistants, **Josep Jujol i Gibert**.

**History**  Towards the end of the the 19C, Count Eusebi Güell decided to create a garden city on the family estate of Can Montaner de Dalt. Sixty houses were planned, and **Gaudí** began work in 1900. In the event, the scheme failed, only two houses were built and one of them was purchased by **Gaudí** for his own use. The municipality acquired the site in 1922 and since then it has been a public park.

● *Continue ahead from the bus stop. First R enter the park and follow the path ahead to the* **Gaudí Museum**. *(Admission charge.)*

The museum is accommodated in the house that **Gaudí** lived in 1904–14. It was designed by his chief assistant **Francesc Berenguer i Mestres** who, until his death in 1914, collaborated with **Gaudí** on several projects.

The gate was brought from Casa Vicenç in 1965.

● *Enter the museum.*

Furnishings include items designed by the architect and brought from other houses.

**Gaudí**'s bedroom contains his original iron bed and wardrobe.

● *Exit from the museum L and continue ahead.*

There are good views over the city.

● *Descend the steps R and proceed to the entrance that faces c d'Olot.*

Cast-iron gates are designed with the usual spikiness favoured by Gaudí.

Stone pavilions, designed by **Gaudí**, flank the gates, their polychromatic 'gingerbread house' appearance being reminiscent of Casa Batlló in Passeig de Gràcia.

The mushroom chimneys add to the impression of fantasy.

Originally, one pavilion was intended for the occupancy of the guardian of the estate, the other was to be a communal building which would provide lounges and medical facilities.

The top of the rubble wall is decorated with broken ceramics and glass.

● *Ascend the first flight of steps.*

Immediately L, the building now accommodates a school.

The cave-like structure R was built to provide cover for horse-drawn carriages.

*●* *Ascend the second flight of steps.*

A large reptile clad in ceramics, the work of **Jujol**, provides yet another fairy-tale ingredient.

Ahead, the Sala Hipostile, restored in 1989, was intended to accommodate a market which would supply the families living on the estate.

Doric columns support the roof, above which lies the plaza. The space is known as the 'Hall of 100 Columns' although in fact there are only 84. **Gaudí** delighted in unusual structures, of which he was a master and here, as at Colonia Güell (page 200), set his peripheral columns at angles leaning towards the centre.

The ceiling is set with mosaics and incorporates large bosses.

*●* *Ascend steps to the plaza.*

**Jujol**'s masterpiece, the polychromatic bench balustrade, surrounding the circular plaza, is believed to be the longest in the world.

*●* *Descend to the main gateway and exit R c d'Olot. L av Santuari de Sant Josep de la Muntanya. Third R trav de Dalt. Take bus 74 to c de Balmes (four stops). Continue southward from the bus stop to M Padua. Train to av del Tibidabo (two stops) and transfer to the bus which continues to the funicular station for Tibidabo summit.*

*●* *Alternatively, return to the east entrance and continue to Tibidabo with Tourist Office bus 100. Its ticket price includes the cost of the bus and funicular to the summit.*

This bus also visits **Parc de la Creuta del Coll** (immediately before Tibidabo), with its large open-air swimming pool.

*●* *Alternatively, if not visiting Tibidabo, proceed to trav de Dalt, as above, and take bus 24, 31, 32 or NG to c Carolines (four stops) and follow Route 8.*

| Location 2 | **TIBIDABO** |
| --- | --- |

Although there are some man-made attractions, visitors to Barcelona ascend this 1,650-foot mountain primarily for its views, by far the most extensive in the city. Apart from funiculars, there is no public transport, and those who dislike them will find it necessary to hire a taxi or private car in order to reach the summit.

Mount Tibidabo's name derives from St Matthew's Gospel, where the devil tempts (in Latin): *Haec omnia tibi dabo si cades adoraberis me.* (All this shall I give you if you will but adore me). The view is undoubtedly beautiful, but Barcelona's air tends to be hazy, with fewer than fifteen days a year, on average, being perfectly clear. When they occur it is possible to see Montserrat and even the faint outline of Majorca.

The first road to the summit was laid in 1868 but it was not until Doctor Andreu formed the Tibidabo Society thirty years later that the development of the park began. A funicular link was commissioned and the park opened in 1908.

•● *Exit from the funicular at pl del Tibidabo. Ahead R is the entrance to the Amusement Park.*

| Location 3 | **TIBIDABO AMUSEMENT PARK**<br>**(PARC D'ATTRACCIONS)** |

Plaça del Tibidabo

*Open January to March, Saturday, Sunday and holidays 11.00–20.00; April to June, Monday–Friday 11.00–20-00, Saturday, Sunday and holidays 12.00–23.00; July to mid September, Monday–Saturday 17.00–01.30, Sunday and holidays 12.00–23.00; mid September to December, Saturday, Sunday and holidays 11.00–20.00. Admission charge (to area only). Admission Pass (includes all the attractions). Reduced Price Admission Pass after 20.00 and to holders of Bus 100 tickets.*

Completely remodelled in 1989, the park is of most interest to younger visitors. Its Big Wheel, Helter-Skelter and Aeroplane provide greater thrills than usual, due to their elevated position; the Aeroplane, for example, extending from the escarpment and sweeping over trees far below.

Less heart-stopping pursuits are also provided for small children, including a boating pool.

•● *Return to pl del Tibidabo. Immediately R stands the church.*

| Location 4 | **TEMPLO EXPIATORIO DEL SAGRADO COR**<br>*Sagnier (father and son) 1902–11* |

Plaça del Tibidabo

Although this is Barcelona's attempted answer to the Sacré Coeur of Paris, the church fails to match the latter's symbolic appeal. It is sited much higher, it is further from the city centre and the towering communications aerial subsequently erected beside it interferes with the silhouette of the building (resiting the communications aerial beside the Amusement Park may alter the situation from 1992).

In 1885, Joan Bosco dedicated the mountain to the Sacred Heart (Sagrado Cor) and **Enric Sagnier** was commissioned to build a church on its summit. Like the Sacré Coeur (Sacred Heart) in Paris it was intended that the church should expiate the sins of its citizens.

Flanked by castellated towers the church, apart from its Modernist portal, is a plain Gothic-style structure.

•● *Proceed through the portal.*

Built on two levels, the lower accommodates the crypt, where most services are held.

Unusually, foliage and bands decorate the columns at a low level.

Walls and vaults throughout are covered with mosaics.

A stone frieze illustrates stages from Christ's appearance before Pontius Pilate to his Crucifixion. Some of its panels are realistically gruesome.

*Continue to the church above and take the lift to the statue of Christ (nominal charge). Ascend two flights of steps to the foot of the statue.*

The great figure of Christ surmounts the building but, as has been said, its effect is now reduced by the aerial erected beside the church.

From here, the most extensive views can be gained in all directions and it is usually the coolest place in Barcelona.

*Descend to pl del Tibidabo.*

| | |
|---|---|
| Location 5 | **AUTOMATS MUSEUM OF TIBIDABO** (MUSEU D'AUTOMATES DEL TIBIDABO) |
| Plaça de Tibidabo<br><br>*Open mid June to early September, Monday–Thursday 17.00–01.30; Friday and Saturday 17.00–02.30; Sunday and holidays 12.00–23.00. Check times for other periods.* | This unusual museum includes fairground automats, mechanical dolls and electric trains.<br><br>*Exit and return to the funicular station, proceeding to central Barcelona.*<br><br>*Alternatively, alight at the first funicular halt to view the Observatory (check opening times).* |

# Environs of Barcelona

The region of Catalonia has so much to offer that it is impossible to describe all its attractions adequately within the compass of this book. However, many will wish to visit some of the better-known locations that can be reached easily from Barcelona, and the following summary is given as assistance.

### Colonia Güell
Open Sunday and Saturday evening. Reached by train from M Espanya. Take the FF. CC. Generalitat line to Santa Coloma de Cervelló. The crypt of the unfinished church, by Gaudí, is considered to possess the most impressive of the great architect's interiors. Built 1893–1915, this is Gaudí's supremely innovative structural achievement, incorporating hyperbolic and parabolic vaults of brick, with columns leaning at various angles, dependent on the load that they have to bear. Stained-glass windows are set like jewels in the otherwise monochrome interior.

### Costa Brava
Buses to most resorts leave from Plaça Medinacelli. The 'Wild Coast' of rocky promontories interspersed with bathing beaches stretches northward almost from Barcelona to the French border. Its southern resorts of **Blanes**, **Lloret de Mar**, **Tossa de Mar**, **San Feliu de Guíxols**, **Platya d'Aro** and **Palamós** are all international in nature, with little evidence of being either the fishermen's towns that they were until comparatively recently, or even of being particularly Spanish. Tossa, however, retains a picturesque quality in its old town, protected by 12C walls – if only practically every establishment was not connected in some way with tourism! Surprisingly, no bus service follows the still beautiful corniche road between Tossa and San Feliu and to proceed directly northward those without private transport must use the boat service.

Once Palamós has been passed, things improve dramatically, the delightful small towns of **Calella de la Parafrugell**, **Llafranch** and **Tamariu**, with their beaches of fine sand rather than gravel, following in quick succession. Boasting fewer discos, but incomparably greater charm, these are the resorts favoured by the discerning. All are reached via Parafrugell, which itself may be approached from Gerona.

Further north lie the Graeco–Roman excavations at **Empuriés** and the picturesque but beachless fishing village of **Cadaquès**, popularized by Salvador Dalí. These may be reached from **Figueres** (on the main railway line from Barcelona to France), where the **Dalí Museum** is located.

### Costa Dorada
The 'Golden' coastline of fine sand beaches lies south of Barcelona, continuing past Tarragona. Its resorts are easily reached from Sants Station (or Passeig de Gràcia), the express from Barcelona arriving at Sitges, for example, in just over thirty minutes. Although **Casteldefels** is nearer, **Sitges** is deservedly the most popular resort for the Barcelonans and, therefore, extremely crowded on fine summer Sundays. Miraculously, the town has protected much of its elegant architecture, with good examples of Modernism, Baroque and Gothic pastiche. Foreign holiday-makers never quite outnumber the locals and, possibly

uniquely in a large Spanish resort on the Mediterranean, the visitor to Sitges can still feel that he or she is actually in Spain. An additional bonus is that prices on the Costa Dorada are significantly lower than on the Costa Brava. South of Tarragona lies **Salou**, a run-of-the-mill beach resort, not worth the journey involved.

### Gerona (Girona)
Trains from Sants Station (or Passeig de Gràcia) provide rapid access to the city. The short taxi ride from Gerona station to Plaça de la Independencia is then recommended, as there is little of tourist interest in the modern city. From the riverside that lies behind the square, romantic views may be obtained of the ochre and cream medieval buildings, reflected in the water. A footbridge from the north-east angle of the square crosses the river Onyar to the old city. Ahead, behind Carrer de la Força, spreads the former **Jewish Quarter**, best preserved around the Centre Isaac El Call.

A little further east stands the Baroque **Agullana Palace**, with its much photographed angular archway. To the north lies the 13C **Sant Domènec Convent**, one of the earliest examples of Catalan Gothic architecture; the complex now houses the **Archaeological Museum**.

**Gerona Cathedral**, the city's greatest attraction, remains open throughout the afternoon, a welcome rarity in Catalonia. Approached by a monumental staircase of 1690, its Renaissance façade is dominated by the Baroque portal, designed by **Pere Costa** in the 18C but not finished until 1962, when the sculptures and gallery were added. The octagonal campanile was completed in the 17C. Work commenced on the apse of the Gothic building, to replace the Romanesque cathedral, in 1312.

Initially, a nave with flanking aisles was proposed, but in 1416 the controversial design of **Guillem Bofill** for an aisle-less nave was accepted; it is the widest clear span Gothic example ever built. Within the choir, the bishop's throne and some stalls are 14C work. Also dating from the 14C are the apse's stained-glass windows and the high altar's silver reredos and baldachino. Tomb chests of various bishops and of Berenguer II, d.1082, and his consort, are outstanding examples of medieval craftsmanship.

The treasury and cloister (joint admission charge) are approached from the north doorway. Exhibited within the treasury is the unique *Tapestry of Creation c.*1100. Well-preserved figure capitals, typically Romanesque, decorate the cloister, *c.*1180–1210. Overlooking the cloister is the so-called 'Charlemagne Tower', the only surviving feature of the 11C Romanesque cathedral. Its name commemorates the first cathedral on the site, built for the Emperor Charlemagne in the 8C.

Concentrated in an area to the south-west of the cathedral are four buildings dating from the Romanesque period: **Sant Feliú**, with its Baroque façade, the **Arab Baths** (Banys Arabs), the cloistered monastery of **Sant Pere de Galligants** and **Sant Nicolau**.

### Tarragona
Also reached from Sants railway station (or Passeig de Gràcia), this ancient Roman capital of the Iberian peninsula is visited primarily for its Transitional style cathedral and Roman remains. Virtually three towns in one, most of interest in Tarragona lies

within its medieval centre, built around the cathedral. The coastal road leads to the **Balcó de Mediterrani**, at the east end of Rambla Nous, with its extensive coastal views, which include the ruins of the third-century **Roman arena** built into the hillside to accommodate 24,000 spectators. It was here that Bishop Fructuosus and his two deacons were burnt at the stake.

The first-century **Praetorium** was blown up by the French in 1813, but much of its Roman structure has survived. By tradition, this was the birthplace of Pontius Pilate and the palace where the Emperor Augustus spent the winter of 26BC.

The adjacent **Archaeological Museum** displays Roman finds in Tarragona, including the famous mosaic depicting Medusa with hypnotic eyes. Picturesque streets and alleyways radiating from here once formed the **Jewish Quarter**. The great wall, part Roman, part Iberian, stretches northward, skirted on its north and west sides by the **Passeig Arqueológic** walkway, which runs between it and the perimeter wall built by the English in 1707, two years after they had captured the city in the War of Succession. At the southern end of the walkway, the city is entered via the Roman gateway, **Portal del Roser**, which may have been the principal entrance to the **forum**, remains of which have been revealed. Medieval streets continue uphill to the cathedral.

**Tarragona Cathedral**, built 1171–1331 on the site of a mosque, is a mix of Romanesque and Gothic styles. Unlike the cathedrals of Barcelona and Gerona, the main façade, which faces south, was constructed in the medieval period. Although planned, pinnacles were never built. The combination of deep archivolted portal and large rose window, designed by **Bartomeu**, gives the façade a strength that is unmatched by any other cathedral in Catalonia. Figures on the portal and flanking buttresses are original Gothic work.

Internally, while the massive piers of the nave are typically Romanesque in style, the vault is Gothic. It is almost twice the height of the flanking aisles, a feature more Northern European than Catalan. Within the choir, the bishop's throne and the oak stalls are 15C. The high altar's alabaster reredos, dedicated to Saint Tecla, patron of the city, was made by **Pere Johan** in 1434. Immediately R of the altar is the 16C Italian tomb of the Infante Don Juan of Aragon. Apses at the north end of the cathedral are Romanesque in style, as is the Portal de Santa Tecla doorway.

Unusually large, the cloister, c.1215, is also basically Romanesque, but its design exhibits Moorish influence and the vaults of the passages are Gothic. Situated in the former chapter house, the treasury displays amongst its exhibits the *Tapestry of the Good Life*.

Immediately north of the cathedral, the mid-13C **Sant Pau Chapel** marks the point where, by tradition, Saint Paul preached in AD60. South-west of Rambla Vella is the **Paleo-Christian Necropolis**, dating from the 3C. Its museum includes the well-known 'lion sarcophagus'. Situated 2½ and 3 miles respectively from the city centre are the great, double-arched **Roman aqueduct** 'Las Ferreres' and the 4C **Centelles Mausoleum**, its cupola decorated with early-4C Christian mosaics.

**Montserrat**
Clear weather is essential for a visit to this world-famous

monastery, perched just below the unique serrated peaks of the Montserrat range of mountains. The best approach is by FF. CC. Generalitat train from Espanya station (Manresa line) to Aeri Montserrat, from where cable cars swing dramatically up to the monastery. Trains leaving at 09.10 and 11.10 (current times) are preferable; the 13.10 is not met by a cable car as its operators refuse to interrupt their lunch period. A daily bus direct to the monastery leaves from Plaça d'Espanya and there are, of course, excursions: much more expensive and inflexible.

For many, the cable car approach to the 'organ pipes' mountain will be the high point of the visit, as the over-commercialization and unexceptional architecture of the monastic complex is disappointing. Devout Catholics, however, frequently make the pilgrimage, solely to pay homage to the 'Black Madonna'. It is said that Montserrat so inspired Wagner that he adopted it as the setting for *Parsifal*, under the name Monsalvat.

Those arriving by the 11.10 train may wish to proceed immediately to the church, where the famous boys' choir sing the *Salve* at 13.00.

Monastic buildings erected in the present century dominate the main square, although two sides of the 15C cloister have been preserved, approached through a doorway designed by **Puig i Cadafalch**, the Modernist architect. Passed on the way to the church are Renaissance sepulchres and the Romanesque doorway of the 11C church, that preceded the present building.

Fronting the church is a cloister-like courtyard, constructed in the early 19C. Although the church is a Renaissance building, consecrated in 1562, its façade was re-faced with Montjuïc stone and marble in 1901. A slow-moving queue proceeds, via the sacristy, to the **Black Virgin of Montserrat**, 'La Moraneta', sited above the high altar. By tradition, the figure is a contemporary likeness of the Virgin, brought to Montserrat by St Peter in 50AD, hidden from the Moors and rediscovered by shepherds in 880. However, it is now believed that the Virgin is Romanesque work and does not pre-date the 11C, when the Benedictine monastery was founded. Candle smoke accounts for the blackness of the statue. The figure of the infant Jesus was restored in the 19C, and the throne of gold and silver made in 1947. Venerating Catholics generally kiss the hand of the Virgin as they file past.

The church itself is entered from a separate doorway, also facing the courtyard, but virtually all decoration is 19C work or later, and of little artistic value. The internationally renowned boys' choir of the Escolania sing during Sunday Mass at 11.00, and the *Salve* daily at 13.00.

Other points of interest nearby are reached by funicular or mountain paths. **The Santa Cora Chapel** is built in the cave where, allegedly, the Black Virgin was discovered in 880. Extensive views are obtained from the **Sant Joan Hermitage**, but the finest are from the **Sant Geroni Belvedere**, over 4,000 feet high, where to the north lie the Pyrenees and to the south the Balearic islands (only visible on the clearest days).

Other outstanding attractions in Catalonia include the monasteries of **Poblet** and **Santes Creus**, in the direction of Tarragona, and the snow-capped Pyrenees mountain range with its delightful villages, many boasting Romanesque churches.

Private transport is necessary to reach these outlying locations with ease, but trains and excursion buses make day trips to the small tax-free country of **Andorra**, on the French border.

# Food and drink in Barcelona

**Food**

Due in part to general prosperity since the nineteenth century, Barcelona, like Paris, is a city of restaurants. The full range, from Michelin-starred luxury establishments to picturesque, if somewhat down at heel, bodegas, waits to delight the gourmet. Visitors who know Catalonia only from its 'international' Costa Brava resorts are unlikely to have sampled the true Catalan cuisine, apart from seafood, and will be pleasantly surprised by their discovery. All Spanish regions have their own specialities, few of which are available elsewhere, and Catalonia is no exception. In addition to the abundant supply of fish from the Mediterranean, the lush pastures of the Pyrenees and the hot fertile plains to the south ensure that Barcelona has direct access to a wide range of fresh produce.

Although the Moorish occupation of Barcelona was brief, the Arab taste for adding fruit and nuts to meat and fish plays an important part in Catalan food, as do unusual combinations of meat, fish and fowl, and the use of honey and unsweetened chocolate to thicken sauces.

Wild mushrooms may be found, even in mid-summer, although, naturally, the selection is much greater between autumn and spring: rovellones are the local favourite. During the cooler months game is plentiful, whilst fresh rabbit, generally served with a strong garlic sauce, appears on most menus throughout the year. A *calçotada* is held in many towns in the Tarragona region, particularly Valls, from January to May, the feature of which is the delicious large spring onions, barbecued over an open fire: eating the blackened vegetable without giving an impersonation of Al Jolson is quite an art, even though large bibs are provided. Coach parties to *calçotadas* are arranged from Barcelona in season – avoid Sundays which are too crowded.

Spanish charcuterie, particularly hams and sausages, is a revelation, certainly rivalling, if not surpassing, that of France or Italy. However, the province of Catalonia is not noted for its hams and the better varieties will almost certainly have come from elsewhere in Spain, particularly the exceptional Jamon Jabugo, possibly the finest cured ham in the world. Botifarra is a juicy pork sausage which will stir those English memories that can hark back to the years before the Second World War; they are generally accompanied by kidney beans cooked with garlic. When returning to England, Botifarra sausage from Palamós, Jamon Jabugo and Fuet de Vic (a long cured sausage eaten cold) are good buys, all available from the Boqueria market on La Rambla. Americans, not permitted to take home fresh produce, are able however to buy tinned foods, including varieties of shellfish, marinated in the delicious escabeche sauce; mussels or clams probably being the most favoured.

It is extraordinary that whilst neighbouring France produces hundreds of distinctive cheeses, almost every Spanish cheese that is readily available, no matter what its name, generally manages to taste of the ubiquitous Manchego. An old (viejo) Manchego can be very tangy but one does long for something different. A noteworthy exception to the rule is the delicious Cabrales, a blue cheese from Asturias with great character. Distinctive local cheeses, such as La Garrotxa from Gerona, exist, but are presumably made in small quantities, as they are rarely to be found in Barcelona. The only French cheeses usually available are Roquefort and Camembert. Cannes Bar, 4 Doctor Joaquim Pas (just north of Avinguda Catedral), specializes in Spanish cheeses, often providing an opportunity to taste up to thirty-five varieties. Handmade Catalan cheeses are sold in Placa del Pi at the artisans' market, on the first Friday in the month.

First courses in restaurants frequently comprise soups, often fish-based and, in summer, the iced gazpacho of Andalusia is added to the menu. Shellfish, in a seemingly endless variety, is the most favoured starter, although no longer cheap. Canelons, as may be guessed, is the Catalan version of canelloni, the pasta dish, and is claimed to be even finer than its Italian progenitor. Numerous fillings have been devised, one restaurant even going so far as to serve the dish with a truffle sauce. Luxury vegetables, such as avocado pear, asparagus and artichokes, are international favourites that are generally available in season. Charcuterie of all types forms another popular first course, generally accompanied by bread coated with tomato and sprinkled with oil and salt. (*Pa amb tomaquet.*)

Meat throughout Spain is excellent, generally much better than in France, although only specialized restaurants in Barcelona offer the suckling pig or baby lamb, which are features of menus in Castile. Roast kid, however, is often to be found. While pork is uniformly tasty, the most sensational meat is fillet steak from the toro de lidia (fighting bull). Uniquely, this combines tenderness and strong flavour, and is the finest steak that I have ever eaten. Certainly, the best 'speciality' steak restaurants in London and Paris cannot match it, in spite of 'genuine Aberdeen Angus' and 'well-hung' claims. Spain provides one of the last European outposts of the free-range chicken and, although not up to the supreme standard set by Portugal, the birds retain an 'old-fashioned' flavour. They may be spit-roasted and purchased to take away, whole or in sections; Barcelona's finest chickens come from Prat.

Seafood, as might be imagined in a great port, plays an important role in the city's cuisine, and Barcelona offers the full range of specialities, not only from the Mediterranean, but from Galicia and the Basque country, where it is based on the cold-water fish from the Bay of Biscay. Dried salt-cod, imported from Norway, is a surprising favourite, found throughout the Iberian peninsula, and many Catalan methods of preparing it have evolved. Zarzuela, a Mediterranean fish stew flavoured with herbs, is possibly the most typical Catalan marine dish, whilst Paella Parellada, although similar to the usual Paella Valenciana, is made easier for the diner by the removal of shells and bones. Fish is often accompanied by Romesco, a 'secret' sauce from the Tarragona region, based on crushed pine nuts, peppers and tomatoes.

Whilst Barcelona's markets stock a vast range of fruit and vegetables, as throughout most of continental Europe, only a very limited variety is offered in catering establishments. 'We don't pay good money in a restaurant to be served a load of vegetables' explained a puzzled Catalan friend. The Englishman, used to his meat and two or more veg may, therefore, feel deprived. Potatoes are rarely offered and when they are, generally take the form of chips. White beans seem to be the favourite vegetable served in restaurants.

Desserts are less than exciting throughout Spain, and while there are a few Catalan specialities the selection is very limited. Rare is the menu that doesn't offer Crema Catalana, a large crème brûlée, with a caramelized crust that can adopt, if well burned, a slight flavour of kippers – quite a culinary surprise! Fresh cheese with honey, and an almond-milk pudding flavoured with cinnamon, just about round off the short list of local specialities. Ice-creams are generally very good, being naturally flavoured and sweetened.

Without doubt, Catalan bakers produce some of the finest bread in the world, but for some reason it never seems to get into even the most luxurious restaurants, rolls or the standard baguette being the rule. A magnificent and economical al fresco lunch can be had by obtaining, for example, a small onion-flavoured loaf of bread from the baker to accompany a slice of Cabrales cheese and some Serrano ham. The many saints' days celebrated in Barcelona are each marked by a special type of pastry that is available at no other time, and they will be displayed in the bakers' shop windows throughout the city. Apart from these, it cannot be said that cakes and pastries in general throughout Spain have the interest of those found in the French- and German-speaking countries of Europe; the same may also be said of confectionery.

Most of Barcelona's luxurious restaurants are to be found in the Eixample, clustering conveniently round the commercial areas where their business-lunch clientele is based. The old city also has a few restaurants in the upper price bracket, but most are economical and aimed to serve the tourists and shoppers rather than those with a hefty expense account. It is also, of course, where the oldest-established restaurants, most of which specialize in traditional Catalan dishes, are to be found.

While lunch is rarely taken before two o'clock, most Barcelonans eat dinner rather earlier than elsewhere in Spain, many of them sitting at about nine o'clock, a good hour before their counterparts in Madrid. On Sunday, particularly in summer, it is *most* fashionable to eat lunch in one of the fish restaurants in Barceloneta: practically all of these will be closed Sunday evening. Most Barcelona restaurants shut for lengthy periods in summer.

Catalans do not regard tapas (small portions of food served in bars) as highly as other Spaniards, always preferring three-course meals, generally consumed twice a day. However, most bars in the city do provide food of some sort and there are enough non-Catalans to ensure that they are busy. If a large portion of tapas is required it is necessary to demand a 'racion'. Unfortunately, with the dramatic rise in the price of shellfish, the major component of a good tapas selection, it is no longer a particularly cheap way of eating, and care must be taken by those on a tight budget. Two linking streets in the city centre, Carrer d'Avinyó and Carrer de la Mercè specialize in tapas bars, the latter in particular, and a tremendous range is on offer. A word of warning: the Catalan taste is for heavy seasoning, and salt should never be added until the dish has been tasted; this is particularly so in tapas bars where, it has been suggested, the proprietors have found that saltier food promotes higher drink sales.

Although Barcelona's street names and signs have now been standardized in the Catalan language, the same does not apply to menus. Roughly, the higher class the establishment the more likely it is that the menu will be displayed in Catalan, and without a Spanish version. Conversely, cheaper restaurants, tapas bars and bodegas practically always display menus in Spanish. To avoid this dichotomy becoming a nightmare for the visitor, I have included separate Catalan and Spanish vocabularies of restaurant terminology at the end of this section. There are, of course, omissions, but in general this will enable anyone without a knowledge of either language to order most dishes without confusion. Emphasis is given to local specialities, and to the bewildering variety of seafood.

The restaurants described in the following pages have been selected so that all categories are represented. There are many hundreds of establishments in the city; obviously I have only visited a small percentage of them and the inquisitive visitor will no doubt discover outstanding examples that have been omitted. Emphasis is given to the old city, as this is where tourists will spend most of their time. Some of the restaurants referred to specialize in regional cuisines, particularly Basque and Galician, and the visitor is recommended to take the opportunity of sampling some of these dishes; the establishments featured all provide menu translations. As in France, the most economical restaurants often expect the diner to use the same knife and fork for the first two courses.

**Drink**
*Wine*
Catalonia is one of the top wine-producing provinces of Spain, more méthode champenoise sparkling wine being bottled here, for example, than anywhere else in the world, including France. It is Catalan wines that visitors are almost certain to drink most of the time during their stay in Barcelona, as, apart from sherry and rioja, few from other regions of Spain are widely stocked. Cava probably holds the greatest interest for visitors, as it provides the opportunity of drinking champagne-type wine much more economically than elsewhere. Most will prefer the brut (dry) version, although the Spanish seem very fond of the semi-sweet pink, known as rosada. It must be said that even the best cavas lack that unique, slightly dusty aroma provided by French champagne but they can be very enjoyable and certainly make lethal cocktails when combined with heady Spanish brandy. There are many cavistas, including the internationally known Cordoniú and Freixenet. Juve y Camps and Raimat are other reliable names to look for. Cavas come from the Penedès region and it is here also that the majority of Catalan table wines are produced: dry, sweet, white, red and rosé. As with most things, price is a good indication of quality. Recommended whites are produced by Marquès de Monistrol, Jean Leon Chardonnay and Marquès de Alella from the Alella region. Maria Bach Viña Extrísima Reserva, De Casta, Sangre de Toro and Gran Coronas Etiqueta Negra are all formidable reds.

*Beer*
Spanish continental-type lager is always available, draught or

bottled, and some of the more expensive bars also hold a range of foreign beers, including British. Draught Guinness from Dublin, at not too high a mark up, is sold in some of the Plaça Reial beer houses.

*Spirits, liqueurs and apéritifs*
Virtually all overseas brands, apart from Scotch, are made in Spain, no matter what the label may at first glance imply. This dates back to the Franco period when, short of overseas currency, the Spanish forbade the import of foreign goods, forcing their manufacturers either to set up production units in Spain or forgo the market. The results were rarely a success, possibly due to variations in the water. A blind testing of most well-known brands of gin, white rum or vodka would leave many visitors foxed as to what spirit they were drinking, yet alone the brand. However, *Negrita* is a very drinkable rum, of medium colour, and the better bars now stock the higher-priced *Tanqueray* gin, imported from England, which is, for easily guessed reasons, indistinguishable from the Gordon's Gin that is made in the UK.

French and Italian brands of liqueurs and apéritifs suffer a similar fate, generally being slightly sweeter and lacking the character of the original. Campari (made in Barcelona) is, however, a fairly good impersonation. Even sherry (Jerez or Xeres), undoubtedly a Spanish drink, often appears to be made to a lower alcoholic strength than the exported version – it is, however, more acceptable in this form as an accompaniment to food.

*Brandy*
As cava is not champagne, brandy is not cognac, but in all fairness it has never pretended to be. In general, Spanish brandies are heavy and tend to sweetness, some from the south even developing a thick caramelized flavour. Lovers of French brandy will probably prefer a 103 (ciento tres), the Torres range or, lightest of all, the locally produced Mascaro. It is common in a bar to ask for a 'carajillo', which involves pouring a generous slug of brandy into black coffee. A combination of brandy and anisette in equal measures is a *sol y sombra* (sun and shadow).

*Alcoholic long drinks*
Ask a foreigner what he knows about Spanish drinks and he will probably mention Sangria, which originated in the Costa Brava. Consisting basically of orange juice, red wine and brandy, care is generally taken to ensure that tourist versions are not too overwhelming. Cremat, basically rum and lemon served with coffee beans as a very hot punch, is a splendid late-night comforter, probably at its best supped with fishermen on a quiet Costa Brava beach, not too many paces from bed.

*Non-alcoholic long drinks*
In summer, the Spanish soft drink specialities suddenly appear, having been replaced in the cooler months by hot chocolate and coffee. Try the horchata (or orxata), a sweet milk shake based on ground tiger nuts (chufa) and served just below freezing point. It is delicious, thirst quenching and incredibly high in calories. Weight-watchers are probably better advised to concentrate on granizadas made from fruit syrups or coffee, drunk with a straw through crushed ice. As is general in continental Europe, soft drinks are much better than their British equivalents, tastes are more natural and artificial sweeteners unknown.

*Hot drinks*
Although it is still difficult to get a sufficiently strong cup of tea outside the British Isles, things are marginally better in Catalonia than elsewhere, probably due to the long-established British demand in the Costa Brava resorts. 'English' tea is available in most supermarkets, but the importance of immediately using boiling water is not always appreciated by caterers. Coffee is pretty uniform, always expresso, as in France, but at least flavoursome. Nowhere are instant varieties offered. Hot chocolate is usually very thick, sometimes almost like a hot chocolate mousse. Spaniards in general like to dip their breakfast churros (long crisp strips of deep-fried dough) in the chocolate, but the Barcelonan appears to prefer a simple croissant and coffee for his start to the day.

## Restaurants

LUXURY RESTAURANTS – OVER 7,000 PESETAS

1 **Cuineta (La)** (map page 3, 29, 55, 70) *4 c del Paradis (315 01 11)*
Converted from an antique shop in 1981, Catalan cuisine with a modern touch, particularly innovative sauces, is served.
*Specialities:* artichoke pâté, truffled goose liver, duck with pears.

2 **Gran Café (El)** (map page 28, 54, 70, 90) *9 c d'Avinyó (318 79 86)*
*Closed Sunday.*
Catalan food served in a turn-of-the-century setting.
*Specialities:* fresh cod with snails, gourmet set menu.

3 **Neichel** (map page 169) *16 bis av de Pedralbes (203 84 08)*
*Closed Sunday.*
An outstanding restaurant in Barcelona's most fashionable residential area. French cuisine is featured.
*Specialities:* lobster, home-made pasta.

4 **Orotava** (map page 148, 158) *335 c del Consell de Cent (302 31 28)*
*Closed Sunday.*
Founded in 1930, classical French and Catalan cuisine is served in luxurious surroundings.
*Specialities:* game, venison, fish 'Cobonoff' (marinated in cava).

5 **Quo Vadis** (map page 28, 54, 70, 90) *7 c del Carme (317 74 47)*
*Closed Sunday.*
Generally rated the old city's finest restaurant, outstanding Rioja wines are served in Burgundy-style balloon glasses.
*Specialities:* fighting bull fillet steak, wild mushrooms, fresh foie gras, bass with fennel, sucking pig, baby lamb.

6 **Reno** (map page 148) *27 c Tuset (200 91 29)*
*Closed Saturday.*
Barcelona's highest-rated restaurant and one of the best in Spain, the cuisine remains basically international, but with increasing Catalan emphasis in recent years.
*Specialities:* the menu Reno, from which six of the restaurant's dishes may be sampled: available at lunch or dinner, for its quality it is a bargain; canelloni, smoked salmon.

7 **Via Veneto** (no map page) *10–12 c Ganduxer (200 70 44)*
Art-nouveau style elegance provides the surroundings for the

diner in this restaurant, that rates second only in Barcelona to Reno.
*Specialities:* the humble Botifarra sausage at its definitive best, stuffed pigs' trotters with wild mushroom sauce.

EXPENSIVE RESTAURANTS – 4,500–6,000 PESETAS

**8** **Amaya** (map page 110) *20–24 La Rambla (302 10 37)*
One of the city's liveliest restaurants, particularly Sunday lunchtime. An excellent tapas bar fronts the three dining-rooms. Perfectly translated menu in English (the work of the author of this book!).
*Specialities:* Basque dishes, Gerona duck with prunes, bream cooked '*à la donostiarra*' (in a Basque oven), txakoli, a dry white wine with a pink tinge that gives it the appearance of a very large pink gin.

**9** **Brasserie Flo** (map page 71, 91) *10 c Jonqueres (317 80 47)*
A sister establishment to the Paris brasserie of the same name, Barcelona's version offers many of the Paris specialities but the dining-room is much more austere – no Belle Epoque here. French cuisine with some Catalan touches.
*Specialities:* salmon *en rillettes*, game, bouillabaisse, profiteroles with hot chocolate sauce and ice-cream.

**10** **Cal Pinxo** (map page 184) *10 ptja Sant Miquel, Barceloneta (310 45 13)*
*Closed Sunday evening.*
A famous beach-side fish restaurant, absolutely packed Sunday lunchtime. To me, the quality of the fish offered seems to be uniformly high in Barceloneta, but I am assured by connoisseurs that this is one of the best.
*Specialities:* rice dishes, paella parrellada, squid.

**11** **Casa Bach** (map page 136, 149) *15 pl Revolució de setembre 1868 (213 30 44)*
*Closed Thursday and Sunday evening.*
For those unwilling to travel to Valls, in Tarragona province, this restaurant provides an opportunity to taste the famous *calçots de Valls* (spring onions) barbecued on an open grill (January to May only).
*Specialities: calçots*, veal and mushrooms.

**12** **Casa Costa** (map page 184) *124 c del Baluard, Barceloneta (319 50 28)*
*Closed Sunday evening.*
Generally the top-rated Barceloneta restaurant. Fine marine views from its first-floor dining-room – try to reserve a window table.
*Specialities:* paella, zarzuela, seafood stews.

**13** **Casa Leopoldo** (map page 90, 110) *24 c Sant Rafael (241 30 14)*
*Closed Sunday evening and Monday.*
Formerly a bodega, Señor Leopoldo converted the beamed and tiled area to a restaurant in 1929 and, now in his nineties, continues to survey his customers with a benevolent eye.
*Specialities:* fried fish, pan parillada-bread toasted, with tomato, ham and anchovies.

14 **Casimiro** (no map page) *84 c Londres (410 30 93)*
   *Closed Sunday.*
   A varied menu, but with fish dominant.
   *Specialities:* lobster in cava, roast beef with port.

15 **Dorada (La)** (map page 148) *44–46 trav de Gràcia (200 63 22)*
   *Closed Sunday.*
   This is a branch of the chain of gourmet fish restaurants, now
   represented in several Spanish cities – and Paris.
   *Specialities:* Gilt-head fish baked in salt.

16 **Eldorado Petit** (no map page) *51 c Dolors Montserda (204 51
   53)*
   Nouvelle cuisine is applied to French and Catalan dishes and
   many consider this to be the finest restaurant in Barcelona
   outside the luxury bracket.
   *Specialities:* Palamós prawns, stuffed peppers, seafood stews.

17 **Gorria** (map page 159) *421 c de la Diputació (245 11 64)*
   *Closed Sunday.*
   One of the finest regional restaurants.
   *Specialities:* Navarre and Basque dishes, particularly fish.

18 **Guría** (map page 148, 158) *97–99 c Casanova (253 63 25)*
   The city's most important Basque restaurant.
   *Specialities:* hot crab in its shell, green peppers stuffed with
   squid.

19 **Hostal del Sol** (map page 136, 149, 158) *44 pas de Gràcia
   (215 62 25)*
   *Closed Sunday evening.*
   International and Catalan food is served in this smart, first-
   floor restaurant overlooking Passeig de Gràcia.
   *Specialities:* rare duck breasts with tarragon, artichoke hearts
   with seafood and caviar sauce, salt cod in spicy pil-pil sauce.

20 **Jaume de Provença** (no map page) *88 c de Provença (230 00 29)*
   *Closed Sunday evening and Monday.*
   Clinically cool ambience for nouvelle cuisine variations to
   traditional Catalan and international dishes.
   *Specialities:* salmon, duck foie gras, set gourmet menus,
   desserts, French cheeses.

21 **Odisea (La)** (map page 29, 55, 70, 91) *7c Copons (302 36 92)*
   *Closed Sunday.*
   Noted for its unique cuisine, combining French and Catalan
   dishes.
   *Specialities:* marinated fish, rabbit stuffed with apples and
   honey allioli.

22 **Puñaláda (La)** (map page 136, 149) *104 pas de Gràcia (218 47 91)*
   This traditional style restaurant was established in 1918 and
   continues to serve fine Catalan dishes.
   *Specialities:* turbot in Chartreuse sauce, wild mushrooms,
   botifarra sausage.

23 **Perols de l'Empordà (Els)** (map page 148, 158) *88 c Villaroel
   (323 10 33)*
   *Closed Sunday and Monday.*
   Cuisine from the Empordà region of Catalonia.
   *Specialities:* black rice, botifarra Perols.

24 **Roig Robi** (map page 149) *20 c Séneca (218 92 92)*
*Closed Sunday.*
Catalan cuisine is served on the terrace in summer.
*Specialities:* hake Rob Roig, black rice, noodles.

25 **Via Claris** (map page 136, 149, 158) *2 ptge de Permanyer (318 36 08)*
Imagine dining outside in a Spanish version of a Chelsea mews – plus palm trees. This is the chief attraction of Via Claris, and the food is good too.
*Specialities:* sole with three sauces, salt cod with honey and nuts, dessert crêpes.

MEDIUM PRICE RESTAURANTS – 2,500–3,500 PESETAS

26 **Can Culleretes** (map page 28, 54, 70, 110) *5 c Quintana (317 64 85)*
*Closed Sunday evening and Monday.*
Founded as a sweet shop in 1786, this claims to be Barcelona's oldest established restaurant – don't be put off by the 'girls' outside, they will not cause embarrassment. No concessions to modern food fads are made, virtually everything is traditional Catalan home cooking.
*Specialities:* rabbit, Botifarra sausage, veal and mushroom stew, pigs' trotters, plats du jour.

27 **Caracoles (Los)** (map page 28, 54, 70, 90) *14 c dels Escudellers (302 31 85)*
*Service until midnight.*
Very picturesque and very popular, this is the Barcelona restaurant that every visitor must go to – at least once. Outside, the chickens turn on the spits, their aroma making them hard to resist. Within, on two levels, photographs of internationally famous clients decorate the walls; they often include the restaurant's late patron, Bofarull, evidently a man of great character, who is also depicted in a large bacchanalian mural. Habitués lament that Los Caracoles is not what it was during his lifetime. A table in the gallery overlooking the chefs at work is much sought after, but the restaurant is not air-conditioned and in summer the heat can be overpowering at this level.
*Specialities:* snails, spit-roast chicken, paella, mussels.

28 **Casa Joan** (map page 110) *12–14 La Rambla (301 10 89)*
An undistinguished interior, but good value for money considering its tourist location at this, the port end of La Rambla.
*Specialities:* outstanding Jabugo ham, garlic soup, black rice.

29 **Camembert (El Vel)** (map page 148) *272–74 c Còrsega*
*Closed Sunday.*
Fronted by a tapas bar, the restaurant, as its name implies, concentrates on cheese dishes.
*Specialities:* raclette, fondue, canelloni stuffed with fish and cabrales cheese, cheese board.

30 **Egipte** (map page 90, 110) *12 c Jerusalem (317 74 80)*
Behind Boqueria market, this bistro-style restaurant serves good-value food to a bohemian clientele.
*Specialities:* Catalan dishes, an unusually innovative dessert list.

**31 Garduña (La)** (map page 90, 110) *19 c Morera (302 43 23)*
*Closed Sunday.*
Another economically priced restaurant behind the Boqueria
market.
*Specialities:* ham, zarzuela.

**32 Henry J Bean's** (map page 148) *14–16 c La Granada del Penedès (213 29 98)*
*Service continues until 01.00 but on Friday and Saturday extends to 01.30.*
Lovers of American food will find that the ubiquitous Mr Bean
here serves almost identical food to that in his other
establishments.
*Specialities:* chilli con carne, pizzas, barbecued spare ribs.

**33 Reco de l'Arnau** (map page 110) *21 c Tàpies (329 81 53)*
*Closed Monday lunch.*
A pianist entertains nightly and on Saturday there is a cabaret,
when a set meal is served – then of little interest to non-Spaniards.
*Specialities:* charcoal grills, cream of garlic soup, stuffed squid.

**34 Retiro (El)** (map page 148) *200 c Paris (237 78 43)*
*Closed Saturday.*
A good-value restaurant offering Galician as well as Catalan
dishes.
*Specialities:* Jabugo ham (bellota), selected sausages, very
economical set lunch.

**35 Set Portes** (map page 71, 91) *14 pas d'Isabel 11 (319 30 33)*
Food is served daily, throughout the year, non-stop 13.00–
01.00 – but it is still advisable to book. Set Portes (seven doors)
is a Barcelona showpiece that has been running since 1836.
Many Catalan dishes, particularly fish, are offered.
*Specialities:* paella Parellada (shells and bones removed), rice
dishes, Vic sausage (fuet).

INEXPENSIVE RESTAURANTS – BELOW 2,500 PESETAS

It is still easy to find a three-course lunch with wine in Barcelona for
as little as 600 pesetas in small restaurants, bars or bodegas; in the
evening expect to pay a little more. Standards seem to vary little,
but it is generally best to keep to simple dishes – can one expect a
gourmet experience from paella on a 600 peseta menu? Particularly
good value is offered along Carrer d'Avinyó, Carrer de la Mercè
and the two main streets of the Barri Xinès: Carrer de Sant Pau and
Carrer de Hospital. I also found that the bodega, Portalón, in the
heart of the Gothic Quarter, offered consistently good cheap food
in a bohemian 'Old Barcelona' atmosphere (see pages 99 and 216).

**36 Agut** (map page 55, 91) *16 c d'en Gignas (315 17 09)*
*Closed Sunday evening and Monday.*
I have never eaten in a better-value restaurant anywhere in the
world. How can Agut still (in 1989) offer a three-course à la
carte meal with wine, including smoked salmon and duck in
orange sauce, for less than 1,600 pesetas? Unfortunately,
everyone knows about it, and reservations are to be
recommended if dining later than 21.00 or at any time for
Sunday lunch – otherwise join the queue outside.
*Specialities:* plats du jour, chicken with prawns, preserved
(confit) goose, duck.

**37 Carriejas (Los)** (map page 71) *7 pl Sant Agustí Vell (319 53 99)*
*Closed Sunday evening, Monday (and when the proprietor feels
like it!).*
Set in one of Barcelona's prettiest old squares, it is hard to know
what to say about this one. I intended to eat there and the
patron's young daughter took my order, but after wasting forty
minutes at the incongruously 'woody' bar I was told that as
there were no other customers the restaurant was closed. In
spite of this, my two glasses of wine at the bar were not 'on the
house'. However, the menu seemed remarkably cheap and
others recommend it. Good luck!
*Specialities:* fish, particularly monkfish with romesco sauce.

**38 Morera (La)** (map page 90, 110, 148) *1 pl Sant Agustí (318 75 55)*
An extremely smart little restaurant, particularly so
considering its value. Very friendly staff.
*Specialities:* ever-changing menu featuring fresh, seasonal
produce.

### Bars

Many gain the impression that Barcelona acquired its name due to
the multiplicity of bars in the city! Certainly it is possible to walk
through much of the old quarter and find that every other
establishment is offering alcoholic refreshment. The problem is
that most of them fall into the categories of seedy, girlie or luxury:
the 'typical' bars of gleaming mahogany, ceramic tiles and
decorative ironwork, found in such profusion in Seville, for
example, are rare. Virtually all, except cocktail bars, offer food of
some description. Most of the luxurious examples are really night
spots, with few customers before midnight. A great drawback to
most Spanish bars is that customers and staff alike find it hard to
keep their eyes off the mandatory television, with its bleak
repetition of sport, game-shows and dubbed foreign films. Don't
expect conversation, however good your Spanish. The following
television-free selection gives only a flavour but, hopefully,
includes the bars of most interest to visitors. Ask around for
current favourites as the situation is (excuse the second pun) fluid.
**Warning** It is now common for red wine to be served ice-cold in
Spanish bars. If the usual room temperature is preferred, always
specify *non frio* or *normal*.

**39 Amarcord** (map page 136, 149, 158) *92 pas de Gràcia (La
Pedrera building)*
Handy for visitors to Gaudí's masterpiece. Unusually, it is
lively mid afternoon.

**40 Azulete** (no map page) *281 Via Augusta*
Elegant, with a fine terrace. In addition to the bar there is a
restaurant, and charcuterie is sold to take away.

**41 Barcelona-Jabugo (Mesón)** (map page 148) *175 c de Paris
Open Monday–Saturday 09.00–01.00.*
Excellent charcuterie, particularly Jabugo ham.

**42 Bar Libreria Cristal-City** (map page 148) *294 c de Balmes*
As the name suggests, the establishment also sells books. Tapas
usually includes the famous Canary Islands ham – like York
ham but very tender and almost white in colour.

**43 Berimbau** (map page 71, 91, 185) *17 pas del Born*
A late-night bar specializing in Brazilian cocktails. Attractive
rear garden.

**44 Boadas** (map page 70, 90, 110) *1 c Tallers (La Rambla corner)*
The most popular cocktail bar in La Rambla.

**45 Casa Esteban** (map page 71, 91, 184) *22 c de Montcada*
*Closed mid-afternoon, Sunday evening and Monday.*
One of the prettiest old bars in the city and handy for the
Picasso museum. Its official name is not displayed. Fish tapas
predominate. Good cider. Described further on page 87.

**46 Cerveceria** (map page 70, 90) *127 La Rambla*
In spite of its humble name (meaning beer house) this bar offers
the most luxurious tapas selection in the city. Described further
on page 112.

**47 Folie (La)** (map page 136, 149) *169 c de Bailén*
Cava cocktails are a speciality. Attractive décor.

**48 Jijonenca (La)** (map page 148, 158) *35 rbla de Catalunya*
A smart establishment in one of the Eixample's most attractive
shopping streets. Delightful terrace on the central promenade.

**49 Mesón del Café** (map page 3, 29, 55, 70) *16 c de la Llibreria*
*Open 08.00–24.00. Closed Sunday.*
Although famed for its coffee, this is also a bar, the prettiest in
the city. Very small and toy-like. Fine selection of brandies.
Extremely limited food.

**50 Miramelindo** (map page 71, 91, 184) *15 pas del Born*
Late night bar, one of three in a row. Some food available.
Occasional jazz.

**51 Portalón** (map page 28) *20 c Banys Nous*
Barcelona's most picturesque bodega – under threat of
misguided renovation. Great atmosphere, remarkably good-
value meals or tapas. Described further on page 99.

**52 Santos Lugares** (map page 28, 54, 70, 90) *4 c Heures*
A dark, atmospheric basement bar: the seats were formerly
church pews.

**53 Taberna Escoceca** (map page 70, 90, 110) *3 c Sitges*
Several hundred brands of Scotch whisky are stocked, giving
this bar its nickname, 'the whisky museum'. Basically a night
spot.

**54 Velódromo** (map page 148) *213 c de Muntaner*
*Closed Sunday.*
Good tapas and, in the basement, bar billiards. Very busy late.

**55 Xampanyeria (La)** (map page 148, 158) *236 c de Provença*
Barcelona's first cava bar to open. A wide selection of local
wines, including cava, is available.

**56 Xampanyeria-unnamed** (map page 71, 91) *7 c Reina Cristina*
*Open 10.00–22.00 non-stop but closed Sunday.*
Do not miss this one – it is unique. Dry, brut cava is sold at 55
pesetas a glass (1989) and nowhere else can this price be
matched. Charcuterie, grilled behind the bar, is served in
sandwiches. Described further on page 96.

**57 Zurich** (map page 70, 90, 110) *35 pl de Catalunya*
This is where Barcelonans sit on the vast terrace and watch the
world go by. Not the cheapest spot to imbibe, but bills are far
lower than its French or Italian equivalents.

## Night spots

**58 Bagdad** (map page 110) *103 c Nou de la Rambla*
Pure (or impure) porn, some of the most explicit in Europe.
Shows at 23.00 and 01.30. Described further on page 130.

**59 Distrito Distinto** (no map page) *140 av Meridiana*
Delightful terrace. A favourite disco for the trendy younger
set.

**60 Otto Zutz** (map page 148) *13 c de Lincoln*
Very up market – only the smartest gain entry, often following
a lengthy queue, particularly at weekends.

**61 Regine's** (map page 168) *pl Pius XII*
Entered from the west side of the Princessa Sofia hotel,
Regine's follows its successful international formula. Non-
members must look affluent to gain entry. Expensive.

**62 Scala** (map page 149, 159) *47–49 pas Sant Joan*
Superb cabaret, catering for an international clientele. Two
sessions: cabaret and dinner, cabaret and dancing (from
midnight).

**63 Studio 54** (map page 110) *54 av del Paral-lel*
All the modern disco techniques are employed. In summer,
frenetic dancers can cool off in the pool.

**64 Tarantos (Los)** (map page 28, 54, 70, 90) *17 pl Reial (317 80 98)*
Catalonia is not noted for flamenco dancing, an Andalusian
speciality, but as more southerners have moved to the city and
to meet tourist demand, flamenco shows are increasing – this is
one of the most authentic. Best to reserve.

**65 Up and Down** (map page 169) *179 c Numància*
Undoubtedly Barcelona's smartest venue. Gentlemen must
wear a jacket and tie if dining in the second-floor restaurant:
disco for younger clients below. Expensive.

## Food Vocabulary
*Catalan*
*indicates a Catalan speciality

| | |
|---|---|
| Albercoc | Apricot |
| Albergínies | Aubergine |
| Allioli | garlic and oil dressing frequently, but incorrectly, incorporates eggs, when it is then similar to the Provençal aïoli |
| Amanida | salad |
| Ametlla | almond |
| Ananas | pineapple |
| Anxoves | anchovies |
| Anec | duck |
| Anyell | lamb |
| Areng | smoked herring |
| Arròs amb llet | rice pudding |
| Arròs de peix | rice with fish |
| *Arròs negre | rice cooked in black cuttlefish ink with various fish; from Ampordà |
| Arròs Xat | rice cooked with stewed fish |
| Avellana | hazel nut |
| Aviram | poultry |
| Avocat | avocado pear |
| Bacallà | salted dried cod (Norwegian) |

| | |
|---|---|
| Bacallà fresc | fresh cod |
| *Bacallà a la Llauna | salt cod with garlic and paprika |
| Bisbe | black pudding |
| Boles de Picolat | meat balls |
| *Bolets | mushrooms |
| Bou | beef |
| Bullit | boiled |
| *Botifarra | lean pork sausage, only seasoned with salt and pepper: particularly renowned from Palamós |
| Cabrit | kid |
| Caca | game |
| Calamar | squid |
| Calamars farcits amb salsa de xocolata | stuffed squid with chocolate sauce (unsweetened) |
| *Calçot | large, sweet spring onion blackened over an open fire |
| Calent | hot |
| *Canalons | filled rolls of pasta with sauce, as the Italian canelloni |
| Cansalada | streaky bacon |
| Cap i Pota | stewed calf's head and foot (like brawn) |
| Cargols | snails; from Lleida |
| Carn | meat |
| Castanya | chestnut |
| Ceba | onion |
| Cervell | brains |
| Cérvol | venison |
| Cigales | small crayfish, 'Mediterranean prawns' |
| Cigrons | chick peas |
| Cirera | cherry |
| Ciureny | 'cepe' mushrooms |
| Coc | coconut |
| Coca | flat pizza, savoury or sweet |
| Cogombre | cucumber |
| Col | cabbage |
| Colom | pigeon |
| Conill | rabbit |
| Cor | heart |
| Costella | cutlet |
| Cranc de mar | crab |
| *Crema Catalana | vanilla custard with caramelized sugar crust: similar to French crème brûlée |
| Cremat | burnt (or a punch) |
| Datil | date |
| Enciam | lettuce |
| *Escalivada | baked aubergines, peppers and onions, sprinkled with garlic and usually served cold |
| Escarxofa | artichoke |
| *Escudella de payes | white beans, cabbage and charcuterie |
| *Escudella i carn d'olla | served as two courses: noodle soup followed by meat, potatoes and sausage |
| Espinac | spinach |
| *Esqueixada | salad with shredded salt cod |
| *Estofat de bou | stewed beef |

| | |
|---|---|
| Faisa | pheasant |
| Farcellet | pork and cabbage dumpling |
| *Faves a la Catalana | broad beans, pork, black pudding |
| Fetge | liver |
| Fideos en cazuela | noodle soup with sausage, pork and grated cheese |
| Figa | fig |
| Filet | steak |
| Formatge | cheese |
| Fideus | thin pasta in the form of short noodles |
| Forn (al) | baked |
| Fred | cold |
| *Fricando | veal stew with mushrooms and vegetables |
| Fruita | fruit |
| *Fuet | long dry thin sausage, a speciality from Vic, eaten cold |
| Fumat | smoked |
| Galldindi | turkey |
| Gamba | prawn |
| *Garrotxa | goat cheese from Gerona |
| Gel | ice |
| Gelat | ice-cream |
| Gerdó | raspberry |
| Guatlla | quail |
| Julivert | parsley |
| Lima | lime |
| Llagosta | spiny lobster or large crayfish |
| Llagostí | large prawn |
| Llebre | hare |
| Llegum | vegetable |
| Llenguado | sole |
| Llenties | lentils |
| Llet | milk |
| Llimona | lemon |
| Llobarro | sea bass |
| Llobina | haddock |
| Llonza | chop |
| Lluc | hake |
| Maduixa | strawberry |
| Mahonesa | mayonnaise |
| Mangle | mango |
| *Mar i Muntanya | chicken and prawn ragoût |
| Mantega | butter |
| Mariscos | shellfish |
| *Music | nuts and dried fruit |
| Manxego | ewes' milk cheese, varies in strength and texture with age |
| *Mel i mato | honey and fresh cheese |
| Mena de torrons | nougat |
| *Menjar blanc | almond paste, milk and cinnamon |
| *Mongetes | beans |
| Mostassa | mustard |
| Muscó | mussel |
| Nap | turnip |
| Nata | whipped cream |
| Nou | walnut |

| | |
|---|---|
| Oca | goose |
| Oli | oil |
| Oliva | olive |
| Orada | gilt-head (fish) |
| Ostra | oyster |
| Ou | egg |
| | |
| Pa | bread |
| *Pa amb tomaquet | both sides of bread rubbed with tomato, sprinkled with olive oil and salt |
| Paella | saffron rice, cooked with fish, meat, shellfish, vegetables |
| *Paella Parellada | as above, but with all shells and bones removed |
| Panet | bread roll |
| Pansa | raisin |
| Pastanaga | carrot |
| Patata | potato |
| Patates fregides | fried potatoes (chips) |
| Pebre | pepper |
| Peix | fish |
| Peix espasa | swordfish |
| Pera | pear |
| Perdiu | partridge |
| Pernil | ham (for Serrano and Jabugo ham description see Spanish listing under Jamon) |
| Pèsol | pea |
| Peus de porc | pig's trotters |
| Petxina | clam |
| Pintada | guinea fowl |
| Pinyol | pine-nut |
| Plàtan | banana |
| Pollastre | chicken |
| Pollastre al ast | spit-roasted chicken |
| Poma | apple |
| Poncem | grapefruit |
| Pop | octopus |
| Popets | baby octopus |
| Porc | pork |
| Porc senglar | wild boar |
| Postres | desserts |
| Préssec | peach |
| Pruna | plum |
| Pruna seca | prune |
| | |
| Raïm | raisin or grape |
| Rap | monkfish |
| Rave | radish |
| Refresc | any cold non-alcoholic drink |
| Remolatxa | beetroot |
| *Romesco | sauce with Moorish origins, speciality of Tarragona: almonds, pine-nuts, dried sweet peppers and tomatoes |
| Ronyo | kidneys |
| Rostit a la graella | grilled |
| *Rovellone | wild mushroom |
| | |
| Salsa | sauce |

| | |
|---|---|
| Salsitxe | long thin sausage eaten cold, or small sausage |
| Saltejats | sautéed |
| *Sarsuela | mixed fish and shellfish cooked in deep pan with almonds, parsley, herbs, sherry, rum: speciality of the Costa Brava |
| Setas | mushrooms |
| Sipia | cuttlefish |
| *Sobrassada | soft sausage-spread from Majorca |
| *Sofregit | onion and tomato sauce |
| Sopa | soup |
| Sopa de peix amb fideos | fish soup with noodles |
| *Suquet de peix | seafood stew with onions, tomatoes and potatoes, a Costa Dorada speciality |
| Suc | juice |
| Sucre | sugar |
| Surenis | wild 'cepe' mushrooms |
| | |
| Tapes | tapas |
| Taronja | orange |
| Tiller | lime |
| Tomaquet | tomato |
| Tonyina | tuna |
| Torrada | toast |
| Tripa | tripe |
| Truita | omelette or trout |
| | |
| Vapor | steam |
| Vedella | veal |
| Verat | mackerel |
| Verd | green |
| Verduras | vegetables |
| Vieira | scallop |
| | |
| Xai | lamb |
| *Xamfaïna | Catalan version of ratatouille |
| Xirivia | parsnip |
| Xocolata | chocolate |
| Xorisso | see Spanish listing as chorizo |

*Spanish (Castilian)*

| | |
|---|---|
| Aceite | oil |
| Aguacate | avocado pear |
| Ahumada | smoked |
| Ajillo | garlic |
| Albaricoque | apricot |
| Albóndigas | meat balls |
| Alcachofas | artichokes |
| Almejas | clams |
| Almendras | almonds |
| Arana | spider crab |
| Arenque | smoked herring |
| Arroz | rice |
| Atún | tunny fish |
| Avellana | hazelnut |
| Aves | poultry |
| | |
| Bacalao | dried and salted cod |
| Bacalao fresco | fresh cod |
| Berberecho | cockles |
| Biftek | steak |

| | |
|---|---|
| Bocadillo | sandwich |
| Bogavante | lobster |
| Boquerones | fresh anchovies fried |
| Butifarra | pork sausage |
| Caballa | mackerel |
| Cabrales | blue goats milk cheese from Asturias, with a strong flavour; probably the most characterful Spanish cheese generally available |
| Cabrito | kid |
| Calamares | squid |
| Caldo gallego | a light soup; generally inspired cabbage water |
| Callos | tripe |
| Carne | meat |
| Camarónes | tiny shrimps |
| Cangrejo | crab or crayfish |
| Cangrejo de mar | seawater crayfish |
| Cangrejo de rio | freshwater crayfish |
| Caracoles | snails |
| Castaña | chestnut |
| Cebolla | onion |
| Cerdo | pork |
| Cereza | cherry |
| Champiñon | mushroom |
| Chanquetes | whitebait |
| Chipirones | baby octopus |
| Chorizo | spicy sausage, eaten cold, or hot in stews; sometimes made with chillis and then very fiery |
| Cigalas | small crayfish, 'Mediterranean prawns' |
| Ciruela | plum or prune |
| Coco | coconut |
| Conejo | rabbit |
| Corazón | heart |
| Cordero | lamb |
| Dátil | date |
| Dorada | gilt-head (fish) |
| Embutido | varied sausages |
| Ensalada | salad (variada – mixed, sin tomates– green) |
| Entremèses variados | hors d'oeuvres |
| Escabeche | marinade of oil, vinegar and herbs: usually for preserving fish or poultry |
| Espárragos | asparagus |
| Espinacas | spinach |
| Fabada (Asturiana) | casserole of butter beans, pork, chorizo and spicy black pudding |
| Filete | fillet (meat) |
| Frambuesa | raspberry |
| Fresa | strawberry |
| Frio | cold |
| Gamba | prawn |
| Gazpacho | iced soup: tomato, cucumber, olive oil, vinegar, garlic, pimento and croûtons: speciality of Andalusia |

| | |
|---|---|
| Haba | broad bean |
| Hamburguesa | hamburger |
| Higado | liver |
| Higos | fig |
| Horno (al) | baked |
| Huevos | eggs: duro – hard, escalfado – poached, frito – fried, revuelto – scrambled |
| Huevos a la Valenciana | fried eggs with peas, tomato, chorizo, asparagus, red pepper, diced ham |
| | |
| Jamón | ham |
| Jamón en dulce (or York) | boiled ham |
| Jamón Jabugo | the best Serrano ham: wild boar and domestic pig are cross-bred. Those fed exclusively on belottas (acorns) are considered the finest. Many are matured for several years. |
| Jamón Serrano | lean, dry-cured ham |
| Judia | bean |
| Judia verde | green bean |
| | |
| Langosta | spiny lobster or large crayfish |
| Langostino | large prawn |
| Leche | milk |
| Lechon | sucking pig |
| Lechuga | lettuce |
| Legumbres | vegetables |
| Lenguado | sole |
| Lentejas | lentils |
| Lima | lime |
| Limón | lemon |
| Lliebre | hare |
| Lomo | loin |
| Lubina | sea bass |
| | |
| Manchego | ewes' milk cheese; varies in strength and texture with age |
| Mantequilla | butter |
| Manzana | apple |
| Mariscos | seafood |
| Mejillones | mussels |
| Melocotón | peach |
| Merluza | hake |
| Miel | honey |
| Morcilla | spicy blood pudding |
| Mostaza | mustard |
| | |
| Naranja | orange |
| Nata | whipped cream |
| | |
| Oliva | olive |
| Ostra | oyster |
| | |
| Paella | see Catalan listing |
| Paella mariscos | paella made with seafood only |
| Pan | bread |
| Parrilla (a la) | grilled |
| Patatas | potatoes |
| Patatas fritas | fried potatoes (chips) |
| Pato | duck |

| | |
|---|---|
| Pavo | turkey |
| Pepino | cucumber |
| Pescado | fish |
| Pez espada | swordfish |
| Pimienta | pepper |
| Pina | pineapple |
| Pinchito | kebab |
| Plancha (à la) | grilled on a hot plate |
| Platano | banana |
| Platos combinados | dish of several components at an inclusive price |
| Poco hecho | rare, e.g. steak |
| Pollo | chicken |
| Pollo asado | roast chicken |
| Pomelo | grapefruit |
| Postres | desserts |
| Pulpito | baby octopus |
| Pulpo | octopus |
| Puréde patatas | mashed potatoes |
| Queso | cheese |
| Rape | monkfish |
| Raya | skate |
| Repollo | cabbage |
| Riñones | kidneys |
| Rodaballo | turbot |
| Romana (à la) | fried in batter |
| Sal | salt |
| Salchicha | pork sausage |
| Salmonete | red mullet |
| Salsa | sauce |
| Salsichón | hard salami-type sausage, eaten cold |
| Sépia | cuttlefish |
| Sesos | brains |
| Solomillo | sirloin steak |
| Sopa | soup |
| Sopa de ajo | soup of garlic, paprika, bread |
| Ternera | veal |
| Tocino | streaky bacon |
| Tortilla | plain omelette |
| Tortilla Española | 'Spanish' omelette, with onions and potatoes, firm textured, eaten hot or cold |
| Tortilla Francesa | omelette French style, soft textured |
| Trucha | trout |
| Uva | grape |
| Venera | scallop |
| Verde | green |
| Zarzuela (see sarsuela in Catalan) | |
| Zumo de fruta | fruit juice |

*Restaurant queries and requests (all in Spanish)*

| | |
|---|---|
| Ashtray | cenicero |
| Beer | cerveza |
| Bill | cuenta |
| Bread | pan |
| Butter | mantequilla |

| | |
|---|---|
| Cheese | queso |
| Coffee – black | café solo |
| Coffee – white | café con leche |
| Cold | frio |
| Cream | nata |
| Credit card | carta de crédito |
| Cup | taza |
| Drinks | bebidas |
| Dry | seco |
| Fork | tenedor |
| Glass (for water or beer) | vaso |
| Glass (for wine) | copa |
| Hot (temperature) | caliente |
| (flavour) | picante |
| Ice | helados |
| Knife | cuchillo |
| Lemon | limón |
| Medium | regular or mediano |
| Menu | carta |
| Mustard | mostaza |
| Nothing | nada |
| Oil | aceite |
| Pepper (condiment) | pimienta |
| Plate | plato |
| Rare | poco hecho |
| Roll | panecillo |
| Salad | ensalada |
| Salt | sal |
| Sandwich | bocadillo |
| Serviette | servilleta |
| Set menu | menú del dia |
| Speciality | especialidad |
| Spoon | cuchara |
| Sugar | azúcar |
| Sweet | dulce |
| Tea | té |
| Travellers cheque | cheques de viajes |
| Vinegar | vinagre |
| Waiter | camarero |
| Water (tap) | agua corriente (*or* del grifo) |
| Water (gassy mineral) | agua con gas |
| Water (flat mineral) | agua sin gas |
| Well-done | muy (or bien) hecho |
| Wine (white) | vino blanco |
| Wine (red) | vino tinto |
| Wine (rosé) | vino rosado |

# Designers

Outstanding architects, sculptors and decorators whose work is featured in this book.

Abiell, Guillem (?)–1420
Alemany, Pere 15C
Arnaudies, Jaume 1609–1702
Arvey, Pere 14C–15C

Barguès, Arnau 14C–15C
Bassa, Ferrer 1285(?)–1348
Bassa, Tomàs 16C
Bassett, Francesc 15C
Berenguer i Mestres, Francesc 1866–1914
Bermejo, Bartolomé 15C
Bertran, Pere 18C
Blay, Miquel 1866–1936
Blai, Pere (?)–1620
Bonafe, Matias 15C
Bonifaç, Lluís 1683–1765
Busquets Sindreu, Xavier 1917–

Ça Anglada, Pere 14C–15C
Carbonell, Antoni 16C
Carbonell, Guillem 14C
Casas, Ramon 1866–1932
Celles i Azcona, Antoni (?)–1838
Claperós, Antoni and sons Antoni and Joan 14C
Costa, Pere 18C

Domènech i Estapà, Josep 1859–1917
Domènech i Montaner, Lluís 1850–1923

Enrich, Joan c.1744–c.1795
Escuder, Andreu (?)–1463

Fabre, Jaume 13C–14C
Falguera i Sivilla, Antoni 1856–1947
Falqués i Urpi, Pere 1857–1916
Ferrer, Arnau 14C
Ferrer, Pere Pau 16C–17C
Flaugier, Bernat Josep 1757–1812
Florensa, Ferrer Adolf 1889–1969
Fontamet, Gil 15C
Font i Carreras, August 1846–1924
Fossas i Martinez, Juli 1868–1954

Galtes (or Galles), Charles (Carlí) 15C
Gallissà i Soque, Antoni 1861–1903
Garcia, Pere c.1600
Gargallo, Pau 1881–1934
Garrido, Joan 17C
Garriga i Roca, Miquel 1804–88
Gaudí i Cornet, Antoni 1852–1926
Granell i Manresa, Jeroní 1867–1931
Grau, Francesc 17C–18C

Gual, Bartomeu 14C–15C

Huguet, Jaume 1415(?)–92

Johan, Pere 17C
Jordi de Déu, Joan 14C–15C
Jujol i Gibert, Josep 1879–1949
Juli, Josep 17C–18C

Llimona i Bruguera, Joan 1860–1926
Llimona i Bruguera, Josep 1864–1934
Llobet, Pere (?)–1441

Martorell, Jeroní 1877–1951
Martorell i Montells, Joan 1883–1906
Martorell i Puig, Bernardi 1870–1937
Mas i Vila, Josep 19C
Mateu, Pau 15C–16C
Mestres Esplugas, Josep Oriol 1815–95
Mies van der Rohe, Ludwig 1886–1969
Miró, Joan 1893–1983
Montanya, Pere Pau (?)–1803
Montegut, Berenguer de 14C

Nesjar, Carl 1920–

Ordoñez, Bartolomé (?)–1520

Paredes, Francesc 18C
Passolles, Llorens 17C–18C
Perello, Miquel 17C–18C
Picasso y Ruiz, Pablo 1881–1973
Pla, Francesc 'El Vigata' 1743–92
Porcioles, Ramón 17C–18C
Puig i Cadafalch, Josep 1869–1956
Pujol, Agusti 1585–1643

Ribas, Damià 18C
Ribes, Josep 18C
Riquer, Bertram 13C–14C
Roca, Bernat (?)–1391
Rodriguez, Ventura 1717–85
Rogent i Amat, Elias 1821–97
Roig, Bernat 17C–18C
Roncali, Count Miquel de 1729–94
Rovira, Domènec 17C–18C
Rovira i Trias, Antoni 1816–89
Rubio i Bellver, Joan 1870–1952

Safont, Marc 15C
Sagnier i Vilavecchia, Enric 1858–1931
Santa Creu, Francesc de 17C–18C

Sert Lopez, Josep Lluís 1902–83
Sert i Badia, Josep Maria 1876–1945
Soler i Faneca, Joan 1731–94
Soler Rovirosa, Francesc 1836–1900
Subirachs, Josep Maria 1927–

Tàpies, Antoni 1923–
Tramulles, Francesc c. 1717–1771

Valeri i Pupurull, Salvador 1873–1954
Vergura, Ignasi 1715–76
Viladomat i Manalt, Antoni 1678–1755
Vila, Francesc (?)–1837
Vilaseca i Casanoves, Josep 1848–1910

# Architectural terms

Only the lesser-known terms in this book are generally included.
*Aisle* Parallel areas subdivided by arcades.
*Ajimez* Romanesque or Gothic windows divided into lights by colonettes. Probably developed by the Visigoths.
*Altar* Table of stone at which Mass is celebrated in a church or chapel. The most important altar, generally situated at the east end, is known as the high altar.
*Altar frontal* Covering of the front of the altar facing the worshippers.
*Altar rail* Low structure protecting the area in which the high altar stands.
*Ambulatory* Passageway in a church formed by continuing the aisles behind the sanctuary.
*Apse* Semi-circular or polygonal extension to a building.
*Architrave* Internal or external moulding surrounding an opening.
*Archivolts* Inner bands of an arch, tracing its curve.
*Art Nouveau* An art style, *c.*1890–1910, developed in England and popular on the Continent and in the USA. Adopted sinuous, organic lines. Gaudí was its greatest architectural exponent.
*Ashlar* Large blocks of smoothed stone laid in level courses.
*Atrium* Roofed courtyard of a building.
*Attic* Low top storey of a building.

*Baldachino* Dome-shaped cover to a high altar, revived in the Baroque period.
*Baroque* Exuberant development of the Classical style.
*Barrel or tunnel vault* A curved vault.
*Bay* Compartment of a building divided by repeated elements.
*Bay window* A straight-sided window projecting at ground level.
*Boss* Ornamental projection covering the intersection of ribs in a roof.
*Buttress* Structure attached to a wall to counter an outward thrust.

*Capital* Top section of a column or pilaster, usually carved in the distinctive style of a Classical Order.
*Castellated* Battlemented parapet. Usually Mudéjar work in Catalonia.
*Catalan Gothic* Influenced by Italian Gothic, the style arrived in Catalonia in the late 12C. Emphasized the horizontal line externally, and wide undivided areas internally. Unlike North European Gothic, pointed arches were generally reserved for religious buildings and less use made of large windows.
*Chapter house* Meeting area for the clerical hierarchy (the Chapter).
*Cladding* Material added to a structure to provide an external surface.
*Classical* Styles following those of ancient Greece or Rome.
*Cloister* Covered arcaded passageway, usually four sided and created beside the main nave of a monastic church.
*Coffering* Recessed ceiling panelling.
*Convent* A complex housing a monastic community, male or female.
*Corbel* Wall bracket, generally of stone, supporting e.g., a beam.
*Corinthian* Greek Classical Order. Columns are slender and their capitals intricately decorated with carved leaves and small spiral scrolls (volutes).

*Cornice* A projecting decorative feature running horizontally at high level.

*Crossing* Where the nave, transepts and chancel intersect in a church.

*Cupola* Small domed roof often surmounting a turret.

*Cusp* Decorative feature of Gothic tracery. The intersection of foils (or lobes) forms a pointed projection.

*Dado* Lower section of wall, often tiled in Spain.

*Doric* Classical Order, the oldest and sturdiest. The capitals of Doric columns are virtually undecorated.

*Dormer window* Window protruding from a sloping roof.

*Eave* Horizontal edge of a roof overhanging the wall.

*Fanlight* Oblong or semi-circular window above a door.

*Finial* Decorative terminal to a structure e.g. spire or gable.

*Flamboyant* Waved lines of tracery producing a flame-like effect. Popular in 15C Catalan Gothic architecture.

*Fluted* Vertical grooving.

*Fresco* Painting on a freshly plastered wall to obtain greater permanence.

*Gable* Upper section of wall at each end of a building.

*Gallery* Storey added to an upper level, always open on one side, and usually arcaded. Alternatively, a long room for displaying works of art. See also roof gallery.

*Gargoyle* Decorative, protruding spouts that drain rain water from roofs. Often carved as beasts or demons in Gothic buildings.

*Gothic Revival* Attempt to reproduce the Gothic style.

*Grisaille* Grey monochrome decoration.

*Ionic* Classical Order. Columns are slenderer than those in the Doric Order and capitals are decorated at corners with spiral scrolls (volutes).

*Keystone* Central stone at the apex of an arch or where the ribs of a vault intersect. Frequently enlongated to form a boss.

*Light* Section of a window filled with glass.

*Lintel* Horizontal section of stone or timber spanning an opening to distribute the weight that it bears.

*Lobe* Petal shape formed by Gothic tracery.

*Lombard frieze (or arcade)* Distinctive element of Catalan Romanesque style, in the form of a blind arcade of curved arches forming a frieze. Often used to decorate a roof line.

*Misericord* 'Mercy' seat provided by a shallow surface for resting purposes that protrudes horizontally when the seat itself is tipped up. Supporting brackets are often richly carved with various subjects, not always religious. Generally in the form of Gothic choir stalls in monasteries.

*Modernism (or Modernisme)* Architecturally, not a style but the application of functional planning and new structural techniques, combined with craft materials. Catalan Gothic Revivalism had an early influence on the appearance of the buildings, but styles became eclectic. Evolved in the 1880s, the movement began to peter out *c.*1914.

*Moulding* Decorative addition to a projecting feature, such as a cornice, door frame, etc.

*Mudéjar* A continuation of the Moorish style, by Moorish craftsmen, who remained after the gradual Christian reconquest of Spanish regions.

*Nave* Body of the church housing the congregation.
*Newel post* Post supporting the handrail at the head or foot of a stairway.
*Noucentism* Architectural return to Classical themes in Barcelona that followed Modernism. Its high point was the 1929 Great Exhibition when most buildings adopted this style.

*Order* Classical architecture where the design and proportions of the columns and entablatures are standardized.

*Pier* Solid structure supporting a great load.
*Pilaster* Shallow, flat column attached to a wall.
*Pinnacle* Vertical decorative feature surmounting a Gothic structure.
*Portal* Important doorway. Wide round-headed portals were a feature of medieval Catalan architecture.
*Portico* Classical porch of columns supporting a roof, usually pedimented.

*Quadriga* Sculpted chariot drawn by four horses.

*Refectory* Dining hall, usually monastic.
*Renaissance* Rebirth of art following Classical modes. Developed in Italy in the 14C, the Renaissance came late to Catalonia (as in England) and Classical themes were generally applied to Gothic buildings. Renaissance principles were rarely followed wholeheartedly in Barcelona.
*Reredos* Decorative structure usually standing behind the altar in a church or chapel. Generally made of wood but occasionally stone. On the Continent, confusingly referred to as a retable.
*Rib* Protruding band supporting a vault. Occasionally purely decorative.
*Rococo* Last phase of the Baroque style in the mid-18C, with widespread use of detailed ornamentation.
*Romanesque* Style of architecture featuring semi-circular arches. Popular from the 9C to *c.*1250.
*Romantic* A style developed in the second half of the 19C, distinguished by heavy terracotta decoration.
*Roof gallery* A popular feature of medieval Catalan mansions. Originally open on two sides and arcaded. Provided roof insulation from summer heat, shade for taking the air and drying facilities for agricultural produce and laundry.
*Rose window* Circular window used in Gothic architecture. Its tracery pattern resembles a rose. Introduced in the mid-13C.
*Rustication* Use of stonework on the exterior of a building to give an impression of strength. The jointing is always deep.

*Sacristy* Room in a church for storage of sacred vessels and vestments. Generally used for robing. Also known as a vestry.
*Sanctuary* Area reserved for the clergy, in which the high altar stands.
*Sarcophagus* Carved coffin.
*Sgraffito(i)* Scratching a plaster surface to reveal another colour on the layer below. Late 17C to early 19C in Barcelona.
*Spandrels* Roughly triangular areas in the wall on either side of, and outside, the curve of an arch.

*Terracotta* Unglazed earthenware used as tiles and decorative features.
*Tracery* Intersecting bars that create a decorative pattern in Gothic architecture.

*Transept*  The area that runs on either side of the nave of a large church forming the cruciform (cross) plan. Rarely extends from the nave on the continent, as it does in England.

*Transitional*  The merging of Gothic with Romanesque architecture *c.*1150–*c.*1200.

*Triforium*  Blind passage that runs above the roof of an aisle within a church.

*Trophy*  Decorative sculptured arms or armour.

*Tuscan*  Classical Order. Roman adaptation of the Greek Doric.

*Tympanum*  Semi-circular or triangular space between the lintel of an opening and the arch above it.

*Vault*  An arched structure forming a roof.

*Venetian window*  Window of three openings, the central, large section being round headed.

*Vestibule*  Entrance hall or anteroom.

*Visigothic*  Adaption of Roman architecture by the Visigoths (in Barcelona 5C–7C).

# Index of locations

Catalan names are given preference, as these will prove to be more useful than their English translations when searching for a location. In some instances, however, the English version is also given. A few buildings are better known by their nicknames, eg. 'La Pedrera' for Casa Milà, and these, therefore, are indicated as well. Location descriptions – palace, street, etc., always precede the name. The most commonly used, with their translation, are as follows: avinguda, avenue; baixada, lane; borsa, exchange; capella, chapel; carrer, street; casa, house; cine, cinema; collegi, college; escola, school; farmàcia, pharmacy; font, fountain; fundació, foundation; galeria, gallery; jardins, gardens; Llibreria, library; mercat, market; monestir, monastery; monumento, monument; museu, museum; palau, palace; parc, park; passatge, passageway; passeig, major thoroughfare; plaça, square; portal, gateway; puerto, port; sant (or santa), saint; teatre, theatre; templo, temple; torre, tower.